Animal

Sara Pascoe

Animal

The Autobiography of a Female Body

FABER & FABER

First published in 2016
by Faber & Faber Limited
Bloomsbury House
74–77 Great Russell Street
London WC1B 3DA

Typeset by Faber & Faber Limited
Printed in the UK by CPI Group (UK) Ltd, Croydon, CRO 4YY

A CIP record for this book
is available from the British Library

ISBN 978–0–571–32522–1

305·40207

FSC
www.fsc.org
MIX
Paper from
responsible sources
FSC® C101712

2 4 6 8 10 9 7 5 3 1

For Rosa, Hollie, Violet and all the other flowers.

Contents

Too Many Introductions

Meet the Book

Writing a book is an arrogant thing to do.

I do stand-up for my main job, and that's pretty arrogant too. At work, I'm the only person in the room who is allowed to talk, I'm the only one who gets to have a microphone and essentially I make everyone sit there and listen to me going on about myself and my thoughts and ideas. A book is an even longer version of that, but I have so much to say that a gig wouldn't be long enough to fit it all in.

For a while I've been researching various theories of female sexuality. I thought that if I could learn to understand hormones and desire and brain functions then maybe I could make better life decisions, maybe I wouldn't be so confused by myself. I had this idea that just like dogs and pigs and dolphins, human beings are animals. And so, like other animals, we should have a programmed set of instinctual behaviours, but no one seems to agree what they are. I wondered if perhaps our cultures, religions and societal pressures had concealed our animal natures, even from ourselves. I kept visualising the modern human as a battleground with inherited instinct pulling us one way and learned propriety pulling us another and all of us struggling to understand or like ourselves.

I wanted to unravel us.

When I researched more around this topic, I realised there are two distinct investigations currently going on. There are the excellent scientists who are deciphering the codification of behaviour written in our genes, the physical shaping of our bodies by evolution and the emotional capacity of our brains. And separately, there are the cultural commentators; the sociologists, philosophers and feminists who write about society and media and modern reality, who discuss how women's bodies are treated, fetishised, worshipped, denigrated or controlled.

I wanted to bring these two separate conversations together. To highlight some of the aspects of womanhood I am struggling with, to discuss what science can teach us and how culture can hurt us. I want to tell you fascinating things about our ancient ancestry and the terrors of recent civilisation, and to ponder the relevance for us alive guys, us now-timers. I want to show you that for every woman in the world, knowledge* and communication are the finest form of self-defence. That empowerment lies in comprehending ourselves as beasts and in accepting ourselves as we were built.

---

* I'll be suggesting lots of further reading for you at the end.

Meet Me

Hello! My name is Sara* and I am thirty-four. I am English, Caucasian. I live in London in a flat that doesn't allow pets. I have no religion but a lot of faith. I have always wanted to write a book.

When I was eighteen years old I decided to apply for Cambridge University. I'd read somewhere that being part of the Footlights drama society was a great way to become a famous actor, which had been my ambition since realising I did not want a proper job. I put Cambridge as the top choice on my UCAS form. My predicted grades weren't good enough, so I had a chat with my kindly teachers and begged them to predict me As rather than Cs. Geoffrey, my psychology tutor, said I wouldn't be properly prepared for the interview without coaching. I explained that my aunty Juliet had seen a news programme saying that there was pressure on Oxbridge to admit more students from working-class families and so I reckoned I'd be alright, then I worked my class right out of there.

AND I GOT AN INTERVIEW! They have to interview everyone who applies, and I was thrilled to be one of those lucky 'everyone'. My mum decided to take the day off work and come with me. I borrowed some of her clothes to wear. My sisters had no one to drop them at school so they came too. The four of us went for breakfast in Cambridge city centre.

---

* My name doesn't have an 'h' on it, but it's pronounced Sarah not Sah-rah. Make sure you are pronouncing it correctly in your head.

My mum talked about how we'd all move there to live some day, while I ate egg muffins. We got lost on the way to the college. It was called Corpus Christi, which like all Latin means 'you don't belong here'. I was fifteen minutes late for a twenty-minute interview, but I didn't let that upset me. I was from a working-class family, raised in Dagenham then Romford. I had an Essex accent and my mum's suit on. I was exactly what they were looking for.

I was interviewed by the Oldest Man in the World. His office was full of piled-up books. 'This is just like my bedroom,' I told him, 'except in my bedroom it's clothes.' He creaked a question: 'Why do you want to study philosophy at Cambridge?'

SARA
I want to come to Cambridge so I can be in Footlights.

OMITW
Why philosophy?

SARA
I think it's really really good.

OMITW
Who have you read?

SARA
Jostein Gaarder. *Sophie's World?*

OLDEST MAN IN THE WORLD shakes head and speaks very slowly as if recalling an awful war.

OMITW
I was concerned this would happen, but so far you are the first one.

Then I pronounced Plato and Socrates exactly as you do if you've only ever seen them written down: 'Plateau is mega good. As was So-crates.' Then I left.

It took me a decade to realise what the old man's comment about *Sophie's World* had meant. I'd loved that book because it introduced me to some really complicated concepts, because it summarised philosophers and their ideas so simply. And of course that was the Cambridge don's problem: it gave Essex girls in their mum's clothes the audacity to think they might understand anything.

But I didn't know that yet. I was so exhilarated being in that ancient churchy building, and I had another interview that I wasn't late for. I told this much more Normally Aged Man that I wanted to be in Footlights and then famous and, hopefully, friends with Stephen Fry.

NAM
Anything else? Apart from acting?

SARA
I'm going to write a book about sex and my generation.

NAM
Why?

SARA
I just think it's really interesting.

NAM
Why?

SARA
It's *really* interesting.

In the back of the car on the way home I tried to read a book about Wittgenstein, but I kept getting distracted by my own excitement at how well I'd nailed the interviews and how much fun I was going to have being in Footlights. And it would be scary to move away from home, but I would expand my mind and learn to ride a bike and have a little bed in a little room and fall in love with an intellectual boy who was homosexual and I was VERY surprised to receive a rejection letter two weeks later. Clearly they weren't as hungry for commoners as Aunty Juliet had led me to believe.

'At least you got an interview,' my mum kept telling me.

That was half my lifetime ago and look at me now, curled up with you and Stephen Fry, reading a book I wrote about sex and my generation. I think it's really interesting and I hope you find lots to think about too.

Dream big, kids. May all your rejections quickly become laughable, because anyone who says no to you is an idiot. Xxxxx

Important question before we start . . .

Are You a Woman?

When I do my job, I'm referred to as a 'female comedian'.
With most occupations, being a doctor or teacher or chef or
whatever, you are defined by the type of work you do. But my
job title also includes my gender. I don't do it any differently
to the non-females, I stand there speaking words, sometimes
walking from side to side or throwing a hand in the air. My
boobs don't get in the way or make me fall off the stage or
anything, yet 'female' pre-empts my 'comedian'. Like a dis-
claimer. I don't hate this and I'm not angry, but it's made me
notice gender more than I would have otherwise.

Lots of jobs have feminised titles: wait*ress* or mer*maid*.
There are women who work under a male title, firemen or
postmen, a lazy catch-all that maybe they get annoyed about?
Sometimes I am called a comedienne, which I like, because
it makes me sound French and cooked. The thing that's odd
about people noticing or commenting or presuming as to my
gender is that they do; notice and comment and presume. I
never told anyone. I didn't ring up for my first gig and announce, 'Hello there, I'm a *woman*, could I possibly have five
minutes of your stand-up comedy next Tuesday?'

I was twenty-six when I started doing gigs and I'd been female all of my life. I'd been dimly aware of that from pregnancy scares and the difficulty of urinating standing up but
it'd never been commented upon when I entered a room. I'd
always identified as a person. Human being. Ordinary. But
when I began to perform at stand-up nights, bookers would

say, 'It's always nice to have a woman on.' They might warn the audience, 'The next act is a woman,' so they wouldn't be shocked and topple their chairs. People might wait afterwards to tell me that I was 'good for a girl' or that they 'usually hated female comedians'. Or they would give me helpful advice like 'You shouldn't talk so much about lady stuff.' No one was cruel or nasty. No one explicitly told me, 'This is a man's job, you are not welcome.' But I was baffled. Why did my being a woman seem so noticeable to everyone else? Why was it the first thing that they saw?

When I became more successful, after a few years on the circuit, I would do interviews for radio stations or local papers. They would ask me, 'What's it like being a female comedian?' and I never knew how to answer. Did they want logistics? I travel to shows on a train, I write words down in a pad. 'It's such a male industry,' they might helpfully clarify. 'What's it like to be a woman?' When I really think about it, I have no idea what it is like to be a woman. I've no experience of gender or species apart from my own. I've nothing to compare it to. I cannot fathom anything other than being inside *my* mind and body. That question is asking me to extend my subjective experience to all women, to speak universally and comparatively of a gendered condition, and that's an existential ask for someone promoting a Wednesday night 'Chucklefest' above a pub in Norwich.

Whenever someone wants a gender comparison, I remember the Greek myth about Tiresias. He was a man, but then he got turned female for seven years after hitting some snakes. And because he had experienced shagging as both sexes, Zeus asked him whether men got more pleasure from sex, or did women enjoy it more? Tiresias said women got ten times as much pleasure as men. But of course this is MYTH not science. You cannot compare the genders in any quantifiable way. You just can't. We can't understand the world from anyone's perspective but our own.

So I've become hyper-aware of my womanhood and that's made me think a lot about what gender even *is*. I have daydreams where I wonder: what if I woke up with a penis? Would I still be a woman? Imagine someone as a horrible prank has sewn a penis on me, and I have to walk about with it in my trousers, but – I'd still feel like a woman, I'd just be a woman with a penis. So it's not my genitals that define me . . . so what then? Ovaries, womb. If they were removed, I'd still be a woman. I'd be a wombless woman. With a penis. If I took lots of testosterone, had my breasts removed, had a deep voice and a beard and short hair . . . at what point would I drop the 'female' and become a comedian? I have decided it's my mind that's woman. It's my narrator. It's my relationship to myself, and oddly, nothing at all to do with my body.

To return to my question 'Are you a woman?', the only person who can answer that is you. You define for yourself what gender means and how you fit within it, if at all. For a long, boring time, gender has been a binary with sweeping fictional stereotypes. 'Men are physically stronger than women,' an idiot shouts. No they're not. If you took all the strongest women and pitted them against the weakest men, the women would thrash them. *All* men are not stronger than *all* women, there's about a hundred million exceptions, and if there are that many exceptions then it's not a rule. Ditto boys don't cry, girls are nurturing, women aren't hairy, blah blah blah, it's a prison. An invisible trap we've unknowingly lived in while wondering why the boys are so frustrated and aggressive and the women spend so much of their energy hating themselves and we're all so needlessly unhappy. Every time you hear someone say 'men are like this' – or 'women are like that' – they're wrong and you should stop listening. There is no statement that is irrevocably and absolutely true across an entire gender through culture and time and geography. Except male toilets always smell worse, but apart from that—

A lot of negative things have been allowed to happen because we believe our gender defines us, or that there is a correct way of being male or female. If you are reading this book it means you are one of the luckiest people in the world – I can presume that you live in the first world. You are educated to a high reading standard; you have leisure time and a little money and live under a government that allows you to think your own thoughts.

We can free ourselves from invisible prisons. We escape from old ideas by replacing them with new ones.

The book I have written is about the experience of growing up in a female body and with the physiology of a female body, and this excludes the experiences of many women. But gender is a mere idea. It's a spectrum, you can slide up and down on it or stay solidly placed – what I'm trying to say is that it's likely your way of being a woman is completely different from mine. I identify as female and I'm heterosexual. And I'll always be white. My subjective world-view cannot speak for all women's experience or reality. I forgive myself for this, and hope that you will too. I'm not attempting to be the last word in a conversation, I just want to be part of it, and then I'll sit back and listen some more.

Falling into Love

I often think about how effortless my life would be if I was a mouse; running between cupboards, shagging all the time and doing tiny poos. I would respond instinctively to my environment and never question or analyse. I wouldn't need horoscopes or psychology. If something is scary, run away; if something smells nice, have a bite. Unfortunately, tens of thousands of years ago, my ancestors developed a complex awareness and intelligence that made responsive simplicity impossible for me. And for you.*

Here is a *rough* timeline of where we come from:

2.5 billion years ago: The first organisms utilise oxygen.

1.5–2 billion years ago: The first cell with a nucleus.

510 million years ago: Fish invented.

300 million years ago: First mammally things.

245 million years ago: Dinosaurs all over the place.

220 million years ago: First proper mammals.

65 million years ago: No more dinosaurs (phew).

20 million years ago: Our great ape ancestors diverge from old-world monkeys.

5 million years ago: First humanoid ancestors, the *Australopithecus* guys.

2.8 million years ago: *Homo habilis* start getting more people-y, using stone tools etc.

* I'll be presuming you're a human for the entirety of this book.

1.8 million years ago: *Homo erectus*, based in Africa. Brain size
74 per cent of ours.

200,000 years ago: Anatomically modern *Homo sapiens* arrive
– let's party!

60,000 years ago: Human migration from Africa.

40,000 years ago: Our cousins the Neanderthals die out.

35,000 years ago: Evidence of cave art: we're getting
creative.

10,000 years ago: Agriculture begins: we're getting
organised.

5,000 years ago: Written language: using symbols to
communicate/do tax returns.

4,500 years ago: Pyramids built. Humans will continue
to cover the earth with architecture as well as creating
computers, aeroplanes, acid rain and the Vajazzle.

400-odd years ago: Shakespeare writes plays so good they
have to be explained to you.

22 May 1981: Sara Patricia Pascoe is born. Evolution is
complete, humanity is perfected.

I've taken the approximate dates above from people who
seem to know what they're talking about/have written books
with good Amazon reviews. But there are elements about
which experts disagree, not to mention people who have a
fundamental religious belief.* My ex-boyfriend's mum used
to say that evolution was 'all a bit far-fetched' and I used to
laugh and laugh, which is more enjoyable than arguing with

---

* If, in the future, the theory of evolution is proved to be a massive prank by the
Christian God to test our faith I'll be the first to apologise and beg to get into
heaven. I want to live forever**

** I want to learn how to fly***

*** high.

someone. I haven't spent my life studying fossils, all my knowledge is secondary. If you prefer a different explanation for how human beings came into existence then you're welcome to read the following as a fable and we can still be friends.

Evidence for the gradual shaping and sudden mutations of human evolution comes from our own DNA structure and skeletons* found underground. Scientists use recovered bones to find out about our ape and *Homo* relatives that are no longer around, and to trace our species's physiological development from tree-dwelling, plant-eating idiocy up to our bipedal, less hairy, super-brainy current state.

I'd like to give you a compliment now: YOU ARE SO CLEVER. So clever. No matter how you did in your GCSEs, no matter how often you've forgotten where you put your tea and knocked it over, you are exceptional. You have a HUGE brain. It's too big. It's embarrassingly large. It's proportionally massive, roughly three times bigger than an orang-utan's or chimpanzee's, twice as big as a gorilla's. And it's not just insanely huge, it is brilliant at communicating with itself. It's adaptive. If you became blind as a child, your brain can map the world using non-visual spatial awareness. If you're deaf, your brain reorganises to comprehend language via visual stimuli. If you're a black-cab driver you'll have a phenomenal, muscular memory while if you're an alcoholic you'll suffer protective blackouts. Our brains change how they function in order to be as efficient as possible according to how we use them. This process is called neuroplasticity and it takes place continually throughout our lives.

Your large and elastic brain allows you to interpret the

---

* Spooky.

world in a way that your ancient ancestors couldn't. It was developed over thousands of generations as a survival tool, for mapping landscapes and predicting behaviours. For hunting and pretending and cooking and protecting. It makes empathy possible as well as the ability to manipulate empathy in others. From the second you were born, your brain has been collecting information in order to make you stronger and more prepared for whatever you might find in the world. Your brain interprets and encodes everything that happens outside and inside of you into what we call 'meaning'. It translates vibrations into music, reflected light into scenery, the movements and vocalisations of other *Homo sapiens* into friends and enemies; it literally creates your world, and you alone live there.

As strange as it sounds, some of our brain's 'thoughts' are unconscious. We all have instinctual impulses and these are inherited because they enabled our survival. A good example is hunger. No one needed to teach you to want feeding; your body responds that way because for millions of years the mammals who were impelled to eat periodically were far more likely to successfully breed than those malnourished losers who felt no impetus. You have the genes of the hungry. It's inbuilt inside you, you're pre-programmed. The conscious part of the brain is the bit that gets you fed. That's how your ancestors knew where to forage, or how to track an animal. It's how you manage to ask directions to the nearest supermarket and select a baguette filling you think you'll enjoy.

Perhaps your conscious mind is working away right now, thinking, 'UM, excuse me lady but I *don't* actually *feel* hunger. I never know when to eat, I'd starve to death if someone didn't tell me to have a banana occasionally—'

Well okay then you: throughout this book I will be making sweeping, generalised statements that are true for the majority of the human race. Not for everyone. There will always be exceptions and abnormalities. We are a very varied species; every generation displays a wide range of possibility. If we were all exactly the same, certain environments or circumstances would've wiped us out in our uniform unsuitability. The outliers and the unusual are our species insurance: curiosities and anomalies have enabled us to survive. So you're unique and unusual, well done, now pop off and eat your banana.

The desire for sex could be called instinctual, it's a—

YOU AGAIN
Not for *me*, I'm asexual.

Please don't speak with your mouth full. For the *vast majority* of adult people, the desire to have sex appears as an instinct. No one has to sit you down and encourage you: 'Look at that guy over there, doesn't he have lovely arms?' But with sexual instinct, the interplay of desire and its satisfaction is more complicated than having a sandwich or reheating lasagne. It involves other people, both as objects of desire and as possible sex partners. I cannot have sex with everyone I want to. I cannot have sex every time I feel the urge. I have to hide the majority of my sexual feelings due to social expectation, cultural education and politeness. We all laugh when a dog humps someone's leg; his life is free of rules and shame. He does not ask himself, 'Does this leg fancy me back? Will it be insulted or offended? Is it a married leg? Or underage?' No, he jumps on and grinds away as his body instructs him. The dog can't get the leg pregnant, so we can just laugh – what an idiot – but the instinct he's obeying will mean sometimes that leg *is* another dog and puppies will be made. So it works, it's a great system. The dog's urges result in more dogs for the world, HOORAY!

Unlike a dog, you'll have been taught about sex, whether in detail or implicitly. From your parents, school videos, watching *Dirty Dancing* when you were eleven and not quite understanding it, you'll have absorbed a trillion messages about what sex is and how you are meant to feel about it. And now, my friend, you're a tug-of-war. Pulled one way by your unconscious desires, pulled back and restrained by the rules of behaviour that your society and upbringing have foisted on you. Instinct on one shoulder, expectation on the other. Add this to the false construction of female sexuality that's flung at you from porn, TV and women's magazines and you're all set for ~~difficulty orgasming~~ confusion.

You'll have heard phrases about humans being a 'higher' species, but interestingly only from other humans. COINCIDENCE? We arrogantly believe we're the best animal on the block. We even categorise ourselves separately. People assume they're superior to chimps and zebras because those guys don't keep diaries or go on yoga retreats. Humans can wear clothes and learn the saxophone and of course this differentiates us, but we're also warm, furry and don't know when to stop eating; we're conscious animals, but beasts none the less. While we might feel in control of the decisions we make, while we might be able to justify every single thing we do, underneath our behaviour, simmering away, are our evolved predispositions. We are overly proud of our consciousness and it causes us to ignore our nature, or to misunderstand it.

Love exists in many species but is classified as 'pair bonding' or 'mating behaviour'. In non-human animals we view it very simply as a 'reproductive trait', an inherited behaviour that aids breeding. Yet when it happens to US, when we feel it for ourselves, jeepers creepers, we don't shut up about it – I've got an exercise book filled with quotes I copied out during my teens. Pages of them; Germaine Greer, Oscar Wilde, Dolly Parton, Glenn Hoddle, my sister Kristyna and my friend Siobhan scribbled alongside Chinese curses, sections of the musical *Rent*, Paul McCartney, Kriss Akabusi and William Wallace via Mel Gibson. As you'd expect, most of the quotes are about love. About how it's worth dying for or fighting for and life is not worth living without it. That it is immortal, priceless, liberating, courageous, comforting and—

Love is described like GOD.

Thinkers, novelists, poets and musicians use religious language about a basic and fundamental emotion. The effect is to mystify rather than decipher. Sure, romantic love can be an overwhelming and powerful experience but, you know, so can desperately needing the toilet, and we comprehend that in a totally unsophisticated way. No poems or songs about the anguish of looking for a bathroom; the torture of a locked door, the urinal that got away. Love has a PR team, and we've been left with two choices, worship or doubt. Either we subscribe to the scriptures and believe love is metaphysical quasi-wizardry or we atheistically spurn it and screw like earthworms in the mud.

OR we could investigate why it feels so huge. We could learn about hormones and neurotransmitters, evolved behaviours, cultural norms and the effects of environment. We could, as objectively as possible, consider ourselves animals for a little while and see if our emotions begin to make more sense.

How We Fall

If you were an alien visiting Earth from outer space and you had to fill in a quick form about how different species procreate and rear their young, most animals would be easy. You'd whizz through them.

Salmon: Female lays eggs in riverbed and male sprays them with sperm. Female protects nest until she dies about a week later.

Giraffe: Males compete to court a female in oestrus. She raises calf with little involvement from father.

Cat: Female mates with local male, gestates for sixty-three days, has kittens. Feeds them for five or six months until they head out on their own. No male involvement in rearing.

Until you got to us.

Human: Female has a bath, puts on a nice dress and goes to All Bar One . . .

Hmmm, you'd think, chewing a pencil with one of your mouths, these human beings don't seem to have predictable behaviours. They *say* they mate for life, except very few of them do. Most claim to be sexually faithful, yet many aren't and all find it extremely difficult. They *say* that children are brought up by their two parents, except loads are adopted or brought up by one parent or a step-parent or a grandparent or, very occasionally, wolves . . . and then you think,

'Sod it, it's too complicated, I'll leave that one blank,' and so you get a C on your Visiting Planet Earth assignment and now you'll never make the electronic egg that birthed you proud.

If all animals have a natural mating and bonding pattern, what is ours? I'm not even an alien and I'm confused. Are we supposed to be monogamous, but culture and modernity have made it very difficult? Or was monogamy foisted upon us by religions in the olden times, and that's why we struggle with it now? What I've been TOLD by, you know, soap operas, cartoons, rom-coms, women's magazines, novels, pop music, dating websites, sex education and every single episode of *Friends* is that the *ideal* relationship occurs between two people, is emotionally and sexually committed and should last for life. Anything shorter than 'for life' is a false start, any infidelity means things are 'not right'.

Looking at species more closely related to us for answers, we find a wide range of sexual and social behaviours:

Gorilla: Several females live together accompanied by one male that they mate with. He gets overthrown when a younger fitter male comes along.

Chimpanzee: A group of males and females live together and practise lots of social mating. Females are most attracted to dominant males, and males are most attracted to older females who have already successfully reared offspring.

Orang-utan: Female lives alone on her territory and is visited periodically by a male. He may visit several females.

Gibbon: Both genders are social but exhibit very strong pair bonds and are often described as monogamous.

So here's a question. WHY such a range? They're all apes, shouldn't they be more similar?

All animals procreate and cohabit in the way that's most suitable for their environment, or rather, environment dictates the most profitable breeding patterns for all animals. Factors like food scarcity or predators will determine whether working as an extended family group is the best reproductive strategy, or whether daddy needs to stick around and help out. And remember this is not conscious. Gorillas don't have AGMs where they sip tea and discuss the benefits of a male-led harem. They have evolved this behaviour over hundreds of thousands of years, because the genes of those who preferred such an arrangement were more likely to survive and be carried through subsequent generations. The best mating strategies proved themselves in numerous offspring and over generations this creates predictable behaviour.

Modern humans were shaped by exactly the same process, and so you, alive right now and riding a motorcycle, are physically equipped for life in the African savannah around forty thousand years ago. Your psychology, hobbies and dress sense will have changed in the meantime, but your instincts haven't. Your culture has transformed but not your nature; you're the same animal in different trousers. So in order to find out whether we should be staking out a territory or getting a gang together for a sex party, we need to investigate what our ancestors did relationship-wise.

CANCEL THE ORGY! The science books say we lived in social groups but with strongly bonded pairs raising their own children.

It is obviously very difficult to be absolutely sure about the behaviours of our long-dead ancestors. Until someone invents a time machine, working out what the *sapiens* of a hundred thousand years ago were up to is supposition. Some behaviours leave physical traces – we know when humans were using tools and cooking food because evidence has been found and dated – but we know little about the sex lives of those primitive people. There are no fossilised love letters demanding fidelity or cave paintings depicting nuclear families, so how have the scientists reached their conclusion?

The strongest evidence is 'body dimorphism'. This is what they call the size difference between genders and it is indicative of alternative mating strategies. Throughout nature polygynous mating results in males that are bigger than females. (Polygynous = males having multiple female partners, but I am sure you knew that already.) When there is competition amongst males, being larger makes it much easier to dominate your opposition and anyone you're trying to get off with. And if larger males are more successful at mating, more of their genes will be replicated in offspring. Here's a human analogy: imagine that massive male wrestlers were each impregnating hundreds of women while preventing any weedy non-wrestlers from getting their leg over – what a sexy story! After several hundred generations the genes for smallness would be much rarer. So when mating is competitive, all males become larger. The females do not increase in size, as this does not have an impact on their ability to reproduce. In human terms, a lady wrestler does not insist that all males only have sex with her and prevent weedy non-wrestler ladies from ever getting any, although I have to say I would have to respect her position if she did.

SO, gorillas have a large body dimorphism, with males being 1.5 times bigger than the females, and orang-utans even more, with males being twice as big. Both these species are polygynous – it's all adding up so far, well done science. With chimps, who are also polygynous, there is less dimorphism, with males being only 1.3 times larger than females. This is because chimpanzee females mate with a lot of males, so while being big is still an advantage for the males, it's not *as* important. Basically, the females put out more so there's a wider gene spread; keep it up, ladies. And then you have gibbons, who are monogamous and have genders almost exactly the same size, with a dimorphism of only 1.02. Which is what we were expecting from this theory, excellent.

We're all excited to find out: what about humans? What is our dimorphism? My current boyfriend is much taller than me, but my ex-boyfriend was almost the same height. Should I take my shoes off before you measure me? Oh, they've already worked it out – PREPARE THE ANNOUNCEMENT TRUMPET:

Human males are ON AVERAGE 1.1 times larger than human females.

So that's more dimorphism than gibbons, less than chimps. If we extrapolated purely from the evidence of gendered body size we'd believe that it's in our nature to practise monogamy rather than polygyny. Our ancestors utilised a mating system where everyone gets paired up, even the skinny and tiny. We use this measurement to indicate that our male ancestors were not competing for females in a way that would make size an advantage. Perhaps a very slight advantage, or maybe females preferred *slightly* bigger men, hence this small disproportion.

There is another possibility to consider when it comes to explaining our dimorphism, but we need to understand something else first, something scientists can be sure about.

We bond. You'd agree with that? In whatever form it finally takes, however long it lasts, we have evolved to love the socks off each other. Hopefully you'll have case studies in your own life to verify this. I certainly have; I loved my first person at sixteen and have been crazy for loving people off and on ever since. But let us stroke our beard thoughtfully and ask *why?* Why do some species of animal pair-bond and others don't? Cats and giraffes and salmon aren't bothering, so why are we?

Is the answer:

a) Boredom.
b) Guilt.
c) Fear of being alone.
d) Parental investment.

That's correct! The amount of parental investment required in raising a baby human is the reason we love so deeply.

A salmon hatches and can swim and feed and go about her business without any need for her parents. A baby giraffe is born able to run around and fight and play, and can reach up and suckle from her mother without assistance. Kittens are physically restricted for the first few weeks of their lives. They are suckled by their mother, and when she goes out to hunt she leaves them well hidden. She is able to protect and feed them by herself until they are strong enough to do it for themselves.

Now let's imagine a human baby, a few minutes old. She cannot swim off and live her life like a salmon; she needs looking after. She can't nurse without assistance like a giraffe, so she needs an exceptionally nurturing and caring parent who does everything for her. Let us imagine her mother, a human woman: she can lactate to feed her baby but she has to hold the baby while she suckles. She can't put her child down as it is exceptionally vulnerable. Babies know this. It's why they cry so much, it's like an alarm going off: 'NO ONE'S HOLD-ING ME I'M ABOUT TO BE EATEN BY SNAKES AND FOXES.' It is tricky for a mother to forage or hunt while carrying her baby and for a few days after birth she may find any movement difficult. How is she going to create a warm place to sleep? Or protect herself and her baby from wildebeests? Imagine you, an hour after childbirth in the African savannah . . . could you put up a tent? Could you run from a scary ~~zombie vampire~~ predator?

A cat is equipped to successfully raise her kittens alone, but a human woman isn't. She needs help. And this brings us back to that big brain of ours.

Remember when I was complimenting that immense organ you keep under your hat? Well, its development radically adapted our bodies. As the human brain increased in size, the female frame had to accommodate producing it. Millions of years ago we evolved a much wider, flexible pelvis in order to birth the huge skulls of our babies, skulls that have to remain soft and flexible themselves in order not to kill mummy on the way out. At some point in the last million generations, the human brain became so big that it couldn't complete its growth *in utero*. Human women give birth to part-baked, premature babies. It's an evolutionary compromise. If human babies developed to the same point as newborn chimps, they'd need to gestate for two and a half years and all women would die giving birth. That means no children would have mothers, and they would be much less likely to survive into adulthood. Women who gave birth earlier, to smaller, less developed babies, were more likely to survive, and although their newborns needed more attention and nurturing, their children had better odds of becoming adults. Thus it was those 'premature birth' genes that were carried into future generations. As you'll be aware, even with a gestation of only nine months, giving birth is still a precarious, critical undertaking. Over three hundred thousand women die in labour every year, even in countries with advanced maternity practices and western medicine. Making a baby is the most dangerous thing a woman can do, and that is the cost of our minds.

Human babies need more parental investment than any other animal on the planet; we require feeding, protecting and educating much, much longer than any other ape. We are born completely incapable and take years and years of growth before we can keep ourselves alive without assistance. A woman cannot raise a child all by herself. I'd be annoyed at that statement if I was reading this – I come from a single-parent family where my mum did everything. Perhaps you did too? My mum probably *could* put up a tent in the African savannah with a baby on her tit and placenta dangling between her legs, she's that kind of lady. When I say that one parent isn't enough, I'm talking about pre-civilised times in a hunter-gatherer society. We have stocked fridges now, and pizza delivery and hardly any wolves, so it's easier – although, if my mum's temper was anything to go by, still really really hard.

Being born so (comparatively) early means human babies spend all their early life lying about growing their brains. They make a MILLION new brain cells every twenty seconds and this can use up to four fifths of their body's energy. If I was going to design baby clothes I'd put the slogan 'Mind-growing is mind-blowing!' on the front in neon, and then on the back a flashing LED screen showing the brain's gradual expansion with a trail running underneath saying 'Five times larger than expected for an animal our size!!!!!!' People would say those clothes were unsafe for young children and prohibitively expensive, and they would be right. So I'd go out of business, having lost all the savings I'd invested. I'd have to go back to temp work, where I'd cry at my desk and eat yogurts. This sad story is just one example of the great things brains can come up with!

So human babies are rubbish at taking care of themselves. They can't hold their own head up for about six months and they have a hole in their skull where the bones are growing together called the fontanelle. They require CONSTANT and INTENSE attention which is super-demanding. When a chimp gives birth, her baby can grip immediately, so she can chuck it on her back and swing away through the trees straight to ~~the cocktail bar~~ some other trees. Human mothers are encumbered by the care their offspring need, and in pre-civilised times would require the assistance of a family group. The families who helped each other and worked together in childrearing would have been much more likely to have their kids reach adulthood. Hence we've evolved to have strong, loyal feelings towards family members. The genes of the isolated were lost.

The greatest factor affecting whether a child survived her

infancy was mothering, and so much mothering was needed – more than one mother could give. Human babies needed at least two mums, and thus our species evolved a new, second kind of mum, a boy one, sometimes referred to as a 'dad'.

It works like this: a baby with two caregivers has a much higher chance of surviving. Just like a male's large size being a strength in polygynous species, the ability to bond with sexual partners and their offspring is a strength in ours. And the more our ancestors bonded, the better they did. The more they loved each other, the harder they worked to provide and keep everyone alive and stop baby falling in the river and things like that. The genes for pair bonding have strengthened generation upon generation for millennia. The parents who wanted to be together with their partners were the evolutionary victors. And it's a huge set of emotions and compulsions. It's not a muted 'Oh, I should probably help out, that's the right thing to do' but a bellowed 'I WILL DIE WITHOUT THIS PERSON THEY ARE BETTER THAN ANYTHING ELSE THAT HAS EVER EXISTED I CAN WATCH THEM GOING TO THE TOILET AND STILL WANT TO KISS THEM OH GOD OH GOD MY BODY IS NOT BIG ENOUGH TO WITHSTAND THE FORCE OF MY FEELINGS.'

Love.

The difficulty of keeping human infants alive has necessitated the deep, terrible way we fall in love with each other; you have to *really* like someone not to run away into the forest when they're holding a crying shitty baby. None of us would be here without love, our species would have diminished and disappeared. There is no fate, there are no souls or stars crossing or 'The Ones'. Our powerful emotion is an inbuilt survival tactic. It's a primordial glue, sticking us together to continue the species. You're correct, I *should* design Valentine's Day cards.

I know it's more magical and less sciencey when you *feel* love, but that's why it works. Reduce the power, turn the volume down and humanity would have died out. Imagine a world with no human beings: the planet would be unpolluted, there'd be no SeaWorld, no factory farming, no animal testing, thousands fewer extinctions and many more rainforests – who'd want that?

So we bond, we love each other, and now we know *why*, it is time to ask *how*.

Let's talk about magnetic resonance imaging, often referred to as an MRI or sometimes as an *f*MRI (the *f* stands for 'functional', I know that because I asked someone). If you've never had an MRI, you just get in a big tube and lie down at the hospital. They tell you they can see your brain and which parts of it you are using at certain times and the machine makes a lot of cranking noises and you feel claustrophobic and you want to move but you're not allowed or your brain pictures will be blurry and you get quite frightened and think, 'I wonder if this was a clever trick to kill me? Pretend to be an experiment on comedians' brains and then zap me while I'm in here?' Then you think, 'OH SHIT, could they see me having that thought?' and then 'Could they see me having that one?' and then you think, 'I'd better not picture anything rude,' and so you think about bottoms non-stop for twenty minutes until they let you out again and you're not dead which is a relief and they show you pictures of your brain and it's all there, which is another one.

Here is a picture of my brain thinking about bottoms. It is my favourite photo that has ever been taken of me:

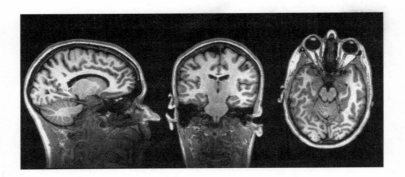

Scientists have conducted experiments in MRIs to find out what parts of the brain are activated when we feel love. They showed participants pictures of their lovers and WHOA their brains lit up like a brain in an MRI. The two most active areas were found to be the caudate, which is involved with cravings, and the ventral tegmental, which produces dopamine.

Dopamine is a neurotransmitter you should know about. It affects pleasure and motivation. Technically it is a chemical reward from your brain, but it just feels like happiness. Imagine natural highs: helping a frail old man across the road, finding £5 on the floor, flying a kite while a cute puppy kisses you – these things cause dopamine to be released and then you feel chilled and amazing. Drugs like cocaine also release dopamine, which is why some people like putting it up their nose so much and don't realise how boring it makes them at parties.

The MRI experiments revealed that when people are in love, the interaction of dopamine becomes heightened; it gets *greedy*. The ventral tegmental floods the caudate with dopamine and the caudate signals the ventral tegmental to send it more dopamine please in a delightful cycle and the result is intense elation.

> *Roses are red,*
> *Violets are blue*
> *I get a big hit of dopamine*
> *When I see you!*

This all-encompassing, delicious, dopamine-fuelled romantic love is experienced as something you crave and can't get enough of; you'll never be full, you'll never be sated and you'll never feel more alive. It's a cascade of chemicals that makes you *need* to be near your chosen person. It is the exact same brain process as addiction, and that's how it's experienced; consuming your attention, taking over your dreams and all your waking thoughts in between. Behaviour may verge on the obsessive and it can be physically painful to be separated from your love – bodily reactions don't get stronger or more compelling than this. Such feelings may arise during a sexual relationship or inspire you to start one, and TA-DA, you've been paired up all nice and ready for child-rearing.

'Er, Miss Pascoe,' says Laura with her hand in the air, 'but I'm on the pill actually so my body doesn't need to bond me to sex partners.'

This is the interesting thing: we have sex all the time that we know won't result in children – because we're using contraception, or we're post-menopausal, or our boyfriend is a woman – but our body doesn't recognise that. Our brain will produce neurotransmitters and hormones and all of the accompanying physiological cacophony because this is what evolution has programmed it to do. We have not evolved a 'non-reproductive sex' switch, because there would have been no genetic advantage in doing so.

'What about unrequited love?' asks Stephanie sadly, drawing a picture of Ronan Keating.

If you love someone who doesn't love you back or maybe someone you haven't even met, the brain reacts in the same way. Think of it as motivational. You've picked someone to pair-bond with and you're getting dopamine hits as an incentive to solidify the relationship. Although this brain function evolved to influence and strengthen pair bonding, it is often hijacked by non-reproductive loves. The caudate and ventral tegmental areas have been shown all lit up in the MRIs of very religious people talking about their god, and it facilitates the 'relationships' people have with animals or inanimate objects as well as adulation of celebrities. In such instances, the intense emotion and euphoria surrounding the object of love will be as real as for those in consensual relationships with actual humans who exist. Perhaps knowing this should make us more sympathetic to each other and our crazy non-rational love lives. For instance there is a Swedish woman who 'married' the Berlin Wall in 1979. Her name is Eija-Riitta Berliner-Mauer – that's right, she took his name. She's been interviewed talking about her 'husband', and it is easy to laugh at the things she says, like how sexy he was and how much fun they had together. But then I remember that her feelings are as real as anyone else's and how strange it must have been on the day the Berlin Wall was torn down; everyone in the world celebrating her husband's murder and the desecration of his corpse while she alone was—

'Okay then,' asks Poppy, pointedly getting us back on topic, 'if this bonding thing is true, why didn't I fall in love with all the guys I've had sex with?'

Everyone in the class laughs because it sounds like Poppy has done it with loads of people. 'SHUT UP EVERYONE,' I say strictly, 'Poppy has asked a really, really important question.'

If our body thinks all sex could make us pregnant, shouldn't *all* sex make us start pair-bonding? I've had it both ways – not an innuendo – I've had sexual experiences with boys I wasn't really into, but afterwards I got a post-coital crush on them. A bit obsessed. And even years later, if I bump into them I'm very aware of needing their attention and wanting them to like me and I HATE it. It makes me feel vulnerable and rejected and see-through. I might not have wanted them to be my boyfriend, but I needed *them* to want to be my boyfriend, or at least to see me again, and I was a bit hurt when they didn't. I would ideally list the full names of the boys who rejected me here and I'll be honest, I thought the whole point of getting to write a book was REVENGE ON THOSE WHO HAVE WRONGED ME but apparently this has LEGAL RAMIFICATIONS and I'm not allowed. I'll save it for my Oscars acceptance speech. If I happen to die before I win my award for Best Actor in a YouTube Video, there is a list of men hidden inside a spotted teapot in my kitchen. Find it, read it out at my funeral and ensure the whole event is televised. Please. Or I'll haunt you.

I'll tell you about one guy from ages ago. I worked with him at the Millennium Dome, which gives you a clue of exactly how ages ago it was. I hadn't really noticed him but he asked me out on a date and I had never been on a proper date before so I said yes to be grown-up. We went to a bar and then for a long walk and I enjoyed myself fine and we went back to his flat because it was nearest. I was on my period but didn't find a good time to mention it, one never wants to seem presumptuous –

ROB (*casual*)
Would you like to have another drink at my place?

SARA (*smiling*)
Yes please, and also, in unrelated information, my womb is currently shedding its lining.

Later in his bed, once it was clear that we were going to have sex, I was too embarrassed to say anything, because we were already having sex and he didn't seem to notice, then we fell asleep. In the morning bright sun shot between the blinds and onto the murder scene. A bloody hand print on the wall. Streaks on his white covers and sheets. 'Ha ha ha,' I laughed encouragingly and alone. He asked me to leave so I asked if I could stay and he said no. And all of a sudden I really liked him, and I checked my phone constantly that day, and that night I sent him psychic messages to text me. But he didn't and when I saw him at work he ignored me and a week later he started going out with someone else in our department. She once told me her boobs were getting bigger from all the sex she was having and I had jealousy about her breasts and her boyfriend. A few years ago I would *still* think about him occasionally so I friend-requested him on Facebook and he must still have been thinking about me too because he replied, 'Where do I know you from?' So I'm glad I ruined his bedsheets, good old bloody womb. And now I don't care about him at all and can't even remember him and what was I even talking about?

Oh yes, the point I am making is that I liked him so much more *after* sex than before. He felt really important and relevant and I suffered seeing him and being blanked by him and watching him kiss someone else. But I've had the same experience reversed as well. Make yourself comfortable as Old Sara P. reads you another tale from her *Sexual Anecdotes* (Volume One, 1998–2002).

I lived in a big shared house with nine other people, one of whom was Italian and couldn't speak English. His name was Tomaso, and whenever I passed him in the corridor he would giggle because he was stoned and say '*Ciao bambina*,' which was super-hot. We started holding hands when we watched television, and we wrote each other letters that we translated sat side by side with an Italian–English dictionary. One evening Tomaso sat on my bed and drew pictures of Sideshow Bob from *The Simpsons* and they were so good that I kissed him. He then mounted me straight away and started pulling my trousers down. I wanted him to use a condom but was struggling to find the word in Italian, and he laughed and kept repeating '*protezione*', which, if there had been a mood, would have killed it. And then we had sex while my inner monologue congratulated me: 'Isn't it amazing that he seems so into this while you feel absolutely nothing?' He came and went. And the next morning he was back and I was saying '*non*' and he was miming and trying to tell me something. I can't be sure what it was, my best guesses are that he used to be a food reviewer for a magazine *or* he'd given fellatio for money. I avoided him for days as he put letters and Sideshow Bob pictures under my door and when he knocked I pretended to be asleep. Then I arranged to move out, and did; bin bags of belongings in a taxi cab while Tomaso was at work one day.

With Tomaso I liked him a lot *less* after sex than before – I more than disliked him: he repelled me, I wished he didn't exist. And it wasn't just because the sex was of poor quality, I've had rubbish lays that I still fancied madly afterwards. I've had *loads* of those. #bragging

Why do we get attached to some sex partners and not others? Is it:

a) Astrology.

b) God decides.

c) Parental investment.

d) For compatibility take letters of both surnames, give numerical worth from alphabet position then add, divide and show as a %.

Yep, the answer is still parental investment. Having a child with someone is such a monumental drain of time and energy, such a precious and precarious expenditure, that we are very fussy about who we undertake it with, which translates into 'who we are willing to bond with'. Remember you have evolved to have these feelings because sex *can* make babies, not because you *are* literally having them or planning to.

To simplify this using my examples, with Rob my body decided 'Game on, baby daddy, he be a keeper,' and with Tomaso my body yelled, 'Close it down, nothing doing, beep beep beep, this vehicle is reversing.'

There are trillions of factors that influence these unspoken, unconscious decisions and they occur every time we sleep with a new person. We evaluate what our sex partner is worth in a measured equation of resources, traits and genetics – in your face, romance! There are some obvious things that might put you off somebody – ill health, bad hygiene, terrible temper. And there are some very shallow things that you can't help finding attractive – money, the nice things bought with money, and expensive trousers that he got with some of his loads of money. You're not a bitch, this is evolution's fault, it is babies having massive brains' fault. If, after the internal sums of your mate's possible contributions to childcare, your body decides you can do better . . . off you run. Not literally, unless this is a Julia Roberts movie,* but you will be uninterested in bonding with them any further or having sex with them again.

There are tons of qualities (aside from money) that make people attractive for dating past mating** – kindness, generosity, strong arms, wittiness, being great at crosswords; your body will respond positively to many traits. Apparently you'll also be judging your partner/lover/guy asleep on you on the night bus via his pheromones – I say 'apparently' because while some books talk very confidently about pheromones and how they influence our behaviours, other people are equally confident that they are unproven. Not their existence – pheromones are airborne hormones so we'll definitely have them – the doubt is over whether we are able to smell them . . . I know, I'm not a science guy so I can't tell you the truth. And the science guys all disagree, so they can't help us either. Let us be interested but reserved in our enthusiasm while we consider what evidence there seems to be.

In pheromone studies they get people to sniff sweaty T-shirts

---

* I'm worried this reference is too old. You see, Julia Roberts once made a movie called *The Runaway Bride*. It reunited her with Richard Gere after that successful film they made about how fun and sexy it is to be a prostitute. It was different in the olden days, you wouldn't remember, anyway, just insert a film reference from your generation in here – perhaps 'Miley Cyrus' has been in a film?

** I will of course be trademarking that. For my baby clothing line.

and then rate the accompanying photographs for attractiveness and they've found that participants are often most attracted to people whose immune system is different from their
own. It's not conscious, but the smell of certain people makes
your loins go schwing* and it's claimed that this allure is caused
by your body knowing that sex with that partner would produce healthier children with a more varied and effective au-
to-immune system. It's real-life sci-fi: we might be able to *smell*
whether we'd have strong, fit children with someone. Personally, I love the idea of pheromones because it makes sense of
the non-rational lust that some people provoke in me. Also I
really enjoy the smell of my boyfriend's armpits and I'd rather
be a great pheromone reader than super-gross. Dear Scientists, more experiments and human** study in this area please,
Love Sara.

So after sex with someone you might be infatuated with
them or you might never want to see them again, yes Laura,
your hand's up again—

LAURA
If, in pre-civilised, pre-contraceptive times—

SARA
Yes dear, get to the point.

---

* Or appropriate word for arousal from your generation. Do One Direction have
patter? I don't know why I'm so sure you're younger than me. Do young people
even read books now? Aren't they all Wii-ing on their Segways and taking Meow
Meow?
** I say human because quite often scientists do animal studies which are 1) cruel
and 2) non-transferable. If we want to find out about humans, knowing about
rabbits, cats and mice is virtually irrelevant. 'Oh I wonder what effect caffeine
has on the human brain?' 'Well, we just gave one hundred cups of coffee to this
beagle and now it's dead.' 'GREAT, will you write this up for the *New Scientist* or
shall I?' That was a short excerpt from my new theatre piece *Stop the Inanity (and
the Torture)*. It stars me and Brian May.

LAURA

– if all sex could result in pregnancy, wouldn't women have evolved to try and hold on to *any* man they'd had sex with, even if he was rubbish, just in case?

SARA

Not necessarily, not if there were *other* men around to have sex with.

LAURA looks disapproving.

SARA

You can tell your facial expression to shut up, mate. Human beings are mammals, yes? And we gestate our young internally, which means sperm swim in, and nine months later, baby comes out.

Nobody SEES the egg becoming fertilised, which means that if the mother has mated with a few men in a short time-frame, even she won't know who the biological father is. Nowadays you could get a DNA test and go on *Jeremy Kyle* for a good shout, but we're still thinking African savannah 40,000 years BC, and exploitative television hasn't been invented yet.

It's called 'paternity certainty', it's a wonderful phrase to sing or rap and it's vitally important to the evolution of our species. Or rather, paternity *uncertainty* is. It means that a woman might have sex with one man, reject him due to low mate potential, then later (could be minutes, could be weeks) have sex with some other dude. And she likes the second guy cos he has a cool nest and is good at peeling mangoes and they become involved and bonded and then bring up a baby together, which, genetically, could belong to the first man.

But mum has made an excellent evolutionary choice, as no matter who it is related to, this baby will have a greater chance of survival with the father who has higher mate potential. Paternity uncertainty means that, evolutionarily, a woman might do well to have a few fellows around her wondering 'Is it mine?' She ensures more resources for herself that way and is better protected, she—

YOU AGAIN

Excuse me, Mrs Contradictions, but earlier you were going on about how body dimorphism proves we're a monogamous species and now you're saying women do it all over the place and then attempt to sucker some guy with a better flat into bringing up baby—

Well I don't think that's *exactly* what I said, but to go back to dimorphism: the 1.1 difference between human genders suggests that male size wasn't very important for mate selection, BUT there is a complication to this evidence and it involves our colossal brain. Some scientists argue that any body dimorphism that might have existed in humans would have been balanced out when the brain began its exponential growth. Huge male babies would have been impossible to birth, mother and baby would have died, those genes were lost and the sizes of the two genders became more similar as a result. It's very interesting to consider, and either way, it's important to remember that this 1.1 does not guarantee fidelity. It places us somewhere between the complete polyamory of chimpanzees and the definite monogamy of gibbons; human pair bonds are not the end of our mating life, nor are they as sexually exclusive as we might like – which the next chapter will explore.

'But please,' you beg me, with a thirst for summary and conclusion, 'tell us, Sara, what is LOVE?'

It's *so* complicated and obviously we all experience it differently, but here you are – for your quote book:

'Love is a compulsive motivation towards a certain person ruled by evolutionary selection bias and a neurochemical reward system' (Pascoe 2016).

Let me know if you want that printed up on a baseball cap.

What's Mine Is You

For me, understanding love scientifically helps. It makes sense
of something that is otherwise illogical. It doesn't answer all
my questions, but I find its objectivity soothing. For a long
time, I kind of defined myself through my first relationship. I
obsessed about it for years, running over memories for post-
humous clues – what had gone wrong? What had I done? If
you and I were drunk in a Wetherspoon's I'd tell you the long
version, but we're sober in a book, so here's a short account
without me crying:

I was sixteen when I first loved someone. We met in a college production of *A Midsummer Night's Dream.* He played a
small servant part and always made everyone laugh with his
deep bow and flouncy exit. I played Puck, on a skateboard,
which was incredibly ground-breaking. At the after-show party
we kissed and then he told me he'd once seen a man shoot
himself, so we went to talk all night in my mum's garden. I
lost my virginity a week later (same dude) and stopped going
home unless he was with me. I only slept where he slept, I only
went to class if he insisted on going to his. I'd get euphoric sitting in the passenger seat of his car or turning round
to look at him after I'd switched the kettle on. I missed him
when he insisted on going to the toilet alone. He was my Ted
Hughes! My Sartre! My Prince Albert!* We were together for

* The man, not the genital jewellery.**
** Unless penis piercing works as a metaphor here? 'My love was like a small hole
in my—' No, it doesn't work.

ten months and seven days. We only spent one night apart. Then at a karaoke night, while I was on stage singing 'Never Ever' by All Saints, I saw him kissing someone else. I ran out, he didn't follow. He was already going out with the other girl. He quit college to avoid me. I slept in my mum's bed for six months.

I'm too old to keep going on and on about it, it's over half my lifetime ago, it should be hazy and irrelevant. It's a year of memories I wish would fade but they became core bricks in the building of my being. Anyway, I have a preoccupation with cheating, fidelity, faithfulness. I don't trust, and I am ruined. NO, not *ruined*, that's too dramatic. I guess I blame all the failed relationships that followed on that first one. And I shouldn't call them failures, but that's how it feels.

During my grieving process I liked my mum. She never told me to be strong or stop crying and she occasionally offered to give me things, which is how we express love in my family. 'Oh that is *awful*, bloody hell, do you want this dress?' My mum was still angry with my dad and now I appreciated why; the betrayal, the broken promises, the breakdown of certainty. Mum had confronted Dad before the divorce, asked him, 'Are you having an affair?' and he had met her gaze and replied, 'No. No I am *not*.' And then later she found out that he *had* been with another woman and she was so upset:

GAIL
WHY DID YOU LIE TO ME?

DEREK
I didn't lie, I wasn't having *an* affair . . .

This story is recounted as a family joke, a witticism, a funny thing my dad once said rather than the remarkable behaviour of a sociopath:

DEREK

. . . I was having seven.

Now you know my parents' silly names, leaving us to wonder how on earth a man called Derek persuaded so many women to have an affair with him.

I was a child and when all this was happening I hadn't understood the emotions. There's a photograph taken when I was six: I'm in a pink leotard and my sister Cheryl's dressed as a cat and Mum is wearing a silver dress, pregnant with Kristyna. I have my arms up, posing for the camera, but Mum is looking at the floor. She has Princess Diana face, pained but keeping it together. We were having a Christmas party at Aunty Sandra's and my dad arrived with a lady called Janice and I told my mum I thought Janice was *beautiful*, then the photo was taken. I feel very guilty now. I wish I'd realised how sad she was – I'd have tried to give her something.

A decade later and my very first boyfriend, let's call him Colin because that's his name,* Colin had betrayed me. I wasn't a child any more and I got it; Dad was a *bastard*, Colin was a *bastard*. They were selfish, they were liars, they were manipulative and – 'Oh *no*,' said my mother. She stopped me and corrected me. 'It wasn't their fault, they're not *bad* people, they were simply being *all men*.'

---

* He lives in Japan now and hopefully won't find out about this book, but if you do happen to be reading this in Tokyo please tippex out each 'Colin' and write 'Julius' or something. There is also a little piece of legislation called privacy law that means I have to disguise anyone I'm talking about so please can you imagine Colin with a moustache and a beret.

In a series of informal lectures that I like to call 'The End of Hope' Mum told me how men[*] couldn't help being attracted to lots of women, that they were built this way, it was biological destiny.

My mum is really clever, she studied for a PhD about eight years ago and insists on being called 'Dr Newmarch' even in restaurants and at bus stops. She has always been interested in how the body works, genetics, nature versus nurture and all that. She is all at once the stupidest, most intelligent person I know. She'll take a break from studying Chinese economics or the structure of the genome to ponder why it's only European countries taking part in Eurovision, where the stars go in winter and how a *character* in *Coronation Street* is going to cope with an *actor* from *Coronation Street*'s sex scandal.

SARA
I think 'Sally' will be alright, Mum—

GAIL (*worried*)
She's already been through so much.

During 'The End of Hope' my mum excused Colin's behaviour in evolutionary terms. While my ideal parent would have been round his house threatening him with a hockey stick until he agreed to go back out with me, my mum was elaborating about sexuality; how it was the most powerful instinct that humans had, it ensured the replication of genes, the survival of the species, it was responsible for the majority of human social behaviour. Sex was at the heart of everything.

---

[*] Sorry my mum was being so heterocentric here. Obviously loads of men don't fancy women at all.

Obviously no one wants to hear this kind of stuff from their mother, *so* gross, but this was not new information. I was half-way through Psychology A-level, I'd spent a year with Sigmund Freud lecturing me about sex.* The only preparation for your mother shouting 'BECAUSE WE ALL WANT SEX' is to hear it first from a long-dead Viennese man. I'd spent a lot of mental energy trying to disprove Freud. I was desperate to dis-cover human behaviours that were *not* sexually related so that in class I'd be able to go, 'What about ice skating?' and every-one would applaud and Geoffrey, my teacher, would say, 'Oh yes ice skating has nothing to do with sex, Sara is right – let's give her ten certificates!' Except that ice skating is a demon-stration of talent and skill and body strength, all attractive qualities, and Freud believed that all artists were consciously or subconsciously trying to get people to fancy them – so that is not a good example.

Try it, see if you can find something in your life that can-not possibly be connected to sex. You think of huge things like death, and you go, 'Yeah actually, death has *nothing* to do with sex . . . except, oh, I guess sex is how your genes escape death and continue after you have gone. It is our mortal-ity that propels us to procreate and sex is a death antidote and – okay.' So you try little things instead: 'brushing my teeth', 'going to the cinema', 'celebrating Halloween'. None of those things has *anything* to do with reproduction . . . ex-cept that personal hygiene is important in attracting a mate and people go to the cinema on dates and films depict all kinds of amorousness and arousal, but Halloween, there you

---

* I mean I was *reading* Freud, not that he was my actual lecturer, I'm not that old and if I were, I don't think the father of psychoanalysis would've been slumming it at Havering Sixth Form College.

go, that's a fiesta of fear and nothing more and OH GOD
LOOK AT THE OUTFITS I've never seen anything sexier.
You've lost another round in 'Find a Thing That Has No Sex
in It'™.

So while I wasn't surprised at Mum's 'sex is everything' ra-
tionale, her new information, her revelation, was that men and
women had separate and distinct sexual programming. Mum
explained that the strategies that enabled our ancestors to successfully procreate were gender-specific; what we wanted from
each other was different, more than different – contradictory.

We've considered parental investment already while we ac-
knowledged the effort required to successfully raise a human
child. What we have to recognise now is that *becoming* a parent
is different for each of the sexes. Our physiology has given
us very unbalanced roles and this is thought to influence our
sexual behaviour. Mum put it in rather brutal terms: 'Men
shag around, women try and stop them,' she told me, nostrils flaring, like an angry pony. And this wasn't just a jaded
divorcee's personal opinion, this was a crude summary of the
anthropological explanations she'd been reading. Let me try
and explain it in a politer form, while attempting to control
my inherited nostrils.

To be a father, a man needs to deliver some semen inside
a woman. This can take less than a minute – we've all been
there, am I right, ladies? But to be a mother, a woman must
gestate a foetus inside her body for nine months; she will experience sickness, vulnerability and pain before the mortal
danger of childbirth. She will require a high-protein, calorific
diet despite being physically restricted from obtaining one. In
a hunter-gatherer society she will need to breastfeed her child
for three to four years.

Let's have a quick look at the maths there: one minute versus nine months plus four years = a huge injustice of input and effort.

The human form of reproduction makes it possible for a man to get lots and lots of women pregnant. Men make trillions of sperm, it's a constantly replenishing* resource, and they can (technically) have lots of sex with different people throughout the day and night. In evolutionary terms, the human males who had the most sex with the most partners would leave the most descendants. It's a probability game and an evolutionary advantage. The male offspring of these philanderers would inherit genes that made them fancy a huge variety of sex partners and the cycle would continue. Generation upon generation, the sexiest men would be rewarded with more offspring, who would in turn produce more offspring, *hakuna matata*. If we put our modern morality on the windowsill for a moment we could applaud these virile men and their wonderful species-continuing abilities. WELL DONE, LADS, YOU ARE VERITABLE SPERM FOUNTAINS!

What of our female ancestors?

Well, a woman who mates with several men cannot produce more children than a woman who has only mated with one – they both gestate and raise offspring equally slowly. No amount of sex partners can significantly change the number of descendants a woman would leave, so desiring a variety of lovers is not an evolutionary advantage for her. Genes for female promiscuity are *not* passed to female offspring at a higher incidence. Further to this, anthropologists tell us that because pregnancy and childrearing are so expensive in

---

* And delicious.**
** I'm joking.

terms of resources, the woman who is not pair-bonded may be less successful at childrearing. The primitive female who didn't bond with those she slept with, who high-fived and yelled 'Thanks for that' before climbing back into her own tree, her children would have had lower parental investment and thus a decreased survival rate. She was a sex loser, so fewer of her genes were passed on to future generations. Instead the genes for deep attachment were inherited by the female children of women who knew how to successfully hang on to a man – their children's survival rate increasing with parental investment.

Put your hands down, we're not clapping this – it's too depressing.

To reiterate: the ideal mating strategy for men is constant seduction, multiple partners and all round sexy sexing times and the ideal mating strategy for women is 'For god's sake don't let that man go.' I wanted to *protest* this, I wanted to march up and down with a sign covered in expletives and shout at – who? Whose fault is it? Oestrogen? Darwin? Evolution, I would like to speak with your manager. How will any heterosexual people ever be happy? Men have this vibrant, exciting sexuality and woman apparently have nothing but a desperation to curb it.

Remember, my mum was telling me this, I was seventeen – AND I HATED IT yet I couldn't prove it wrong. It *seemed* to make perfect sense. If I scanned my surroundings, Essex *circa* 1998, it was a panorama of girls trying to get boys to like them; we bleached and browned and starved ourselves while the boys clustered outside Threshers or near funfairs waiting to accept or reject us. I was aware of male sexuality being, like, a proper *necessity*. They were open about their libidos, they'd exclaim the need for a wank or shag in the casual way I might express a yearning for an appetite-suppressing cigarette.

So, though distressed, I believed it. This was truth, men and women were doomed to disappoint each other. There were gender agendas, fidelity versus freedom. I'd been naive with Colin, but heartbreak was my education and I would not be fooled again. I began subsequent relationships with cynicism and Armageddon mutterings, slamming down cocktails and exclaiming, '*Well*, it's not going to go anywhere so let's just have fun,' with the un-fun eyes of someone who died inside when the person opposite didn't contradict my 'not going anywhere' statement. I had a few small boyfriends and then a bigger boyfriend but there was no excitement; as soon as a guy liked me back, I prepared myself for the ending. I thought I was being very clever and protecting myself, I thought I was a realist and could now have a great old time without getting hurt.

If this was a film there'd be a montage here: bright lights, loud music, me buying drinks for a succession of fresh-faced men. And then it would cut to me in my thirties, living alone in a flat that doesn't have wi-fi, decoupaging a chest of drawers with the words 'I'm so lonely'. Then a dinosaur would run in and eat me, because this is a really great film. From the dinosaur's belly you'd hear a grumbling sound and then me:

SARA (*O/S in belly*)
MY CYNICISM DIDN'T SAVE ME!

Without hope and expectation things were *not* fun. My flings weren't flippant and pleasure-fuelled, they were pessimistic and miserable, like spending your day at Alton Towers waiting by the exit because you know it's gonna close eventually. There you stand, lying to yourself that you're exactly where you want to be, packed and ready to get out before anyone's asked you to leave.

ALL MEN CHEAT was my mantra; I lectured in it, I warned my friends, I was not invited to *any* weddings. 'It's not failed morality but a reproductive necessity,' I would explain to my boyfriends while they protested their innocence. 'You can't help yourself,' I'd patronise, 'but you must stop lying about it.' You can imagine how great I was to go out with – punishing my partners with mistrust and shouting and no evidence of unfaithfulness bar their Y chromosome. I shook my head when friends insisted their lovers 'weren't like other men'. 'Assume he's cheating and see if you still want to be with him' was my relationship advice. I felt very sorry for my dad's new wife – and for Hillary Clinton. 1998 was a bad year for her too, probably worse because she had the press to contend with. There's such personal shame in being cheated on, like you failed by not being enough for someone. I didn't like the disrespectful way newspapers wrote about Hillary, or how they wrote about Monica Lewinsky like this was her fault. And people seemed so shocked that a PRESIDENT would do it: how could he risk the most powerful job in the world for some heavy petting? But I understood it. 'Monkeys, mate, we're all monkeys,' I said it then, I say it now. How can the president of the United States be immune to his genetic programming when nobody else is?

If we fast-forward ten years of my life we'll see a long on– off relationship interspersed with lots of short relationships speeding past blurrily. We stop briefly: it's late 2007 and I start stand-up after a particularly hurtful break-up. We watch a bit of the gig and it's terrible, I'm bitter and too drunk to be on stage. Fast-forward another five years, we see my work improve but not my romantic life, blur blur blur, now stop – it's 2013 and I'm having a conversation with comedian John Gordillo outside a club in Hampstead. He's smoking a roll-up and I'm watching jealously, trying not to ask for a puff on it. I'm telling him all about how I don't believe in monogamy. He doesn't believe in it either. He recommends a book called *Sex at Dawn*, says it will blow my mind, or something equally emphatic. Skip through a couple of weeks now as I order the book from an ethical tax-paying online bookshop and read it. Play in real time as CGI effects show my skull bursting open and brains and blood spurting all over the room while my eyes roll around on the carpet. Then a dinosaur runs in and from my mouth, which is hanging off, I say, 'Please don't eat me, I have so much to live for . . . I just found out that *women have a sexuality.*' Then my headless body and the velociraptor do it.

It was a totally new idea to me. Despite all my talking and thinking about sex, I'd never considered that women had their own sexuality. I'd assumed it was an accompaniment to male sexuality, a tangent, an offshoot, or worse, something we *pretended* to have in order to turn men on. To begin understanding that women had our own desires that existed only for our own pleasure was – well you saw, my eyes fell out of my face and my mind was sprayed everywhere.

I've no idea how you'll be responding to this information. Perhaps you've fallen off your bus seat being all like 'WHAT? We have a – excuse me? I can't see a sexuality anywhere upon my person, there's certainly no room in my trousers. Where would this *sexuality* be? Surely this is all a silly rumour put about by *More* magazine?' Or perhaps you're the opposite, a

sexually realised and satisfied woman, extinguishing your cig-
arillo in the man you're straddling's piña colada and exclaiming, 'How can this idiot have taken thirty-two years to realise
she was sexual?' But in French.

I regret that I spent so many years fascinated and terrified
by male sexuality while uncovering absolutely nothing about
my own. For a decade and a half I believed that men wanted
sex, and the most that women could want was to let them have
it. Men had horny sex drives and women were the boring gatekeepers, deciding who we let in. I knew that being sexy was
important for women, oh yes, it was completely paramount.
You needed men to fancy you – that was your currency. I spent
my twenties spouting all kinds of shit about a woman's sexuality being powerful 'because she can, like, use it to manipulate
men'. I want to puke in old me's face, I want to fight her and
her docility in a car park. If men have stuff we need or want,
we don't pole-dance around them hoping they'll start whack-
ing off and drop it – we restructure society so that women are
able to achieve everything they want and need for themselves.
But you know that, sorry for shouting. What I'm trying to say
is, for me 'sexiness' was a pretend thing that I did to make
boys like me. I had no grasp of sexual desire, I'd never noticed its absence in my decisions, I never thought about it because I'd only ever wanted to be wanted. I was thirty-two and I
had never successfully masturbated. I had no sexual fantasies.
I enjoyed sex in a detached and reassuring way; 'he still likes
me', 'he's into this', 'this means he won't leave me' and 'this
is what I should be doing', like all the magazines had told
me. Sex often felt like acting – always being super-aware of
whether *he* was enjoying himself and never realising that I was
supposed to.

But now I knew better. Thanks to *Sex at Dawn* I found a teacher, an educator, a substance to lead me through an exploration of the feminine side of the evolution story. My guru, my mentor, my informant, was sperm. YES, it turned out I'd been wasting it previously, mopping it up with my pyjamas or washing it straight out of my hair, when I should have been scooping the jellied off-whiteness up to my face and whispering, 'What is it you have to tell me? What it is that you know?'

It starts with a man, I KNOW ALL SPERM STARTS WITH A MAN, but this man worked at Liverpool University, his name is Geoff Parker and Wikipedia says his birthday is 24 May so we know he's a Gemini. Dr Parker made all kinds of discoveries about how sperm behave when you watch them under a microscope and those findings were developed by science writer Robin Baker into a theory called 'sperm competition'. No it's not Channel 5's new gameshow but a claim that when the semen of different men are mixed together the sperm *fight*. They battle, they go to war and attempt to destroy each other.

ASTONISHED TRUMPET

According to Baker, men have two kinds of sperm: 'egg-getters' and 'kamikaze'. The egg-getters try to get to an ovum and fertilise it, as the name would suggest. The second type, kamikaze, are slightly smaller, their heads are elongated, they cannot fertilise an egg. Instead their job is to stop any rival egg-getters, those that originated inside another man. Some kamikaze sperm work by blocking, curling up in mucus to stop enemy sperm travelling through, and others are fighters, recognising competitor egg-getters thanks to ~~tele-pathy coloured shirts~~ hormonal signals, headbutting them and emitting poisons.

It is baffling to think about and so I can't stop thinking about it. Sperm can live for up to five days inside a woman's reproductive system, so if I had four male partners ejaculate inside me over the weekend a full-scale battle would be raging in my womb and tubes when I caught the train on Monday morning. And I wouldn't be able to *feel* it and nobody could tell by looking at me unless I was wearing my 'Banged Four & Feeling like Agincourt' sweater. Yes of course I will make you one.

There is much debate on the subject of sperm competition and a huge amount of research still to be done on exactly how it works, if indeed it does occur in humans. Some very reputable scientists have argued against it, and it's currently rather an unfashionable subject. Is that because of how it reflects on our species or because the original theorists were not very well respected? I don't know. This is the difficulty with being an interested person with only secondary sources to rely upon; you can read one book and believe one thing and then read another that entirely contradicts the first. I need my own lab, a pipette and a gallon of fresh semen in order to find the truth – I'll set up a Kickstarter page.

Lots of animals do demonstrate versions of sperm competition. Sometimes this involves speedy sperm or congealing fluid or even the volume of sperm produced. It does seem that human males ejaculate more sperm into partners they really like. (Sara fans her face and acts coy: 'Oh my, with that extra 0.2 of a millilitre you're *spoiling* me.') Apparently men's bodies do a subconscious calculation of how many sperm to ejaculate into their partner based on the likelihood of needing to compete with other sperm. Studies have found that men ejaculate more when their partner has been away, when they are with a new (non-virgin) partner, and when they're having an affair and know their lover is sleeping with someone else. So if you've been with your boyfriend* all weekend gardening and watching movies and haven't so much as popped to the shops, when** you have sex he will ejaculate less than if you've just arrived back from three days at a conference called 'How to Admire Male Models'.

It's worth reminding ourselves that such physiological responses are subconscious and uncontrollable. Strategic ejaculation is not affected by wearing a condom and it is not a reflection of conscious mistrust or suspicions about a partner's infidelity. It's clever old nature seizing control and taking precautions.

But why does it need to?

If we understand that some sort of sperm competition exists, we have to accept the ramifications. Evolution is a responsive process rather than an inventive one. Strategic ejaculations and kamikaze sperm do not exist as a back-up, a 'just in case' or designed idea, but because for thousands of generations sperm that could fight and block may have been a reproductive advantage. If Gerald and Bernie both had sex with Doreen,*** Gerald would have a better chance of inseminating her if he had extra sperm. Bernie would have a decreased chance of insemination if he ejaculated less. This

---

* If your boyfriend is a woman, studies have found that she will never ejaculate more than zero sperm.
** If.
*** These names have been changed to protect their prehistoric privacy.

means our ancient female forebears may often have practised multi-partnering. If sperm evolved to fight it was because there were rival sperm to contend with.

So we need to re-evaluate what we've been told about female sexuality. Specifically, we need to forget what my mum told me, because *she was wrong*. And it's not the first time – Mum's been wrong several times before, like when she claimed the live *EastEnders* episode would be the best thing that ever happened to television or when she went out with that guy Paul* who stole our car, but at least in this instance it wasn't her fault.

The scientists who discovered evolution were Victorian men. They wore monocles and top hats. Their opinions and ideas were shaped by their society, as is true for all of us. The platform for communicating natural selection was built by men such as Charles Darwin and it was lopsided with male bias. Women in the nineteenth century were restricted and oppressed, generally dismissed as coy, chattering nurturers. Victorian culture was dominated by ideas of 'propriety', repression and public prudery. The combination of these factors resulted in observations about animals, apes and humans being made solely from a masculine perspective. Males were understood as active, while females were seen to be passive and non-instrumental. Even with examples such as peacocks where female choice in sexual selection had clearly and visibly affected evolution (males have big beautiful tails because peahens fancy the guys with the prettiest feathers) the possibility of female desire as a species-shaping factor was denied and ignored.

* Real name, long hair, lived near a dry ski slope. If you know him, tell him to pay my mum back.

The public construction of sex in Victorian times was that men enjoyed it while women derived their pleasure from conception and pregnancy (lucky us). With this weighted presumption, the results from animal studies met the new theory of evolution and created a model of human sexual behaviour that completely ignored female lust, desire and pleasure as forces that moulded our species. There was no ugly villain masterminding this, no dastardly plot to supress female sexuality, just some fallible and subjective scientists. If you believe without question that female animals derive no pleasure from mating, that intercourse is something they simply endure to beget children, then you'll ignore a jungle full of female animals displaying desire and initiating sex. They'll be invisible, obscured by foliage and preconception. And poor old western civilisation will spend decades entrenched in misunderstanding. We'll accept that sex is something that happens to women, something which is performed upon us rather than by us. Despite being fifty per cent of the cast we'll be props rather than actors. And we have been.

I try not to shout, as I don't think it's useful. People stop listening, they feel lectured. But this is the first point in the book where I have really wanted to open the window and BELLOW. I found the previous paragraph very difficult to write as I kept welling with fury. I wanted to underline things thirty times in red pen, I wanted to hammer it all out in capitals and misspelled swear words. I don't want to be reasonable, I want to insult those Victorian imbeciles and smack them on the bottom with what they've cost us. Modern women have been betrayed by science. We have been lied to and about; they stole our autonomy, they vanished our pleasure and the effects are so embedded, the words of experts so respected that the revolution of reclamation will be slow and difficult. But hey, at least it's started, and you're part of it, so pack some sandwiches and try to think positively.

I am sure Charles Darwin was a nice man. I'm sure if I'd bumped into him on the Galapagos Islands I'd have thought, 'What a decent fellow – and he sure did know a lot about worms!' At university we were always asked if artists could be considered separately from the age they lived in – should a two-hundred-year-old novel with racist language be removed from the canon, or could the author be forgiven as she didn't know any better? There's no answer to this question, by the way, just opinions. Some people say it's detrimental to keep racist ideas floating about by respecting their vessels; others say historical racism mustn't be buried and hidden, we modern guys must recognise and learn from it. Usually an assessment is made of a work's worth and intention and the same has to be true of Darwin and sexism. It's not his fault he was a Victorian, I'm not suggesting we throw his incredible and enlightening life's work in the bin and start again. But I think he and his contemporaries' prejudice has to be flagged because an entire area of science has been built upon it. If we were *literally* going to make a flag I would embroider it with Darwin's list of pros and cons for getting married. It's fun source material for finding out about Victorian sensibilities. You can find the whole text online but highlights include describing a 'nice, soft' future wife as an 'object to be beloved & played with, better than a dog anyhow' and looking forward to the charms of 'female chit-chat'. I doubt those words come from a man who considered women his equal, but – well, he's dead now and we're not, so we win. See below for more female chit-chat!

Since the discovery of sperm competition, scientists, an-thropologists and evolutionary psychologists have been build-ing a more balanced model of human sexual behaviour. They don't all agree and there's loads of conflicting evidence and opinion to be found out there, but it can safely be acknow-ledged that women have a basic biological drive to have genet-ically strong children. Our sexual attractions are our body's attempts to make clever, tactical decisions in regards to future offspring and those attractions do not always lead us towards one man and fancying him and only him forever and ever.

HETEROCENTRIC BIAS KLAXON: of course many women reading this will not fancy men at all. Every living person evolved from heterosexuals or at least from people who had *some* heterosexual intercourse and this means while discussing evolution, homosexuality can often be ignored or considered unworthy of comment. While I'm using these broad strokes of opposite-sex attraction I should make it clear that exactly the same process and instincts are at work in homosexual loves and lusts. The mechanics are identical, you're still choosing possible parents to future offspring in every sexual encounter; the incentives or deal-breakers of cer-tain partners are still assessed via a genetic agenda. Our bod-ies don't understand that not all sex makes babies – like how using contraception or being infertile or post-menopausal does not affect heterosexual sex instincts; it's always poten-tial mummies and daddies we're looking for. I *know*, it does sound gross when put like that, sorry.

We already know that the number of sex partners a woman enjoys won't alter the number of children she could have. But if genetic strength of progeny is considered, we find that while the quantity of offspring may not be increased, the quality could be. Consider this for instance: for a woman in the pre-civilised, harsh environs of ancient Africa, having all her kids with the same father could be risky. With a single gene pool her children will have similar strengths and weaknesses; a disease or environmental factor that killed one might well kill all. Instead, breeding with several different men could work as a form of spread betting – her children would inherit a larger range of genetic traits and dispositions; Jeremy's got darker skin and won't get sunburn, Claire's got longer arms which help with fishing. There would be a higher likelihood that some of her children would survive into adulthood and BANG, sister gone evolved herself a roving eye. Hallelujah and Merry Christmas, suddenly being a woman doesn't look so committed and passive after all. I'm going to put on my sexiest beret to celebrate.

Have a go on my trumpet while I tell you a bit more:

Apparently multi-partnering could have been instrumental in our becoming the empathetic, social creatures we are now. Picture this: a tribe of nine or ten family groups, numbering around a hundred people in total. If all the families are headed by pair-bonded adults who are completely sexually exclusive then there's little incentive for sharing and inter-familial support. Each may well look after her own. BUT if each adult woman is sleeping with a couple of her male neighbours, and each of those males are sleeping with a couple of other local women, then none of those men can be sure if any of those women's children are his. With no paternity certainty there would be a greater incentive for families to work together, to pool resources and to be emotionally invested in each other's success. The children of the tribe would be better protected and more valued, thus increasing their survival rates. The more adult caregivers each child has, the better their chances. Paternity uncertainty and multi-partnering connects people together. Our social groups, our fondness for our friend's offspring and group childrearing can be linked to this system of mating. Cohesive social harmony induced by our horny female ancestors? It is time to don a second beret.

Contrary to what we've been told or what we might expect, women are not programmed to be purely monogamous. But we *do* form strong, chemically enhanced pair bonds, so we're not completely wild and uncommitted either. We exist somewhere between the two extremes and it seems the flexibility of our desires is an ingenious survival tactic. We're able to react to environment and circumstances when seeking a mate or a partner and to ascertain what we most need from him or his genes. But life has thrown us a paradox; raising children requires committed parenting and powerful bonding, while having the healthiest, most likely-to-survive children could require mating outside of that relationship. It would appear that for both genders, an ideal mating state could be a bonded family unit, with some extra sex with external partners.

How do you feel about that?

All morality and personal feelings aside, *your* ideal mating state could be to bag yourself a skilful person who is useful and great at providing, while having the occasional affair in order to deepen your children's gene pool and encourage support from other adults. If you're in a long-term relationship, you

might find yourself attracted to people very physically different from your partner for this reason. You might get crushes
on people who are more successful than them, a reliable signal of smart genes and access to resources. You might have a
crush on their best friend or brother or someone else socially
close . . . the guys and girls you fancy outside of your pair bond
are determined by your subconscious desire to cuckold.

Morality and personal feelings back safely on the table, I
find these theories and explanations of human bonding and
attraction interesting and terribly troubling. It's a relief to
read about non-monogamous evolutionary programming as
I always feel very guilty for fancying people outside of my
relationship. I took it as a sign that my relationship wasn't
working or that I was a bad person. Now I understand that
being in love doesn't stop my body noticing handsome
young men in the vicinity and I can forgive myself. My body
is a baby-making machine honed by millennia and I've com-
mandeered it for bike riding and buying stationery; of course
I'll wobble when I encounter a flat-bellied twenty-four-year-
old who smells of the seaside. But I don't want to provide
excuses for cheating. While we can't control who turns our
head in the street or makes us flush by the photocopier, we
are in charge of our hugging arms and kissing lips. I don't
think biology is an excuse to cheat – but it could provide an
explanation for wanting to, or for trying open relationships
or practising polyamory or any other non-monogamous state
that is built on honesty and makes you happy. Our evolution
has shaped us to have wide-ranging urges and lusts but topped
our brain with a pre-frontal cortex to control ourselves. If
you've promised a lover you'll be faithful, don't you be quot-
ing my book and blaming me while he cries in the bath. You

be kind to that boy. 'We're all monkeys, mate,' is not a good enough excuse for hurting people.

Hang on, why *does* it hurt so much to be cheated on? If multi-partnering and philandering is in our genes, why do I get so jealous? The thought of my boyfriend kissing someone else ignites a volcano of pointless nauseous anger. I cry myself to sleep when he's away, suffering the varied sexual jaunts I send him on in my mind. If we listened to my emotions they would dictate that monogamy is the *only* way, thank you, and couples should all be faithful to each other forever and ever until they die, the end. Even when you've broken up with someone they shouldn't be allowed to go out with anyone else, you should be able to put all your exes in a freezer until some future date when it won't wreck your weekend to find out they've got married from an uploaded photo on Facebook. Congratulations, Christopher, if you're reading this.

I am trying to educate my emotions.

I watched a documentary about polyamory. These were not couples with open relationships, as I had been expecting from the title, but trios who were all in love with each other in committed love triangles. They lived in houses as threesomes. Took care of children together, shared chores and swapped beds. I was very sceptical, keeping alert for a strain of voice or sadness behind eyes that would signal 'they're just pretending to be happy'. One of the groups was made up of two women and a man. He'd had an affair at work and fallen in love. His wife had gone out on a date with his mistress, thought she was great and invited her to move in with them. 'She didn't wanna lose her bloke,' I heckled the programme from my head, 'she'd rather share him than be alone.' I watched as she made dinner for their children while her husband had a night out at the cinema with his girlfriend. 'What a mug,' I judged and presumed, while she explained how well the situation suited her, how she had more time for herself and more love for her husband.

I have to remember that all of my discriminations are hard-wired. I was tutored by my culture to view only two-person relationships as 'normal' and any other formation as an aberration, an emotional freak show. If I'd grown up in a polygamous society, I might consider Aunty Sandra and Uncle Trevor the weird ones. It'd be their love life I'd want to gossip about; why doesn't Uncle get a younger wife to help with children? Why does Aunty not bring a nice local girl in to be her new sister and do the chores? How can they be satisfied only having each other?

In Britain, it's not just rare or unusual, it is *illegal* to marry more than one person and punishable with up to seven years in prison. A couple of years ago I took part in a TV politics show with university students. The discussion was about the affordability of living in London but a question popped up from someone who said he represented the Polyamory Society. He asked the MP I was sitting next to: 'Now gay marriage has been recognised, isn't it time people who want to marry more than one person be given legal rights?' The MP was flustered and I really felt for him. As he stuttered and corrected himself, you could tell how worried he was about replying stupidly to a question he was unprepared for. He was preoccupied with showing his respect and support for the gay movement and he finally announced, 'These kinds of questions make me angry.' People who were against gay marriage had criticised the government, saying their decisions were undermining the sanctity of the wedding ceremony, predicting that people would soon be able to marry animals – or cars and fences. The MP said, 'Bigamy has nothing to do with gay people having equal rights,' and then he stopped talking. The atmosphere in the room was tense and confused and the polyamory man who'd asked the question wanted to speak again. The presenter avoided him and moved the discussion on while the student waved his arm in the air, red-faced and misunderstood.

I thought about it afterwards. Of course a marriage of three or more people is not like marrying a pet or inanimate object, because it still involves consent and love and intentions and promises from all parties. And while most of us in that room considered polyamory a strange and perhaps scary thing, isn't that how homosexuality used to be regarded a few decades ago? 'Normal' is a concept formed by averages but it changes with education and tolerance. I wish we'd been brave enough to investigate what the student was asking us, but we were too scared of offending people. Trying so hard to be tolerant that we were the opposite. I also realised the question wasn't as off-topic as I'd first thought. Perhaps the only way any of us could afford London house prices would be to marry a few dudes and combine overdrafts until we got a deposit?

Human polyamory can be inextricably connected to economics and circumstances. Most countries where polygamy is legal seem to be very poor, like Bangladesh, Sudan and Ethiopia. For women living in countries where their gender prohibits them from a career outside of the home, they are better off as one of a rich man's many wives than as the sole wife of a poor man. It's almost always this way round because, globally, it's men who control access to resources. The Polygyny Threshold Hypothesis posits that a male animal is more likely to have multiple partners when there is an uneven distribution of resources, when one male occupies a safer/more plentiful territory and can protect and provide for more than one female. This hypothesis was based on the behaviour of birds, where (because of the way they breed) females are reliant on males. It is interesting that the countries which allow men to marry more than one woman also seem to restrict the lives of women, for religious or cultural reasons. Female humans in such countries are similarly dependent.

As we've already discovered, a man with many female partners can potentially have more children – so polygamy makes sense as a mating strategy for a wealthy, powerful man. But because no amount of men can significantly increase a woman's brood, cultures where women have more than one husband are very rare. There is a well-documented polyandrous society in rural Tibet. The exhausting methods of farming they undertake and the shared family ownership of land mean that if a woman wants to marry a man, she often has to marry all his brothers as well. In severe conditions with hard work and food shortages, polygamy is a survival tactic; with more bodies to toil and care for children, the extended family is far stronger and more likely to succeed than a lone man and woman would be under such circumstances. In cases like this, multi-person marriages are a response to the environment.

But I'm still biased by my background, my subjectivity is emotively playing the trumpet and I'm imagining this poor Tibetan woman – what if she fancies only one of the brothers but has to do it with all of them? What if they gang up against her and she is bullied and mistreated in her own home? Same with the Pakistani or Saudi Arabian women who share their husbands with younger wives; do they feel rejected and jealous? Do they wish they lived in a country where they could have a

husband all of their own? The problem with a completely prej-
udiced world-view is separating the benefits of someone else's
marital arrangement from how I would feel if it were imposed
upon me. *I* wouldn't want to be married to five brothers in
Tibet, or be part of a harem. But that doesn't mean there's not
lots of happiness, satisfaction, love and joy available to the people who choose that set-up. Marrying three brothers, if that's
completely normal to you, might be super-hot. I'm trying not
to project, and I am failing. I remind myself that a two-parent
family is not 'normal', it could be interpreted as a sign of environmental luxury, access to food and no fear of predators. It's
just one of the ways that humans can choose to live.

I have tried to imagine situations where I would share my
boyfriend, or take another lover into our house . . . they all
involve an apocalypse and I'm not happy even thinking about
it. Two boyfriends . . . yes, I could probably manage that, but
I don't find the idea sexy because I know I'd simply be watching *two* grown men playing iPhone games for seven hours a
day. Unless the electricity has run out because of the apocalypse and then the iPhones won't have battery and if I know
my boyfriend, which I do, he will kill himself. So, forty-five
minutes into the apocalypse and we're back to monogamy.
The opposite way, being *one* of his girlfriends? I know he'd
love it and it upsets me so much I'm crying as I type this.

Sexual jealousy is an ugly trait and I'm ashamed of it. I know
it stems from insecurity, I know that mostly it's irrational and I
wish I didn't care. I wish I could have open relationships and
not be raw at the thought. I can repeat to myself calmly, 'It's
just sex, just genitals, it's just flesh and skin and –' AARGH no
can't do it, my body isn't big enough for these feelings. I hate
my boyfriend's past and I am terrified of his sexual future and

if all the women in the world could just sign here to promise they'll never kiss him then I could relax a little bit:

> I _____ do solemnly swear never to kiss or
> do anything else sexual with Sara's boyfriend no matter
> how much he begs or how good he is at iPhone games.

Thanks guys.

Jealousy evolved alongside pair bonding. They are intertwined and inseparable, ancient and animal. There's a lot to lose when you are investing time and resources into bringing up children – a man who is cuckolded will spend his life ensuring the success of another man's genes. A woman who shares her partner with other women will lose some of his potential resources. If the man with a pie has two wives, they each get half a pie. If the man with a pie has fourteen children with six different women then everyone gets a tiny bite of pie and those children now have a lower survival expectation. If your dad is a jazz musician like mine then he can't afford any pie and your mum will have to work very hard to support you on her own. In terms of genetic inheritance, the suspicious, jealous, possessive types may have ensured their own genes were carried into future generations, and into us. This ugly trait is a mating technique too and another aspect of ourselves to struggle with and hope to forgive.

Our next battle is forever. Eternity. The idea that the only successful relationship is one that never ends. If you've accepted that human beings have an inherited predisposition towards something slightly more flexible than monogamy, let's move on. Even if you haven't accepted it, come anyway, the bottom of a page is no place to be sitting on your own.

Happily Ever After?

I was never interested in Disney princesses as a child. My dolls didn't get married, they got haircuts and amputations. When I was twelve, I was into marbles, gymnastics and the curse of Tutankhamun's tomb. I was unaware of romance, I was too busy running around. Then an injury forced me to sit down – I'd choreographed a cardigan-swinging dance that knocked all the ornaments off my babysitter's mantelpiece. 'The show must go on,' I thought and continued my routine barefoot atop the debris. I couldn't walk for a week after the operation to remove glass from my feet, and my career as a cardigan dancer was sadly over.

While I was recovering, my babysitter and I would watch TV together to distract ourselves from the newly empty mantelpiece. And it was on that sofa that I learned about love, from a daytime movie on Sky. It was about a young, beautiful woman who was seduced by this guy. She shouldn't have had sex with him but he was too sexy and so she had to. And then she found out she was pregnant and he said he would marry her but he had to get some diamonds from the diamond mine first. And she said, 'No it's too dangerous,' and he was like, 'I have to, for you and the baby.' So he went, and he never came back. And so the girl was looking for him all the time, and trusting that he would return. And everyone was like, 'He abandoned you,' and 'He's a loser,' but she kept looking out and waiting by the road to the diamond mine for him. And she had her baby and it was a girl who grew up thinking her

73

father didn't want to see her, but her mum kept telling her he would come back if he could. But everyone else, like her nan, was saying, 'Your dad was a naughty sex man and a user.' And then time passed as it does, and the mum was an old lady and she died. She had never got married because she was waiting for her love. And after her funeral, a man came running down the road from the diamond mine. They had found a SKELETON down there, it was the father of the girl and it was holding a MASSIVE WHITE DIAMOND and they brought it to her, and her dad hadn't run off or found a new woman, he had died when all the rocks fell on him. And now the mum would never know that she was right because she was completely dead.

It was very upsetting, it was so *unfair*. I cried and cried until my mum picked me up and then I continued to cry as I told her about the poor woman and the poor man and then she cried too because she is a very empathetic and passionate woman. And I never forgot the film. I have regularly thought about the story and what I had learned about love. That if love is *true*, if love is *real*, then you will get a diamond eventually so just believe in it, until you die.

I am in love at the moment. His name is John and the first thing I said to him when I met him was 'You need to know I've seen your penis.' It's not a famous penis or anything; he is not a condom model. I was texted a naked photo of him as a joke. He was drunk in a flat at the Edinburgh Festival and had put Tom Craine's new coat on to rub his bum on it or something, and Tom had taken a photo and sent it to Josh Widdicombe, who forwarded it to everyone else, including me. I looked at it and thought, 'That guy is having a great old time laughing in that coat.' And then a few days later I met John at a gig and I was very embarrassed. Eighteen months later we were in a relationship. We had fallen for each other while drinking heavily, just like in the movies.

John has an English degree from Oxford, which I am jealous of. He can quote Philip Larkin and T. S. Eliot and before sleep he relaxes by pretending he is Sherlock Holmes. When he is *really* drunk, he cries about Freddie Mercury while singing along to Queen on YouTube. He is pretty great AND YOU HAVE SIGNED A CONTRACT PROMISING NEVER TO KISS HIM so don't get any ideas. I loved him quickly. It was sudden and thunderous like a waterslide. I walked to the station after my first night at his flat and searched myself for the negativity and loneliness that live in my crease and spider about when I'm sober. Gone. None left, blown away. I bought a packet of bagels and ate them on the Central line, stroking the world and its inhabitants with my eyes. I was calm and I existed and if I was a film I would've ended. John was the resolution, thank you, roll credits. I was happy for fifty-five minutes and it was really enjoyable and I will never forget it. And then the spiders scuttled back.

A couple of months into our relationship, I was falling asleep in John's bed and I whispered, 'Promise you'll never leave me.' He stayed silent, I lay there waiting. I asked, 'Are you asleep?' He said 'No' in a tight voice and I knew I was being creepy and needy. He told me, 'People can't promise each other things like that,' and I knew he was right and I was ashamed. It was a weak moment, but sometimes, in all the rawness of loving, it would be nice to go to sleep wrapped safely in a comforting thought, even if it is a lie or the kind of thing you can't really promise. Another time I asked him if he would consider being frozen if we broke up and unfortunately he thought I was joking. We went on dates where I'd slam down cocktails and say, 'I don't believe in marriage, let's just have fun!' and then I would weep because I didn't believe in marriage and I didn't believe in anything and I was asking him for reassurance that I couldn't define. He finds me very confusing.

I was so grateful I had met John. I was thirty-two, it was sixteen years since I had loved Colin when I was sixteen. I tried to read something meaningful into the numbers. I felt very excited and joyous but the positivity of those emotions was cancelled out by my fear that this happiness would disappear. My elation sat hand in hand with doom. Every wonderful moment reminded me of love's finiteness – this too will pass. All of my previous relationships had finished, so why not this one? That's what relationships do, they end. And you shouldn't worry about the ending at the beginning, it's illogical and it ruins everything, it's like giving birth to a baby dressed as the Grim Reaper. It's like turning up at a job interview and saying, 'Oh what's the point? If you don't sack me, I'll quit.' It's like going to your job interview and just before the boss falls asleep, begging him to promise he'll employ you forever.

I don't even believe in forever but I don't feel safe without forever and this is problematic.

I ruined the beginning. We moved in together and I cried all day. I got hysterical in Ikea imagining all that assembling in reverse when we broke up. Everything we created together, every contentment I autopsied immediately, predicting how I would feel when it was over and all these happy moments were added to my collection of regretted memories.

I blame my parents, which is unfair but quicker than self-examination. It's their fault I don't have an example of a

healthy, committed relationship to emulate. My parents met
when they were teenagers. My dad was in a pop band and my
mum had seen him on TV when she was thirteen. We were
told the story a lot when we were young. We had scrapbooks
of my dad's pictures in magazines. When my mum saw him
on TV she had an *epiphany*, a physiological reaction: she was
flooded with certainty that this was the man she was going to
marry. She just knew it, she knew it! And then to ensure that
happened she stalked him for four years, attending concerts
and recordings and sitting out on his lawn with other teenage
girls. She insisted. She threatened suicide and attempted suicide and she mugged him with her love and eventually she
wore him down. They got pregnant with me, something I will
always feel guilty about, then Cheryl. Then they got married,
then Mum got pregnant with Kristyna, then Dad left for jazz
and other ladies.

I should be grateful to my mum for her persistence. I
wouldn't exist if she hadn't succeeded in seducing my father
and learning nothing about contraception. She told me that
when she saw my dad that first time, the epiphany she felt was
me wanting to be born, insisting on it. And that is *exactly* the
kind of thing I'd do; vibrate through a teenager telling her to
make me.

So John and I are living together and I'm attempting to
control my angst. I become obsessed with historical couples; I
have this idea that if I can find a great example of a pair who
got it 'right' then I can copy them and learn from them and
everything will be fine. I started with Adam and Eve, the original pairing. And they're very typical, sure, at the beginning
it's all magical and staying up late counting each other's ribs
and laughing. But you can't sustain that. The magic fades,

he's boring, she's off talking to wildlife and comfort eating –
then their landlord kicks them out and one of their kids kills
the other one. If they can't make it work in Paradise, what
chance have I got in Lewisham?

I researched all the great love stories: Sylvia Plath and Ted
Hughes, Simone de Beauvoir and Jean-Paul Sartre, Victoria
and Albert, and what I found was: suicide, infidelity, cousins.
They were all *entirely* tragic. My friend Vanessa recommended
I read Napoleon's love letters to Josephine, said they were the
most romantic things ever written, and so I did. And they are
beautiful, I admit it. He is this powerful man, in charge of
most of Europe, and he just misses his wife madly and wants
to kiss her on the heart and 'much lower'. Historical swoon.
Then I found out he later divorced her because she couldn't
have children and married somebody else, the little French
bastard.

Every love story I found wasn't. They were all tragic and im-
perfect. Everyone got hurt, everyone died. This wasn't helping.

Then John and I set off on a walking tour in Bloomsbury
and we stand outside the house where Sylvia Plath and Ted
Hughes spent their wedding night. I want to press my hands
all over the bricks and rub myself on this magical place but
decorum and John's arm prevent me.

'Sylvia Plath didn't mean to commit suicide,' the tour guide
says. 'She put her head in the oven, yes, and she turned the
gas on, yes—'

'She also put milk and biscuits in the kids' room,' I whisper helpfully into John's ear. He looks at me and mouths,
'Shut up please.' The guide is telling us that Plath's downstairs neighbour was due to come up to clean and do chores.

Had she arrived on time, she could have saved Sylvia, but she didn't, because the oven gas had seeped through the floorboards and she'd passed out too.* The tour guide pauses and shrugs.

I think he's trying to persuade us that Sylvia Plath's death is even sadder than we'd realised, because maybe she didn't mean to die. I'm trying to absorb this when the idiot moves on to the next building and a funny story about advertising slogans. 'Ha ha ha,' laughs everyone as tension is dispelled. And this is *my* epiphany. I grab John's hand and in a loud voice explain, 'I've just worked out that Plath and Hughes is NOT a love story at all. I'd always thought that they were the most *romantic* framework: meet tall intelligent guy; bite his cheek at a party; poems, passion and Ouija boards ensue; he deserts you so you kill yourself – I thought that's what love was, that pain is how you prove your devotion and if it's not so extreme that you would die for it then it's not worth living for and—' John's eyes beg me to stop talking, so I do. He continues to listen to the stupid old tour guide but my mind is too noisy now. Maybe it's the *story* that's the problem. The way our minds collect information into a narrative.

Stories are how humans comprehend things they don't understand, like all the ancient creation myths trying to explain away what's scary: 'Oh, that river is there because some god ejaculated,' and 'Oh, the sun just hides at night because the moon is her ex and she doesn't want to bump into him.' And even with all our modern knowledge, the feeling of love, the too-big HUGENESS of how it *feels*, reduces us all to mystics.

* I have looked this up – it's not *quite* true. Sylvia had left a note asking a (male) neighbour to call a doctor, but he didn't see it on his way to work as planned, because the gas had knocked him out.

We idealise the relationships of celebrities, we fetishise the lovers in films and novels and we rationalise the chaotic explosions of feeling that happen to us.

The human mind does not allow events that affect us to remain mysterious; our consciousness requires the firmest relationship between cause and effect in order to function. When our conscious mind does not 'know' why or how something has happened, it guesses. It predicts or assumes based on previous learning and WE DO NOT EVEN KNOW THAT THIS IS TAKING PLACE. The process is called 'confabulation', it's when your mind takes over, provides an answer, and you, the person thinking, feel it like truth. There is a wonderful example that illustrates how this works: in the nineteenth century the German psychiatrist Albert Moll instructed a hypnotised patient to put a book back on the shelf when she awoke. The lady woke up, took a book from the table by her side and placed it on the shelf. Moll asked her why she'd done that and she replied, 'I do not like to see things untidy. The shelf is the correct place for a book and that is why I put it there.' Her conscious mind was unaware of the instruction she had received and confabulated an explanation that made sense to her; she was a tidy woman, this was the kind of thing she would do.

More recent experiments have involved injecting participants with adrenaline. This naturally occurring hormone stimulates the sympathetic nervous system. You'll have experienced its effects yourself when you've been nervous or very excited – it can be unnerving. It makes your heart beat faster and causes skin to flush and heat. It's a strong physiological reaction that we interpret as emotional. In tests, when people don't know they're being injected with the drug, they attribute the physiological symptoms to something that has happened, some stimulus. 'That man made me angry', 'That film was really funny', 'Certain situations stress me out.' When participants know what they're being injected with and its effects, they tend to understand: 'My body was reacting to adrenaline.' This is huge, isn't it? When people didn't re-alise they'd been reacting to a chemical, they accepted the effects without question. They owned them, 'Yep that's me, that's how I feel because I'm feeling it.' They even reasoned with events and their environment to work out what they were reacting to. They confabulated and it seemed so logical that none of them knew it. This highlights the greatest weakness in our personal psychology: when our body causes us to feel a certain way we rationalise why we have those feelings, we at-tribute causes to the effects. We can never separate ourselves – 'Oh, I feel this way because a gland inside me is releasing molecules into my bloodstream.'

This is relevant to our topic because what we call 'love' is really a variety of hormones and neurotransmitters swishing around our body. These chemicals induce behaviours and stimulate strong emotional reactions. But when we experi-ence it we aren't in a lab, there isn't a scientist waving a syringe and getting us to fill out response forms, so we're unaware of the chemicals, they're invisible. It's left to our conscious mind to justify how and why we feel the way we do. We confabulate, we justify; star signs and toned arms and 'I've always liked a bad boy' – but, you know, we're subconsciously making it up. We create a story.

Thinking about my own body as a responsive meat machine reacting to chemical stimuli makes me feel disassociated and mad, but I'm not going to stop. We've already spent some

time with dopamine; now I'd like to introduce you to my favourite hormone, come here –

Oxytocin, this is reader; reader, this is oxytocin. Every book
I've read about hormones, and you should be aware that is
over *two* books, refers to oxytocin as 'the cuddle hormone',
which makes me think about blankets and middle age and a
huge cushion with a face. Oxytocin deserves a sharper name
to reflect its function: 'the satisfaction after orgasm hormone'
or 'the not abandoning your kids hormone'. I don't want
oxytocin sounding tame when its effects are so gargantuan.*
Oxytocin is released by affectionate touching, stroking and
massaging, holding hands, nipple stimulation and coming.
It is what bonds mothers to their babies after birth and via
lactation and it is a vital part of romantic attachment. It creates blissful, contented feelings towards the object of your
affection, it works to decrease stress and, *I* think, it's addic-
tive. Being completely subjective now, I've always felt like a
cat who wants to be petted all day, circling legs, begging for
more attention. I get irritated with my boyfriend because he
needs space away from me and refuses to play when I want
to sit on him or squash him or wrestle. Yes, I'm very annoying. Apparently a person's relationship with oxytocin is set
in childhood. People with very physically affectionate parents
and carers can become adults with a 'skin hunger' who need
to be touched a lot, while children who were held less can feel
uncomfortable with touching. But I also know people who are
the opposite, they come from physically reserved families and
are desperate for contact as adults, or my friend who has a
really really affectionate mum and any kind of hugging makes

---

* I utilised the thesaurus function of my computer here because I worry I've used
the word 'huge' too much.

her feel smothered and suffocated, so . . . I dunno. We don't have definitive answers.

They sell oxytocin sprays on the internet, they're expensive. I have no idea if they work. I'd thought they were for people like me who feel affection-starved and don't get enough sex but in fact they are for people like me who worry about their partners cheating. There was a study on infidelity where men had a spray of oxytocin up their nose before being let loose in a room full of women. They scientists studied where the men looked, who they spoke to and for how long (welcome to my life) and asked them questions afterwards, and found that those men who'd had the spray flirted, looked and leered a lot less than those who'd had a placebo spray. The oxytocin-sprayed men seemed to notice attractive women a lot less, although I STILL wouldn't recommend you buy one. I think they're taking advantage of paranoid partners and the product feedback on Amazon is a list of one-star 'the bastard still didn't come home for two days' customer reviews.

Also, guess what? Oxytocin makes you forgetful. It's instrumental in blotting out the pain of childbirth, so women don't remember how awful it was and are willing to go through it all again, and it's why we behave foolishly when we are falling in love. If you're going crazy on each other, hands everywhere, PDAs, tons of sex and massive orgasms, your body will be flooded with oxytocin. You'll be drunk on it, making you less sharp. You might ignore the odd warning sign of bad behaviour; it won't seem so important that he stole from your purse or made a pass at your sister. But as the relationship goes on, those early hormones recede and it can feel like waking up to reality. Understanding the science of this should stop us disparaging ourselves for our loved-up decisions. Your body was behaving very cleverly by making you a bit stupid. Falling in love *is* irrational and we have to forgive ourselves for it – but if you're gonna keep seeing him, maybe invest in a safe and don't take him to family gatherings?

Oxytocin plays a massive role in falling in love, as sex and touching promote bonding, but it is also relevant to falling out of love. When you've been with someone for a long time, there is less incentive to connect physically; you may take each other's body for granted. But the less you touch, the less bonded you feel, and the less bonded you feel the less you want to touch, and it's an unfortunate cycle. But knowing about it can help. If you're having a row with your bae, ask if you can hold hands while you shout, and you'll find oxytocin makes you conciliatory and less angry. Vice versa, if you're trying to break up with someone STOP SLEEPING WITH THEM as you're making it more difficult for yourself to leave. Some very mumsy advice there, you're welcome.

So far we've tasted a mere spoonful of the hormones that affect us. But as they fluctuate, rise and plummet, our emotions are powered and shifted and, like the people in adrenaline experiments, we attach reasons to our altered states. When I skateboarded around as Puck in *A Midsummer Night's Dream*, I placed a 'love potion' on the eyelids of sleepers, who woke up and loved the first person they saw. In real life it is dopamine, oxytocin and other chemicals that drug us and we are equally unaware that they've taken over. We feel crazy with emotions and intentions and we can only make sense of all that with story.

Here is a story: Once upon a time in 2001 I worked in a hotel in Nottingham and I had no money, I got paid £100 a week into a bank account where I was so far *over* my overdraft that I couldn't take any out. It all went on fees and fines and I was stuck. I wanted to go home but didn't have the train fare. I'd usually have borrowed it from my mum, but she'd lent me money to get up there and I still hadn't paid her back so we weren't talking. I got free food and a room at the hotel, which was good, and I used Rizla papers to make cigarettes from the fag ends left in ashtrays in the bar. For entertainment I had books that guests left when they'd finished with them. It was a generous system, but the fruits were a poor quality. The hotel was aimed at the over-fifties, it was supposed to be 'cruise-style' holidaying for people who hated boats, and I don't know if it was that demographic or maybe something that happens to the brain after menopause, but Jesus, those women read shit books. The men read hardback sports biographies but never relinquished them, so the Book Swap Box was refilled weekly with the same story, in varying lengths, countries and costume. It could be ballerinas in Russia or camel farmers in Egypt, it might be set in the ancient past or in deepest space, but the plot was always:

Woman very poor and has very thin waist and wrists and long silky hair, she has some talent but who cares? She so poor. Bad rich man notice her and then good man rescue her. Good man marry her, he turn out to be even richer than bad man, ending.

I was as poor as the peasants and slave girls the stories described but with added stinky ashtray hands. Every day my books told me that as long as you are very very beautiful a man will save you eventually. Beauty is your only escape plan. The ideal beauty is a contradictory sensual/virginal look and you can literally exchange that shit for a rich man's money. I didn't believe that I was beautiful, or that I'd ever meet a man at the over-fifties Warner Holidays hotel, but I brushed my teeth and plucked my chin just in case . . . and then one day, just when I had given up hope, I *did* meet a man, Terence Peterson. We would walk together in the grounds, pushing his ageing mother in her wheelchair. He would describe the scenery for her decrepit eyes, adding in kingfishers and raccoons that weren't really there as his mother laughed and I hoped she'd never die. But she did, on a Tuesday, and Terence had to leave. 'Come with me,' he said. It should have been a question, but he was insistent and used to getting what he wanted. 'I'll never touch you,' he added, although my thin wrists were desperate for him to grab them and wave them around. 'We'll just be best friends,' Terence explained to me, 'unless . . . but no, but maybe? My mother has left me two million pounds in her will on one condition – that I MARRY YOU.' I was shocked and surprised and virginal and sensual and I turned to him and swooned while I replied, 'No thank you, I will not marry you, because I'm suspicious about this new will and the circumstances of your mother's death and also, more importantly, because you don't exist.'

If this was a musical I would sing a solo called 'The White Diamond Was Inside Myself' now and you would clap and clap and think, 'That is so meaningful,' and, 'She's a better singer than I was expecting.'

We're not stupid, are we? We're astute and self-aware, we know that the men depicted by rom-coms and chick-lit are invented for amusement and dreaminess. But I worry that being bombarded with these fictional men all the time has caused my disappointment with real ones. It's emotional porn. Even taking good looks and money out of the equation, the men in films and books and television are BRAVE. Even in comedies or when romance is a B-plot, the central male characters are *emotionally* heroic: they pick one woman who they really like or love and then they risk rejection and humiliation and they don't give up and they fight for her and become better men for her and – it's literary Photoshop. No matter what our ideal, fiction feeds it to us and tells us to wait for it. With actual sex pornography, the flip is created. The majority of porn depicts a reality where women are always horny and willing for sex, easily aroused and loud to orgasm from penetration. We should all be fretting about how the repeated consumption of those lies is affecting people, but there is also this other, more common lie being shouted about what we should expect from love. This is the modern world; women lied about by pornography and men lied about everywhere else.

So many romance stories involve a saving, a redemption, a woman floundering until a man steps in and takes control. But dependency on a man is not freedom, it's a rubber ring that could deflate. There are evolutionary reasons why resources are attractive in a mate, so it's appealing to celebrate wealthy men in our fantasies, but I would like to put a warning sticker on every Mills and Boon or *Bridget Jones's Diary*: 'SEEKING FINANCIAL SECURITY IN A PART-NERSHIP IS DANGEROUS!' Yes, dangerous I say; when someone leaves you, they should only be able to take their love with them, not your house or your stuff. Vice versa, you should never be imprisoned in an unhappy relationship because you can't afford to leave. Economics underwrite love – any human who cannot support herself is vulnerable to others, and if we romanticise that vulnerability, if we continue to idealise it, we're permitting the infantilisation of women and maybe even creating victims. Now I would love to brag about how I saved myself from the self-dug debt pit of 2001 but I was actually rescued by Mr Student Loans Company and his non-credit-checked lending policy. And then at university I got into more debt and eventually had to do Mr Voluntary Bankruptcy in 2005, so I am definitely the sort of wise and clever person you should absolutely be listening to.

The idea of 'The One', this belief I've absorbed that there is ONE person who will make me happier than any other, is itself a fairy tale. It is a story format. It has a beginning: the search for The One; a middle: some investigations of authenticity to check if he's The One; and an end: ta-da, a crowning ceremony and a booming voice, 'He hath passed the test and is indeed THE ONE.' It's how we communicate our romances to each other and ourselves and it's an antiquated ideal. In Plato's *Symposium*, Aristophanes explains that in the olden times humans were round like balls and had two faces, four arms and four legs each. And they had double genitals: some had two willies and others had two vulvas, and some had one of each. And they floated and bounced around happily, feeling very content but also super-powerful and making attempts to take over heaven. And the gods were really threatened and decided to split all humans in two, dividing and diminishing their strength.

And now human beings only had one face and a mere two arms and two legs each and one willy or vulva. And Zeus said, 'You guys better behave now or we will split you again and you will only have half a face and you'll be hopping around on one leg,' and the new bipedal humans promised to do their best. But now they missed their other halves and could not feel whole without them. They had lost their soulmates, and would spend their lives looking for them. For some women their soulmate was another woman and for some it was a man, but either way they would only feel happy when they found them again and pushed their genitals together and were complete. THE END.

I don't know if the ancient Greeks took Aristophanes' story literally or if they just enjoyed the poetry of the metaphor. It's a wonderful explanation for how it *feels* to fall in love – an attachment so powerful that it *seems* like destiny. The olden Greeks didn't know that hormones and neurotransmitters are the real gods that rule us. They needed myths for explanation; this was how they confabulated. But for modern me, being told that I'm not whole on my own, that I need another very specific person to *complete* me, is unhelpful. The idea that there's only one correct answer among the millions of wrong ones – doesn't this make us fussy and overly critical? It's the relationship equivalent of spending New Year's Eve travelling between addresses, miserable and imagining everyone else is at some amazing party you can't locate, when in reality they too are in taxis and on night buses wondering where they will ever find happiness.

I've spent my adult life believing that some partner, some relationship, some sort of sex would make everything better. My sadness would leave me, and that's how I'd *know* I was with the 'right' person. I recognise the dissatisfied, incomplete, half-souled being Aristophanes describes and when I've met a guy and those feelings haven't gone away—

SARA

It's the wrong set of limbs. He was NOT the answer!

Oh, I don't know what the answer is, by the way, or even why we have such troublesome questions. This is not a self-help book and I worry I've given too many of my own opinions

already. Like that stuff about not relying on men for money –
do what you like, of course, it's your life. And maybe you have
brilliant New Year's Eves and the observation was not universal, perhaps you're grounded and content and all these words
seem like the overthinking of a woman with too much time
and not enough hard labour on her hands? If that's true, why
don't *you* write a self-help book and I'll read it during breaks
at the gravel pit/heavy-lifting factory.

In my wonderings and efforts to be open-minded I remind
myself that western world assumptions could be wrong. Maybe Aristophanes was on the right track but human beings
actually used to be in big conjoined blobs of four and you
have to find *three* other people to be happy. Or six? What if
the happiest and most fulfilling relationships available to our
species contain the same number of participants as a basketball team? Our closed minds restrict our decisions – are they
cheating us of contentment? Why is it *one* person we're supposed to be seeking? Oh no, here comes a strict old scientist,
all white hair and stern face:

SCIENTIST
You're being very silly.

SARA
I'm not! I'm trying to shake off cultural conditioning—

SCIENTIST
We bond in twos because that's how many people it
takes to make a child.

SARA
Not if you don't know that—

SCIENTIST
But we *do* know that—

SARA
There is this tribe of Native Americans, the Bari, and
they believe that every man a woman has sex with
adds to the child she makes, that all the sperm works
together to build the baby and they all have joint
paternity.

SCIENTIST
And you brought me in just to tell me that?

SARA (*stroppy*)
I AM *TRYING* TO UNDERMINE THE CONCEPT
OF COUPLES—

SCIENTIST
Why?

SARA
I'm scared.

SCIENTIST
Of what?

SARA
That I will never have a relationship that lasts forever,
I'll never find the stupid 'One' and I'll always feel like a
failure.

Pause. SCIENTIST looks smug.

SARA
Okay, I heard myself, I get it, you can go now.

SCIENTIST does thumbs up like she's the Fonz and exits. Yeah, the SCIENTIST was a woman all along and if you pictured a man you're a sexist conditioned to expect males in positions of authority (as are we all).

Why should I feel this pressure for a love that's endless when virtually no one achieves it? When I researched historical lovers the only technically successful relationship was Adolf Hitler and Eva Braun. They got married and stayed together for the rest of their lives – about thirty-six hours, until they took cyanide in a bunker (*drops mic and leaves stage*).

I used to be really judgemental of my mum. After my dad left, she would drink wine, listen to terrible music and wail, 'No one wants a woman with three kids, I'll never meet anyone.' But she did meet men, and I hated them. A new one would be introduced and she'd joke that I was 'the protective one' while I tried to set him on fire with my eyes. And then eventually the man would stop coming round, and I knew that it was our fault, because they didn't want to be part of our awful family. Because me and my sisters were too much to take on. Because we were naughty and never went to bed, because we spilled things and didn't clean them up, because we existed. I hated the boyfriends because they stole, they sucked up any happiness my mum was capable of, and when it was all gone they left and abandoned us to clean up the emotional oil spill.

I wished my mum would stop looking and that we would be enough for her. She would cry and say she had no one to talk to and I didn't understand because she was talking to me *right now*. The music would go on and the wine would be opened and we would hug her and try to make it better or dance and try to make her laugh. But the crying only ended when she met someone new, and she'd ask me to be nice to this one please and Cheryl would sit on his lap and cuddle him and I would stare from across the room and refuse to go to bed so I could keep an eye on things.* When I was little I blamed the bad men for coming into our lives and hurting us, but when I reached twelve or thirteen I started to blame my mum for inflicting them upon me.

The punishment for my adolescent scorn has been to repeat what I'd seen Mum do from the inside. Like *Freaky Friday*, I became her. All the phrases I loathed – 'this time it's different', 'he's the one I've been waiting for', 'I really think this is *it*' – now fly from my mouth. And my poor friend Katie, she has to listen to me and she will kindly and occasionally say, 'Do you remember you said this about Mark/Tom/Steve?' and I say, 'NO I HAVE NEVER FELT LIKE THIS, IT IS A NEW FEELING ALL THOSE OTHER FEELINGS WERE INCONSEQUENTIAL.' As a teenager I despised my mum for needing a man to feel complete, for seeking a happy ending that made sense of all that had been before. Now I'm that way myself and it's me I can't bear. 'Oh this one is The One,' I say, and then it doesn't work out so I go, 'Oh no, he wasn't,' or sometimes 'He *was* and I ruined it,' and then I meet someone else and say, 'Hooray, this is it, The One,' and then it doesn't work out and I think, 'Oh I was wrong again,' and then I meet a new One and I am an idiot. Or I'm an animal. I'm an animal desperate as I begin the end of my fertility and my body is crazy for making babies while my mind is full of romance stories and hope. If there was a switch I could press and not

---

* An eye I was training to START FIRES.

fancy boys any more I would. I wonder what I could have achieved in my life if my thoughts weren't consumed with longing and insecurity. Should I get spayed like a cat, to stop my yowling and nighttime wanderings? I'd be a bit shy after the operation, but I'd soon heal and then I would curl up on a soft chair and whatever was near would be enough. I'm completely projecting onto cats now – maybe being spayed is really depressing? People don't tend to be thrilled about their hysterectomies. Oh cats, tell us your secrets.

If you read articles about divorce rates – always described as 'shockingly high' or 'on the rise' – blame is laid at choice's door. 'Not enough commitment nowadays,' says an old lady on a porch. 'These young people quit too easily,' says an old man in B & Q. Are we romanticising this 'staying and working at it' mentality? The divorce rates are never celebrated. This would be my article about it if I had a newspaper column:

New statistics from the Department of Knowing Things show that nearly fifty per cent of marriages are ending in divorce rather than the cold, honest death promised in front of God/loved ones/a registrar. These figures indicate that many human beings are free and self-loving enough to alter situations in which they have become unhappy. An increasing number of the world's women are no longer trapped by economic dependency on husbands whom they do not love. Historically women could not own property, lease in their own name, borrow money from banks or retain ownership of wealth or assets they inherited. It is only within the last century that British women have gained rights to vote, to work in all professions, control their own finances and be considered 'persons' in their own right. As recently as the 1970s women in the UK could not get a mortgage without a male counter-signature and could be sacked if they got pregnant. Perhaps a proportion of these modern divorces are instigated by women whose great-grandmothers would have been trapped with fewer options? Just saying. Now over to outside with the weather.

Thanks for reading my column. If there was an accompanying picture it would be me and a Labrador, I'm shrugging and he's raising an eyebrow, so the tone would be like 'What a world' but also 'Let's try and stay cheerful'.

I've never been married. No one has ever asked me except the fictional Terence Peterson in a story I wrote sarcastically. I have bountiful respect for those who wed. My past incarnations, old Saras of different ages, feel like different people to me; Sara who got herself into debt or Sara who loved Colin. I wouldn't want to spend the present stuck in irreversible situations I created in the past. Although actually I can't get a mortgage or an overdraft or one of those bank cards that you press on the thing and it zaps money – a contactless card – and that's past me's fault. Imagine if she'd also chosen me a life partner? If I'd married my year 2001 love, I'd be Mrs Amateur DJ with a Substance Abuse Problem.

Agreeing to marry is an overcoming of logic, a pledge: 'I don't care if I change, I'm prepared to stand by the decisions I make today.' Or, or it's more that when you're really deeply in love you can't imagine it will ever recede. Love wouldn't be doing its job properly if it was sane, if you could see through it and make rational assessments. But the loving feelings *do* diminish. The evidence is all around you and in the list of previous sex partners you keep hidden in an unused teapot. I thought I would love my first boyfriend, Colin, forever. I checked myself periodically, through university and jobs and living abroad, and, yep, I still loved him. And then I saw him, we met up, six or seven years later. We went to Brighton for a drink and I felt nothing. It was so odd. He talked and I stared at his face thinking, 'How did I ever kiss you?' I was a sane woman reflecting on insanity. He'd changed his surname and found God and got married and had children. And I politely chatted, wondering if I'd got much more intelligent or just been blind to his clichéd talk. And then we left and he sent me a text about wanting to fuck me and I stared at it wishing it felt like a victory. All the chemicals that go crazy gluing us to someone by loving them, when they're reabsorbed or redistributed or go wherever they go it's like being left beached by the sea. The previous state makes no sense.

There is a brilliant woman called Helen Fisher and I'd really recommend watching her TED talk about love if you haven't already. She's also written about theories of serial pair bonding; she studied divorce rates from countries across the world and found that the median duration for marriage was seven years. 'Seven-year itch is proved real by science,' cried crappy newspaper journalists who are never pictured with wry Labradors. The median time for divorce has to fall somewhere, as is the nature of averages, so the seven-year timespan may not be significant of anything. Also 'seven-year itch' sounds like an old-person cliché, from back in the olden days when they were happy to do things for seven years. If 'itch' refers to a discontentment that makes you reassess your life and want to make changes I have one every thirty-five seconds. I blame mobile phones that can go on the internet #attentionspa—

Fisher's studies found that while the median was seven years, the mode – most common – length of time to stay married was four years. This is more illuminating, considering what we have discovered about parental investment and bonding. A four-year-old child is mobile, communicative and, in our culture, ready to go to school. In hunter-gatherer societies four is the age when children tend to start being cared for by older siblings or outside the immediate family, and on average women give birth about once every four years. The conclusion drawn by Fisher and others is that we've evolved to closely bond with a mate for the period of time that ensures the greatest survival odds for any offspring. After this mating cycle it is natural to detach and move on to a new partner, so that women can have genetically varied children. Fisher's stats also showed that there were higher divorce rates among younger people, which she argued had little to do with modern dissatisfaction and everything to do with their peak of fertility and ability to have a second or third cycle of childrearing with a new partner.

That is the kind of thing I read and go THERE IT IS, THAT'S THE ANSWER: humans have a cyclical bonding tendency of around four years, we intermingle deeply and massively and *painfully*, and then we recover and start fancying other people again. It explains me and my relationships, how difficult the end is, how my feelings change. How hurtful it is to snap away from someone in the early stages, before the cycle is complete. How impossible I find it to like someone I have spent a few years with. But this might not resonate with your experience. I am so keen to find an answer that explains me that I will grasp at anything – not a euphemism.

I think it's worth contemplating the serial bonding theory seriously. I'm not saying that the numbers are exactly right or that the explanation doesn't have flaws and contradictions BUT imagine if, culturally, we expected relationships to finish. If rather than this venerated concept of eternity overshadowing our pairings, we all loved and loved and then moved on when necessary or timely. In that society, anyone who stayed with the same person for too long would be mocked and ridiculed – if you knew an old couple down the road who'd been high-school sweethearts, you'd tell me and we'd go egg their house and shout up at their windows: 'Get dressed! We're taking you speed dating!' We'd march them there ourselves. Maybe you'd get off with the old man to prove a point? I wish you hadn't, that's a bit out of order actually. But imagine if the people who ended up being together for fifty years were like, 'How weird, it was just a fling that went wrong!' If we admired the people who created and kept lifelong partnerships, but considered them a wonderful anomaly, while the lists in our teapots got longer and longer and we judged our loves on our hearts rather than the calendar. Hmm?

I'm imagining myself giving this speech to Sylvia Plath and she is smiling through her tears and getting back into bed. Simone de Beauvoir is texting Sartre that it's over. Queen Victoria is removing her widow's weeds and now she's nude and making a pass at Simone. Eve walks in with a bowl of fruit and we all laugh. Ha ha ha ha ha. The musical finishes with a brilliant finale, I'm singing 'Endings Aren't Failures' and when I get to the rap bit, all the women in the world do the robot dance and we all feel okay about everything. We all agree that pair bonding is the most powerful influence that affects our bodies. Doing it multiple times is an evolutionary strength, we're the winners! We throw our diamonds into the air because we don't need them any more! Terence Peterson tries to propose to all of us and we beat him to death with hardback copies of *A Room of One's Own*!

And then we go home.

We have learnt a little bit so far, I understand some things slightly better – or I have more ideas to ponder. But there is so much about my body and its behaviours that I still want to comprehend. The female preoccupation with looks and youth and body weight; women assessing other women's attractiveness; a beauty industry that grows rich on female insecurity and a society that celebrates a woman's sexiness as her most valuable achievement. I'd always believed these were contemporary challenges caused by commercialism and women's magazines, but it's truer to say they are the residual concerns of ancient mating tactics sent haywire by modern living.

If this were a film there'd now be a close-up on a mouse in a cage. She is grooming her whiskers over and over again. She is agitated and gnawing at her own fur and she doesn't know how to stop. And you'd tut and understand that the director was, quite heavy-handedly, telling you she is you.

Is There Any Body with You?

So, you know glow worms?

If 'no' throw the dice, if 'yes' go forward five pages. COME BACK, I totally pranked you. It feels wrong to suddenly start talking about glow worms out of nowhere but I think about them all the time, I believe we can learn something from them, so let me tell you about it – STOP LOOKING FOR DICE.

I read that glow worms are dying out and that it was because of electricity. Then I looked it up on the internet and found out some people had been claiming for ages that there were fewer glow worms, but there was no definite proof because it's really hard to count them and then, even once you *have* counted all the glow worms, if they've never been counted *before*, you have nothing to compare that number to. So they had to wait and count again, but now it seems certain that glow worm populations are diminishing. Oh dear.

Glow worms are not actually worms, they are little flying beetles and it is only the female glow worm who glows, which is sad for the male glow worm as both of his names are a lie. So the female glow worm lights up, and the male glow worm finds her fuzzy fluorescence very attractive. I'm anthropomorphising, let me be more clinical – the light emitted by female glow worms enables male glow worms to locate them and inspires mating. Male glow worms have been shaped by their evolution and the sexual selection of their species to be 'turned on' by the glow that emanates from the female. And then bastard humans put their clothes on and invented conductive wires and lightbulbs and now male glow worms spend a lot of their time mating with street lights, which they think are massive, super-sexy lady glow worms. Idiots.

Lots of animals have evolved sexual ornamentation to attract mates: bright red bottoms, colourful plumage, handsome antlers – all kinds of visual stimuli that advertise health, great genes, lack of parasites and what have you. In nature ornamentation has been a failsafe and trustworthy way of ascertaining mate potential for millions of years, right up until humans evolved to the point of screwing with everything. There are some interesting experiments that scientists have done, and when I say interesting I mean cruel, but also, yes, interesting. They have artificially heightened the ornaments of certain species, attaching dyed feathers, painting bottoms, sticking on super-massive antlers to see what happens. And what does happen? All the lads or ladies go crazy for the super-sexy sex signals and no creature has a built-in bullshit detector. They don't have a cut-off where they go, 'Surely, Stephen, those antlers are too big, you can barely lift your head and you won't be able to fit through the door of the house I've got even though I'm a deer.' Instead they are like, 'Come over here and rut with me, Stephen, your headgear is flipping amazing.'

As you know, human beings also evolved via sexual selection. Let's just clarify what this is. *Natural* selection is the well-known shaping force that has created our bodies and minds. We adapt to what our environment requires – or rather, those who don't adapt perish. The genes of the ill-suited are lost as their offspring flounder and fail to produce healthy children. To give a rough, crude and made-up example: imagine some *sapiens* living in a forest a hundred thousand years ago, and imagine one family had a genetic mutation that made one arm bigger than the other – the left arm, it's massive. If that bigger arm made them better climbers (to avoid predators), better foragers (they can reach for more fruits and things) and better hunters (they can use their big arm to club things to death) then they will be better fed and safer than other families. Their children have a lower mortality rate, so they go on to have more children with the genes for bigger left arms who also flourish and have more children who survive more successfully than their smaller-armed cousins and, generation upon generation, there are slightly more genes for big arms than small arms. Let's say one per cent more each breeding cycle. Speed this up: over a hundred generations, over a thousand – if the bigger left arm is still an advantage then many more *sapiens* now have the genes for it. There are more big left arms in any community, and now it becomes competitive, perhaps about twenty per cent of all the *sapiens* have this big left arm, but now they are foraging and hunting so well that there is less food for the small-armers, whose children now have an even higher mortality rate, blah blah blah, you can see where this is going, eventually all *sapiens* end up with a big left arm. It takes millennia but it happens.

Sexual selection is just as gradual a process, but rather than improving the spread of certain genes through an animal's fitness, it happens via mating opportunity. Imagine there was the same mutation, a hundred thousand years ago, but that hefty left arm does *not* help with climbing or foraging or hunting. Instead it is super sexy, just plain gorgeous to have a big left arm, and the males from the big-left-arm family have sex with about twenty per cent more females than small-armed fellows, while females from the big-left-arm family have more choice of breeding partners and can select much stronger and healthier males than the average female. Over thousands of generations the genes for this purely aesthetic advantage would have a wider and wider spread. This too could result in all *sapiens* developing big left arms over tens of thousands of years.

And often there's an overlap. Imagine if that big left arm was found sexually attractive *because* it enabled those who possessed it to be better food providers and thus exciting potential mates. With both forces working upon mate selection as well upon any offspring's survival rates and their mating opportunities, genes would be spread even faster. I'm so convinced by my own argument I'm wondering why people don't have a big left arm when they are clearly so great – then I remember that symmetry is an important visual signal of health in humans. It proves – or suggests – that there was no illness, parasites or malnourishment in childhood and adolescence apparently. Maybe that's why the fictional big left arms never stood a chance?

As odd as it is to think about, you are made like any other animal, with ornamentations and attributes that advertise your worth. Your physical composition speaks as to your mate potential. This is an inescapable truth. No matter how civilised we are, typing away in our offices, we are programmed to assess each other, everyone we meet, for indications of health and fertility. This is why beautiful people are more likely to get away with crimes than ugly people, it's why older women find themselves unrepresented on television, it's why disabled or physically unusual people have to fight so much social stigma to gain respect and equal rights. As unfair as this seems, as unfair as this *is*, if we become more aware of our inbuilt animal bias we can improve. We can make better conscious decisions, question our reactions and ~~send good-looking people to prison~~ improve our human interactions.

Just as our judgement of others is based on subconscious evolutionary programming, so is our low-level awareness of being assessed back. It's why feeling attractive is so closely linked to confidence. It's behind our urge to manipulate what others see of us through shaping clothing, padded bras, make-up, Instagram filters and, in extreme cases, cosmetic surgery. It's why being a woman can sometimes feel like being an unwilling shop window – constantly visible and considered an advertisement. Our selfhood is obscured by superficial valuation. Whether we like it or not, women's bodies evolved physical ornaments that signal our ability to conceive children. It is creepy and unfortunate but instinctual. Men look at women and women look at each other; we assess height and hair shininess and face shape – but the most fundamental adornment, our trustworthiest signal of vitality and potential, the hot brightness of our glow, is fat. Fatty fatty fat fat. Body fat enabled our species to survive; it created the energy store to grow our brains. Like the big left arms of my imagination, a high body fat percentage was both naturally and sexually selected in our evolution. If you have ever felt negatively about any fat on your body, I am about to attempt to change your mind. And mine.

Bums, Boobs and Clever Old Fat

Once upon a time a woman was reading a magazine that was aimed at making women feel bad about themselves so that they would buy stuff. It was called You're Fat! *magazine. The woman enjoyed the bright coloured pictures of the publication and the familiar sting of hating herself. And then, across the page, there was a QUIZ! 'What body shape are you?' The woman answered the questions in her fine, calorie-counting mind and the answers revealed that she was apple-shaped. Shaped like an APPLE. Suddenly everything made sense: the fact she always rolled off bus seats and couldn't hold pens. No wonder she couldn't get a husband. Sure, some guys liked her stem and leaf, but all of her boyfriends had found that ash-like grassy patch on her bottom gross. And all women have been shaped like fruit ever since, except hourglass women, they are the happiest women of all as they are filled entirely with sand.*

When I started writing this book I enrolled on a course for Body Confidence. A burlesque performer with a degree in psychology would teach a small group of us to love our bodies. 'This will be great for research,' I told myself, which was a lie. I want to stop hating my body because it is so time-consuming and because it makes me so sad sometimes. I get angry at myself about how lucky I am to be healthy and alive and how stupid it is to cry about how you look in a bikini. I also find the idea of any kind of journey towards self-acceptance utterly repulsive. '#firstworldproblems,' I would say sarcastically if I was planning to go on a course like this for myself, 'maybe you can take a class in vapid self-obsession afterwards.' So here I'd cleverly solved the conundrum, pretending my incentive wasn't my *own* body confidence but the other women on the course – I could write about them and learn things. When you are a great liar like me, deceiving yourself is easy.

To make sense of the statement 'Hating my body is time-consuming' I could describe a simple process like 'getting dressed' or 'preparing to leave the house' and demonstrate how much of my daily thought is squandered on hiding my stomach – but I don't want you to know. I am very embarrassed about how I feel. I'm ashamed that I care about what I look like and I've been aiming since childhood for invisibility. I could never be small enough; my ideal body shape is disembodied voice, radio. And it's a secret. I haven't talked to friends about my body since I was a teenager and I don't confide in my family. My insecurity is more than weakness – I consider it a personality defect. I have always believed it makes me a bad person, a vain, shallow waste of humanity. With all of the awful, terrible things that happen in the world, how dare I spend all my time thinking about my bottom? I have the luxury of being one of the few fortunate women on the planet who are safe and sheltered and fed and watered, and I have the audacity to be unhappy. The only thing I hate more than my bum is my preoccupation with it. A cycle of self-hate: I hate my body and I hate *me* because I hate my body. And seeing all this written down, it is CRAZY that I don't think of my body as 'me' but as something that my 'self' is trapped inside.

Any concern with appearance is a time tax. Conditioning, colouring, scrubbing, plucking and shopping. Apparently Albert Einstein had loads of suits but they were all exactly the same so he never had to think about what to wear.* He went on to use that saved brainpower to do something very brilliant like invent the car.

It's scary how much of my inner monologue is consumed by debating food choices, berating myself for what I've recently eaten and promising I'll do better. Plus the hours in front of the mirror, prodding, sobbing, trying everything on and deciding not to leave the house. My weight has stopped me doing things, has kept me from parties and dinners and award ceremonies because the stress of attempting to look 'nice' has beaten me.

I don't know if the fact that my job involves people looking at me makes it worse. Comedians put themselves down a lot; it's an easy source of comedy. At my early gigs I had material about how physically disgusting I was and how I couldn't get a boyfriend or whatever. And then I saw another woman do the same kind of thing – a brilliant and beautiful comedian who I really respect – and seeing it from the outside, I realised the effects; we were apologising for ourselves while reinforcing to all of the women in the audience that we *were* fat and it *did* matter. And I decided never to do it again. I would never again write a joke about not being good enough because of my appearance. Now I imitate arrogance instead, but in the nervy few moments before every show I wish I had worn something more flattering and fret that someone will heckle me about my weight. No one ever has. My enemy is internal.

When I was fourteen, my best friend Hayley and I would get dressed together at her house before going out. We often planned what we would change as soon as we could afford

* Easier for him though cos he had curly hair, which makes your head seem bigger, which makes your body look smaller. That's general relativity.

plastic surgery. I'd get big boobs and a small nose, she would get liposuction and a six-pack like Peter Andre's. Hayley always told me to do make-up first, get dressed second, because hiding how ugly your face was would make you feel better about your body. I have to get dressed on my own now, but I live with my boyfriend so sometimes he comes in and his face, his facial expression, when I am freaking out and throwing things and being hysterical – he stands there pale and big-eyed and baffled about how this can happen to a grown-up, intelligent woman who just popped into the bedroom to put some trousers on to go to Sainsbury's. 'I'M SORRY,' I yell at him, like yelling ever improved a situation, like an apology ever meant more by being louder and aggressively intoned. He looks scared and I get angrier. A logical me observes from a distance, knowing I'm being completely mad, but can't do anything about it. I'm on irrational and unpleasant autopilot. I don't look in mirrors when I am out of the house because it is too dangerous. My reflection in a shop window can cause me to go home. The memory of a great gig is ruined if I am emailed photographs that were taken.

Since early adolescence I've been ridiculous, but now I had this course. I didn't hope to be fixed, but the act of booking it, paying for it, turning up there, would be the *beginning*. The undoing of nearly thirty years of constant inner negativity. I was going to listen to the other women's feelings about themselves, their journey, and I was going to tell them they were beautiful and mean it and see them start to *feel* it. And I, I would start to feel it too. I could never love myself, no way, but if I could get to a neutral position of not caring, *well*, imagine what I could do with all the time and thoughts I'd reclaim; I would do more charity work, breastfeed the poor, reinvent the car – a better car, one that's made of balloons and pops if you hit any animals or people – I couldn't wait to be more productive!

'Thank you for enrolling in your chosen class: Self Esteem and Body Confidence,' said the confirmation email. 'For the first session, please bring an outfit that makes you feel really sexy.' There was then a list of suggestions; hot pants, mini-skirt, high heels, suspenders, catsuit etc. I cried for a while imagining how great it must be if you have an outfit that makes you feel sexy.

I hope you understand why I didn't go.

Broadly speaking, there are many differences between men and women. These differences will never be universal, never true for every single person, and there will always be a larger variance *within* a gender than *between* the genders. That is a confusing sentence so I'll reword it more simply. Take height. Here is the broad stroke: men are taller than women. But this is not universal, because loads and loads of women are taller than loads and loads of men. Also the height difference between the world's tallest man and the world's shortest man is much more than the difference between the average height of men and women – *comprendos?* On average, as well as being shorter, women are fatter than men. Woohoo for us, the roly-poly tiny guys. On average we're composed of twenty-seven per cent fat while the typical stringy manthing is only fourteen per cent. As I'm sure you're aware by now, nothing about the body's composition is an accident. We are perfectly built; any flaws about our ancestors' persons were thrown into the bin of natural selection. Our doubled body fat means something. Either fat was imperative to our individual survival OR it was sexually selected OR, da da da da da DA, both.

If we were to slip down the hill of time and hang out with the humans of forty thousand years ago we'd find they were physiologically the same as us. If you'd been born then, you would be you – there would be differences in socialisation, you wouldn't have as many shoes, but your brain and body would be identical. Pre-farming, with no domesticated animals or reliable crops, you and your family would have foraged and hunted about for the things you liked to eat/anything edible you could find. The calories contained in the food you ate would likely be burned off during your endeavours to find more food. Rooting, scouting and scavenging would have been your main exercise and the majority of your waking hours would be spent locating the sustenance needed to keep you alive. In any country of the world, in any era of human existence up until the last hundred years, a slow metabolism was beneficial. Storing energy as fat is an insurance policy for the lean times – a long winter, a drought, any time when food is scarce. The skinny, too-fast-metabolismed women of prehistory perished. We can cry for them later.

For post-adolescent women, fat on the body is an announcement. It proves that they are great at finding food and, even better, that they have plenty of energy saved up ready to feed their children. Males who preferred fatter females were rewarded throughout our evolution with a higher survival rate for their offspring. A woman with a surplus of stored fat can utilise that energy even at times of starvation. It is broken down when she needs to breastfeed her babies, so the enriched milk nourishes her children through their most vulnerable years. This incredibly sensitive and reactive storage system saved and enabled our lives. Men have evolved to store only enough fat for themselves – you're wriggling round with a family's worth. And I've been idiotic in despising something I should've been worshipping.

We have to learn more about fat. The word is poisoned by negative connotations: greed, bad health and abnormality. I've considered my fat as a visual punishment, a toxin. And it's not, it's a magnificent organ with the worst PR team in history. Fat is our energy source, our batteries – fatteries? Hmm, yes, fatteries. It's our fillable hamster cheeks. Our fattery cells are storing processed calories, condensed into lipids and waiting there until we need them. If you are an average woman (I certainly don't think of you that way) and I kidnapped and starved you for an experiment (I'm a terrible friend), you could survive for around two months. THANKS, FAT, FOR SAVING YOUR LIFE.

Every single cell of your fat is *amazing*. It's not some numb luggage, it's alive and a vital part of your endocrine system. Adipose tissue (or fat) releases a hormone called leptin which travels via your blood to your hypothalamus and lets your brain know how much you're carrying. If you've got enough your brain will inhibit appetite; if you need more the hormone ghrelin will be produced, which encourages hunger. That conversation is going on constantly as your body regulates itself to maintain a perfect balance, a shape and size that will keep you at your strongest and healthiest, ready for the longest trek or the harshest winter.

Fat also produces oestrogen. Your lovely lady sex hormone is largely provided by ovaries, but supplemented by kindly fat cells. Being super-skinny means a bit less oestrogen, which might result in irregular periods in younger women and a more difficult menopause for older ones. The residual oestrogen from fat is why plump ladies age a bit better and their skin seems a little smoother. And not all fat is the same. During adolescence girls can gain between ten and twenty kilos of adipose tissue. It is mainly located on the bum and upper thighs and is composed of omega-3 polyunsaturated fatty acids. This is the exact same stuff that adverts for butter substitutes are always telling us is 'good fat'. Well, good is an understatement, mate. Omega-3 polyunsaturated fat is a large component of the human brain. The adolescent female body is storing it up ready for any children that will come later. When she breastfeeds, the omega-3 polyunsaturated fat around her hips will be used to fortify her milk and build her baby's most important organ. How can I have been allowed to hate my wobbly thighs when there were brains in there all along? BRAINS! Minds. The things that compose sonnets and invent balloon cars. Our massive brains are about sixty per cent fat, by far the fattiest organ in our body – without fat there would be no thought.

You are correct, that does deserve a 'Congratulations, fat' trumpet:

Here's another thing to consider. If you *were* living forty thousand years ago your only impression of what you looked like would have been from looking down. You could see your hands and wiggling fingers; your arms up to the shoulder if you turned your head; your belly, hairy pudenda, your legs heading off towards the floor with little feet down there in the distance. But no matter how much you craned your head round you could not find your bottom. You could feel it with your hands, squeeze it, you'd know it was comfy for sitting on. You could look at other people's bottoms but you couldn't accurately compare your own to theirs. I assume back then I'd have been bowling about assuming my derrière was as delicious as the nicest ones I saw, and with no mirror to prove otherwise, how happy I'd have been. I'd have patted my own cheeks and thought, 'Yes, that's about right,' and continued feeling fabulous. During our species's entire evolution we would never have seen ourselves reflected clearly. Our assessment of self-worth and status would have been drawn from the behaviours of others around us. We were completely unable to scrutinise certain aspects of our physicality until some bastard invented metal-backed glass two thousand years ago. Our modern silver-backed mirrors have only existed for two hundred years, and this is relevant because they affect our self-confidence. Psychological studies consistently demonstrate that looking in the mirror makes us feel worse about ourselves. For people with body dysmorphic disorder just twenty-five seconds of mirror-gazing can produce anxiety and stress, and for healthy confident people ten minutes can lead to distress and becoming more self-critical. The less we look in the mirror, the happier we could be with our appearance. In fact one study found that women who were blind and couldn't look at themselves were more satisfied with their appearance and dieted less than sighted women. Any mirror-staring sessions are doing us harm.

Until I started researching for this book I'd always assumed that concern about the aesthetics of our bodies was a modern insanity – but it's actually an evolved behaviour that recent inventions are sending into overdrive. We are predisposed; the reason I care about the shape of my hips and the pertness of

my buttocks is that they tell tales about my worth as a breeding partner. The safety and security of my female ancestors
would have been partly determined by their shape. Their value and status within their tribe was connected to their health,
youth and fertility. The same is true for all mammals on this
planet, yet none of them evolved consciousness of it. None of
them invented the mirror and developed enough awareness
of self to stand in front of it fretting.

Our male ancestors made conscious and subconscious
choices about who to mate with and some of those selections
were more successful (in reproductive terms) than others.
A penchant for women too weak to bear children, too old,
too narrow-hipped, led to a dead end for those genes. What
remains worked. There have been tons of studies on what
makes women attractive; you'll be aware of oft-quoted 'ideal'
female body measurements. Out-in-out, boobs-waist-hips. It
seems not to be a woman's size that matters so much as her
proportions. When they've tested male and female prefer-
ences for women's bodies they reliably define 'perfection' as
a ratio of around 0.7 between breasts and waist and again between waist and hips; the classic 'hourglass' shape lauded by
magazines. Whether six foot or four and a half, whether eight
stone or fifteen, it is these proportions that mark a woman as
a wonderful beauty. Interestingly (well I thought so anyway),
when men and women are asked to draw the ideal female
body the ratio stays much the same but men generally draw
a fleshier, wider woman. Heterosexual men have an inbuilt
appreciation for female body fat that is not reflected by the
tastes of modern women – what does this mean? Is it because
our female ancestors bred with men whose body fat percentage was half of ours, so they assume the same is ideal for us?

Are heterosexual women seeking to be like the men they want to attract? Or is our obsession with youth idealising tiny female frames?

The small waist, flat stomach thing *is* related to youth. Remember that until recently, almost any sexually active woman would be pregnant every few years so her stomach would show the effects of childbearing and her waist would widen gradually throughout her life. A 0.7 ratio is nature's way of indicating fertility; the widened hips and breast fat acquired in adolescence alongside the flat, smooth belly of the un-impregnated. It's a body that says 'I'm ready and able'. Even more incredibly, this indication of fertility is not a deception. It appears that women with a desirable waist–hip ratio do conceive more easily than those with thicker waists or slimmer hips. The hormones that have sculpted their physique are the exact same ones necessary for baby-making, lucky bitches. And so male humans are driven to seek curves exactly as their glow worm equivalents are drawn to light.

And this is how women lose twice. Once in being looked at and once in the looking. Women's bodies are compartmentalised. Those feelings you've had since childhood, of being sized up like a prize marrow, being assessed and weighed and eaten up by eyes, are real. The psychologist Sarah Gervais conducted studies in which people looked at photographs of men and women, some of which were digitally enhanced. She found that when there was a woman in the picture the eyes of both genders focused on breasts, waist and genitals. Gervais also tested participants' memories and found both men and women were more likely to recall a woman's breasts than her face. Participants of both genders appeared to view men as whole and women in pieces. It's awful, but it makes sense. In a way it's reassuring – you're not mad or imagining things, everyone is looking at you all of the time (especially if you're young). And you're looking at women too. Why? Don't shout all at once; yes please, Clara, you've got your hand up nicely:

CLARA

Is it because we all secretly fancy each other?

Clara, that's a good theory, and of course *some* of this eye-balling is sexual in nature – women are attracted to each other occasionally or exclusively – but that doesn't explain all of it. Shelley?

SHELLEY

Is it because we hate each other and view each other as competition?

Erm, that's nearly right. We don't hate each other, but we are aware of each other. Sometimes unknowingly aware, if that makes sense – for hundreds of thousands of years before clothing and farming and capitalism, our bodies were almost all we had. We might have had a few tools or that day's food, but no other external signals of status. And status is extremely important to all animals, it relates directly to your power and safety, your resources and comfort. Human beings have evolved to be hyper-aware of their personal position in any group, and to find our place we assess each other. That's why women look at each other's skin, hair and body shape. And that's why our self-esteem is connected to our body image, because instinctually we connect being attractive with high status, protection, usefulness and power. When we feel physically inferior to the women around us it can be very difficult to feel happy and sane. Our big fat brains cannot help

compartmentalising other women and visually dissecting ourselves because we assess our bodies like a product we're selling and it's been that way for millennia.

Let's have a little remember about the modern world now:
it's not just mirrors we're surrounded by but billboard advertising, television and cinema, pornography in every household
and magazines in every supermarket. Women women women,
undressed women, lingerie-clad women, smooth-contoured
sex-faced women, busty, luscious, flat-stomached women,
glowing, poreless, young, unwrinkled women. Photoshopped
women, digitally enhanced women, fifty foot high, staring
right at you, aggressively threatening women. How you coping with that, ape lady?

Both men and women have their attention caught by attractive women, so attractive women are used to catch our
attention. In advertising, that attention means money, with
the wonderful bonus that making women feel insecure makes
them spend even *more* money. Especially on all the crap that's
supposed to make us look better or hide imperfections. Looking at pictures of semi-clad models makes all women's self-
esteem plummet – scientists have tested it. Even model types
downgrade their own attractiveness after viewing the kind of
photos you'd find in any women's magazine. But we know
that, right? I know not to buy glossy-paged rubbish that's going to make me feel inadequate, but what about all the stuff I
can't ignore? What about when they plaster my environment
with images that I can't escape?

I'm not stupid, I know if you're selling a body lotion or
some tiny lacy knickers then a long-legged beauty is the ideal
canvas and even if I cry myself to sleep with jealous rage at
least the advert makes sense. But, BUT so often it DOESN'T.

Like there's this charity, okay, and they're working to high-light the depletion of the world's oceans. And every year they create a celebrity campaign and every year the campaign is naked women holding dead fish. The photos make it on to the front page of the newspapers and the accompanying article is always: here is a naked famous woman, she is holding a fish. The publicity is fuelled by nudity, and there is quite a *lot* of publicity because for a couple of days the papers all have licence to put naked women on the front as this is actually about a really important issue which is – sorry, I thought I saw a nipple, what were you saying?

This fish campaign fascinates me. The photographs are very arresting, existing somewhere between porn and comedy, the airbrushed glamour of the well-groomed, stripped human horribly undermined by the shiny-scaled corpse obscuring boobs and fanny. Last year on a train I saw twenty Helena Bonham Carters topless astride fish, and I tore them all out and took them home. I felt ashamed for her, discarded as she was all over the Northern line. I felt patronised on behalf of all human beings. 'Even *charities* are exploiting nudity now, even the good guys . . . none of us are expected to engage with anything any more unless it's scrawled on or next to bared flesh,' I ranted to John when I got home. 'Let's have a look,' he joked, so I went for a quick cry in the bathroom, watching in the mirror to see how my face looked when I was disappointed with the media.

I feel affronted by female nudity; sometimes I feel attacked by it. On a bad day I'll count how many women in their underwear I see on posters on my way to work, but what am I supposed to do with that information? I might mention it when I arrive at my gig, moan on and on about it if I'm with someone, but there's no catharsis. Bombardment, that's the word that I would use, I am BOMBARDED. Once on an escalator at Oxford Circus station, I passed by fifty-six women in their pants, sleepily cunning and looking through me. Fifty-six against one, that's bullying. And I hate myself for my inability to ignore them. Posters for burger restaurants or shiny Jeeps blur into the background of my journey but not the women. I hate the meat industry and I loathe cars (sorry Einstein) but they don't sadden and dismay me like a Wonderbra ad.

Of course I don't blame the stupid sea charity, this is how the world works and I understand their position; stats on declining fish populations, descriptions of water pollution and insufficient governmental regulation do not make it to the front page on their own. Beautiful women do. Only women do. Because we were built to like looking at women more than absolutely anything else. But doesn't the use of nudity undermine the importance of the message? Since when has a woman with no top on been taken more seriously? We don't pop our bras off before important meetings. From my experience, we tend to feel more pressure to cover up when we want to be listened to because we *know* our body is distracting, which is another shit thing. We should be able to go to work and church and round the town centre wearing whatever we bloody like but we're too accustomed to the assumptions and reactions caused by our bared skin to be truly free. When baring does take place it is brave and raunchy, it has to be owned. I am thinking of Jodie Marsh wearing two belts as a top – look that up if you've never seen her – she embodies this. Any kind of serious underdressing is a visible act of defiance and acknowledgement. When girls go out in tiny skirts or in their bras the message is loud and what they're *always* saying is 'I know you're looking – so look then.'

Anyway, these are thoughts I'm thinking now after years of noticing and reflecting. When I was a child, posters were just posters, magazines were mere magazines, not PROPA-GANDA OF THE PATRIARCHY. But I started feeling fat very young. It was the ultimate insulting adjective at primary school. Cheryl and I called each other fat all the time. My mum would stand in front of the mirror and call herself fat; we'd call her fat too if we were arguing. There is a picture of me at about eleven, I am up a tree, very high up actually because I'm amazing at everything. Someone came over to take a photograph and I asked them not to but they did. I am doing Princess Diana face, shy and ashamed, because I knew I looked fat in my stripy leggings and I didn't want anyone to look and the camera embarrassed me. The girl in the photo is so skinny. At every age I have felt revolting but when I look at pictures of past me I can't believe the slim young woman I was can have felt like that. I've tried to think, 'Future you will look back and think that about you now,' and that did not help, it merely made me realise I'm only going to get *fatter* and *older* until I die.

I was fourteen when I realised I had cellulite. I had been giv-en a red-and-white gingham bikini. There was a girl at school who wore a see-through swimming costume, you could see her bum crack and her nipples when it was wet, and I wanted to check my suit wasn't similarly flawed. I wore it in the bath and then bent over in front of a mirror, only to find I had leg cancer all down the back of both legs. I checked the bath for wicker matting, I moved the curtains in case the dappling was a trick of the light. How could I have been walking around looking like this? From waist to knee (these were the heady days before the big C found my arms and stomach) I was lumpy bumpy broken. 'Orange-peel skin', *More* magazine and *Just Seventeen* would call it, but oranges are delicious and purposeful and my thighs were porridgy idiots letting me down. I couldn't afford any kind of anti-cellulite cream so I didn't buy any. I read an article about how Pamela Anderson massaged her bum and thighs on the toilet for up to two hours a day to keep cellulite at bay, so I tried that for three minutes before giving up and lightly carving 'FAT' on my thigh with a razor blade instead.

(Step behind the curtain for a sec. When I handed in a first draft of the book to Julian, my editor, the above line was focused upon as being, I dunno, I guess harsh? Or a bit shocking – which really surprised me. 'Julian, have you never *met* a teenage girl?' I shrugged off his concern. I explained to him that girls between twelve and twenty spend a great deal of their time hurting their bodies in different ways. He suggested this was not normal, while I thought it was. Everyone I know hurt themselves a bit. Tried it out. Had low points and recovered. Julian then very rightly pointed out that I would have to be responsible in case any young women were reading this and might be influenced or incited – and that is a very good reason not to be flippant about what he referred to as 'self-harm' but I called 'something girls do sometimes'. But it is serious. If I think of a young woman currently feeling alone and self-loathing enough to put a razor on her skin in such a way – even to write a *complimentary* word – I would do anything I could to stop it. I wish I was friends with all the teenage girls in the world because I could cuddle you all and tell you how much better life gets, how much more reasonable and bearable. And that you are never to blame for the pain that you feel and that's why hurting yourself is an injustice. Also, exercise helps: have an angry run or swim, ache a bit that way. And talk to people you know and trust or to strangers who understand and are trained. Big hugs and back we go. Xxx)

I always believed that cellulite was caused by toxins because THAT IS WHAT I HAVE BEEN TOLD, repeatedly, by journalists and copywriters. Cellulite is caused by alcohol and chocolate and coffee and cat videos and joy, they said; deny yourself, avoid all pleasures or you get the thighs you deserve. Turns out they're liars and it's actually hormones. Oestrogen, insulin, noradrenaline and thyroid hormones all affect how fat cells are connected to each other. With oestrogen it can result in some cells bulging out of their little clusters, giving the bumpy-rump look we know and despise. So two-hour rubs aren't gonna help you unless they can erase your genetic predispositions, and any time you see some ointment advertising itself as an 'orange-peel' antidote, ask the man at Superdrug: 'REALLY? Does this fifteen-quid cream that is probably tested on animals *actually* get absorbed inside my body to restructure my hormonal interplay and destroy my fat deposits which, BY THE WAY, are future possible babies' brains, MATE?'

They make so much money off us, you know, so much cash leeched via our self-hatred. Billions a year spent on useless pointless crap. I don't believe in conspiracy theories, I don't think The Man has meetings with other The Mans where they plan how to do this but . . . there is complicity. Think of us, fifty-one per cent of the population all crouching in bathrooms, pummelling our bum cheeks like imbeciles, when we should be taking over this crazy world and stopping all the wars.

BUT IT'S *SO HARD* NOT TO CARE. Or rather, *I* find it hard not to care.

When I was little my mum would stand in front of the mirror, maybe she was getting dressed or into the bath. She would ask me if she had small boobs, she would ask me if she was fat. I thought she was beautiful, with massive tits, and I always told her that for as long as I can remember. What I struggle with now is that it's a body I inherited. The tops of my arms became my mother's at the end of my twenties. My breasts, when they finally arrived, were equally small. 'I don't mind the size,' she would say, 'but you ruined them.' I was the first baby and a big one and I stretched all her stomach skin and drank all her pertness and I always regretted it. I took her body when she was still a teenager, and I scarred her. My father was unravaged so he could leave and seduce other women without my marks of ownership on him. As a child I felt guilty when I was told I looked like my dad, that I reminded my mum of him, but now my face is all my mum's – I am now the age she was when I was fifteen. My smile, eyes, voice, phrasing, thighs, bum, arms and boob disappointment are all inherited. And when I hate my body I feel guilty of matricide. And I wonder how much of this I learned by imitation. And even wondering that, I feel bad for blaming her.

My friend Katherine[*] has a daughter who is currently six. We were all in Australia for work, and after breakfast one day I called myself a pig. 'I'm a piggy, I don't know when to stop,'

[*] Katherine Ryan is an immensely brilliant comedian who you are probably already familiar with and jealous that I know her. You should be jealous: she is the most composed and strong person I have ever met. And generous and compassionate and sensitive. A hero. And her daughter called their cat 'Sara Pascoe' and I get so happy whenever I remember there is a little male cat with my full name.

I said to no one as we walked to the lift. And Katherine asked me, so sweetly and rightly, not to say things like that in front of children: 'You teach them it's wrong to like food.'

Of course, OF COURSE we perpetuate a cycle with what we say in front of children, and of course we reinforce what we believe when we allow each other to call ourselves fat and ugly. So we've got these three routes of attack – the people around us, the messages of culture (people not around us but able to affect us), and then the inbuilt propensity to care. And it is different for women and it *is* emotional. When men and women were shown digitally altered images of themselves in an MRI, only the women's brains showed engagement of the pre-frontal cortex and parahippocampal area. This included the amygdala which is crucial to our emotional functioning. So the female response was emotional while the male counterpart was visual and spatial. Seeing a fatter image of themselves was *felt* by women, but only *seen* by men.

This means something. It restricts how we live our lives. The connection between our body image and our happiness isn't superficial. Seventy per cent of American women were found to believe that being thinner would make them happier – seventy per cent isn't a small problem in a varied society, it's an epidemic. And it affects more than just mealtimes. It influences the choices we make, our energy, our confidence. It's physically restraining – you can't rule the world when you're feeble from starving yourself.

I've eaten variations of a constrained diet since I was fourteen. I have seriously starved myself for two periods in my life and have only stopped skipping meals since I became vegan and gained a different type of control. Veganism helped me break a guilt cycle, and now I eat much more and I reflect on my fainty, light-headed earlier incarnations with much self-sympathy. Both my big starves were heart-related. After breaking up with Colin, I didn't feel hungry very often. It was like a switch went off. But whenever I *did* feel hungry I'd imagine him having sex with his new girlfriend and it would go away. On a 'good day' I would eat two green apples and drink two Diet Cokes. A 'bad day' would mean a sandwich and maybe alcohol. I got skinny. I could afford to buy clothes from Bay Trading with the dinner money I was saving, because the clothes in my new size were all reduced to clear. A teacher at sixth form stopped me in the corridor and asked me what had happened. She told me to 'go eat a burger' and I sulked off after telling her I was vegetarian, but I felt amazing because she'd noticed. I checked myself for symptoms of anorexia – I wanted hairy arms; when you had the hair, you knew you'd made it. I joined a dance class but I had to stop going because I fainted every week; I pretended to be embarrassed but I was proud. I had one friend Hayley who could make herself sick, but I couldn't, and a different friend Hayley (the one who wanted Peter Andre abs) who told me about laxatives you could shoplift from Boots. I took Chocolax because I can't swallow pills. Chocolax you could eat and it just tasted like the worst thing you've ever eaten. That's when my mum started to notice because the bathroom always smelled so bad. I didn't care that I stank. I was sewagey, like a drain full of the dead. My stomach went concave and I got obsessed by the comparative bulbousness of my arse. I was the saddest I've ever been, and yet I was euphoric on skinniness. I looked at myself constantly. I was my own project, I was my own work of art and I owned myself for the first time.

My second starve was after another break-up. His name was

Steve, he smelled smoky and had a concave chest. He was so clever about science and, he warned me, incapable of love. I spent months with him, eroded by how much I loved him and how he cringed whenever I said so. He was a comedian, so when we split I started stand-up, partly as an exercise in combating grief with creativity but mostly as a revenge move. I wanted to understand why he couldn't focus on me properly; why gigs I'd thought he'd done fine at would follow him and bother him for days; I wanted to know where his mind went when I was talking, because afterwards he never remembered anything I'd said. AND I wanted to be more successful than him, and now I *am* more successful than him and WHAT IS THE POINT of being on television if it doesn't make your exes want to get back with you? Maybe when I get that Oscar.

So this was 2007, I started stand-up, I started swimming and I stopped eating. I wouldn't let myself eat anything until evening. Sometimes I would let myself drink calories rather than eating them, get pissed on a large glass of wine and go on stage happy with forgetting. The only time I didn't think about Steve was when I was on stage talking about him. I had to teach myself to swim, because I was scared of getting my head wet since a school trip when I was nine – they took us to Hainault forest for a week, and midway through marched us across fields to a communal shower. This was the term after we'd finished our project on the Holocaust. My teacher ordered me to get undressed as I begged her not to gas us. I have been traumatised by a Nazi/water death certainty ever since, but now I was twenty-six and I was forcing myself to put my head under and provoking myself up and down the pool. I whacked and slapped at the lengths with my arms until I felt too weak to hate and then I allowed myself to get out. There was another woman who went every day and I watched her shrink and wondered what pain she was escaping. I looked out for her at gigs but she doesn't seem to have found the obliteration of stand-up. She also never learned to put her head under.

My new stand-up friends didn't know my real size. Tania once said I was 'naturally tiny', ha ha ha ha. Lou hugged me after a gig and said, 'I didn't realise you were going to be so bony!' and I replied, 'I've put on so much weight recently,' which wasn't true but it felt it. After months I saw Steve at a rehearsal for something. I took a chocolate brownie out of my bag to eat in front of him so he would know I was fine. He said he was worried about me and it was the best day of my life, but I crashed when he left and didn't kiss me or need me and it didn't feel like he was very worried. I had to move out from Katie's house – I lived with my best friend and her mum, and Katie saw, I couldn't deceive her. She knew the food in my cupboards, she witnessed my new drinking habits and the state I came back in. I said I wasn't on a diet, and I wasn't. It wasn't a diet, I wanted to die. Every time she tried to talk to me about it I avoided her more, until she cried and said I hurt her when I hurt myself, and so I left. It is very difficult to accept any claim of love or affection when you are in a hole of worthlessness. You can't trust anyone who tells you are beautiful or lovable or even 'fine'. And that is how the person who loved me best became my secret enemy for many years.

Both the phases I describe above were a few months of what would be called 'disordered eating'. Everyone I know has eaten in a disordered way sometimes. I assume this is a normal part of the modern western woman's experience. It's a side effect, isn't it? Of the constant availability of food, our mother's attitude to food, the daily information about what's healthy and what should be avoided, and the images – acres of tits and ass to cross on every journey, and a lady's heart full of feelings sometimes can't cope with it all.

Anorexia is an eating disorder, but should be considered separately from disordered eating. Most people are familiar with anorexia and will have seen pictures of emaciated bodies with protruding bones, but the disease itself is not well understood. It could be perceived as a step further than a strict diet, a more extreme, committed version, but it's a much more complicated disease. While it might be triggered by emotional stress or media images just like disordered eating, anorexia is far more compulsive. Most doctors would now agree it is a pre-existing condition, a propensity that some people (mostly women) have that can be activated by environmental events or conditions. Anorexia is not a diet, it is a topsy-turvy existence where food and sustenance become 'bad'. Whereas people who are dieting or suffering from disordered eating are denying themselves something that they want, anorexics are protecting themselves from something they believe will do them harm. Does that make sense? It's why anorexia is so difficult to treat – it mutates what the body most needs into an enemy.

Anorexia nervosa was recognised as a condition in the nineteenth century, in 1873 to be exact. By Sir William Gull of all people, do you know him? He was one of Queen Victoria's doctors and was posthumously accused of being Jack the Ripper by many theorists and a film with Johnny Depp. But just to keep this in perspective, every single person alive in 1888 has been posthumously* suspected of the murders,

* I recently learned to pronounce this word and am celebrating by using it twice in one paragraph.

including Victoria herself, so let's not go ringing the *Daily Mail* with 'Jack the Ripper Invented Anorexia' just yet.

It's easy to believe that anorexia is a modern affliction, a response to our visual and terrible culture, but its origins pre-date that. Catholic girls in the thirteenth and fourteenth centuries are recorded as starving themselves to death and have since been sainted for their endeavours. Apparently Mary Queen of Scots displayed symptoms. Early records in many cultures describe purges or self-imposed famines: ancient Roman women punished their bodies by refusing food and old Chinese and Persian manuscripts describe the ailments of eating disorders. Because anorexia frequently manifests during adolescence psychologists surmise that it could be a denial of sexuality: a wish to remain a girl rather than transitioning into womanhood. I've read evolutionary psychologists' claims that eating disorders could be a response to stress, useful as a way of freezing fertility. Because starvation stops ovulation, eating disorders could be a subconscious way of avoiding pregnancy during dangerous times. Nature's brake pedal gone haywire in modernity.

More recent research links anorexia to autism. Some claim that anorexics don't empathise effectively with themselves and that there are similar obsessive behaviours in both groups. There is an interesting theory that there could be a genetic disposition for autism which tends to be expressed differently depending on gender, but there's a lot more research needed in this area – I can't tell you that it is proven fact. I'll just reiterate how complicated this disease is, how irrational it can appear to family members and loved ones who can't comprehend what a sufferer is experiencing and why they won't just eat. Why they can't believe that they are not fat. But imagine if everyone around you suddenly started telling you the sky was green – 'It's green, it's green, it's green,' everyone would say, and you would stop trusting them, you'd be suspicious or you'd feel mad or you'd want to agree with them but how can you distrust your own senses when they are all you have to decipher the world? Your eyes would tell you the sky is blue and that would be your only reality and no amount of conversation could change that.

There is certainly something inbuilt that makes girls more susceptible than boys to eating disorders, something that predates the billboards and pornography. But there is also clear evidence that such conditions are exacerbated by the messages of our media. In the 1990s there was a study in Fiji – a society of people who had no access to television and who celebrated bigger women, *really* big, more than curvy, robust. 'You've gained weight' was a Fijian compliment. Bigger brides were rewarded with bigger dowries and there were even fattening camps to feed up teenage girls. And then TV arrived and within three years the number of girls with symptoms of bulimia rose from three to fifteen per cent, with fifty per cent of girls now describing themselves as 'too fat'. The male Fijians continued to have the same pre-television ideals of beauty for men and women, but the women's changed, and changed quickly.

What seems obvious to me is that we've evolved to be aware of our bodies and those of the women around us but have no protection against the effects of mirrors and images, exactly as male glow worms evolved to be drawn to light but are unable to discern between electric bulbs and real females. Evolution couldn't predict our synthetic environment. My forty-thousand-year-old brain cannot defend itself from women on screens, pages and billboards. While intellectually

I can discern between fictional and actual, my instincts react to all of those women as real, real tribe members, real ideals, real local women that I can't compete with. If I lived in a regular tribe there would be twenty women older and twenty women younger than me and all at different stages of pregnancy or lactation and I would have a middling sense of security and confidence. Instead I am in a tribe of millions and on every surface I lay my eyes I see falsified female perfection. My *Homo sapiens* life should contain five or six goddesses, not thousands, hundreds of thousands, and my conscious brain can't protect me – I know about Photoshop, make-up, lighting, Spanx, botox, chicken fillets, liposculpture, I know Barbie couldn't give birth because of her dimensions, I know TopShop mannequins are only vaguely human-shaped and that cartoons are drawn to satisfy the fetishes of fantasy, but still. I am crushed.

So I would say I have two types of fat, good and bad. Right places and wrong places. There is the fat I dislike and think I have too much of (all that body below bra), and there are two places where I do not have enough. Or rather, I have the correct amount of fat but it's wrongly distributed. Time to meet my boobs.

SARA's boobs enter.

SARA
Hey guys. Should I address you together or as individuals?

LEFT BREAST
Well, we are usually considered as a unit, even though there are two of us, and we are different—

RIGHT BREAST

I am bigger and more optimistic—

LEFT BREAST

Right's right, I'm a bit depressed. And more sensitive.

SARA

So you're twins, but non-identical – like my mum and Aunty Juliet?

BOOBS

Yes.

SARA

Okay, so how is *our* relationship? Is it healthy?

BOOBS

Your main job is moving us around. You help us get from A to B, pop us in a crop top so we don't get too tired—

SARA

You don't need a proper bra.

RIGHT BREAST

We know. And that's fine with us, but you—

SARA (*not fine*)

It's fine. Honestly, I'm used to it.

BOOBS

You wish we were bigger—

SARA

I'm okay about it now.

LEFT BREAST
We swell up when you are due on and you like us more.

SARA
Um, ONE of you does—

From under the table, a booming voice.

BOTTOM (*O/S*)
YOU THINK I AM TOO BIG AND THEY ARE TOO
SMALL!

SARA (*to* **BOTTOM**)
This is not your interview, butt out – THAT IS NOT A
PUN. Stop picking on me, I don't want to be defined by
any of you—

*SARA grabs her boobs and bum and leaves the cafe. Everyone claps
because she is trying so hard to deal with her issues and if that can't
be applauded, what can?*

I read something a man wrote (I'm *very* open-minded)
about women's bodies. He was a bit obsessed with the idea
that evolution had disabled us with the impracticality of our
breasts. 'Can't run naked without pain,' he kept repeating;
'their breasts make running nude very uncomfortable,' he'd
interrupt himself. LET US WEAR SPORTS BRAS THEN,
let us wear sports bras even in your imagination, writer man.
Despite my uneasiness at the book's constant conjuring of undressed joggers, I do acknowledge his point. In pre-civilised
times, before nylon and Lycra, women evolved unnecessary
appendages on their chests that would make hunting and escape far more difficult for us than for boobless men.

Yes, you heard me right, 'unnecessary appendages'. The year-round chest fat that adult women have is not needed for milk production and bigger boobs do not mean (as I would've presumed) that you can make or hold more milk. All female mammals have nipples, all female mammals feed their young via lactation and none of them have surrounding fat deposits the size of ours. That's why they can sprint about happily without clothes on.

So why is this, please, nature?

If you look in an anthropology book from the 1970s, it will tell you that breasts developed as a result of human beings walking upright – which doesn't answer our question, which was *why*? And then Desmond Morris or one of his peers would come in to tell you:

DESMOND
To emulate the buttocks.

YOU
Are you insane?

DESMOND
No. You know how breasts look like buttocks—

YOU
Not in any way.

DESMOND
Yeah they do, this is science. So anyway, the buttocks were the main sexy area—

YOU
Why?

DESMOND
Because we had sex from behind.

YOU
We did not—

DESMOND
Human beings did, so men liked looking at bottoms.
They found bottoms arousing, associated them with
sex—

YOU (*dubious*)
Okay . . .

DESMOND
Uh-huh, and then once we were walking about, four
million years ago or whatever, we started having sex face
to face—

YOU
Why was that?

DESMOND
Logistics? Politeness? Anyway, then the bloke needed
something to look at, and so women grew breasts.

YOU
We grew them so that men could like them?

DESMOND
Yes. For sure.

YOU
And where is the evidence?

DESMOND

The *evidence* is that men like breasts.

YOU

So men* find breasts sexually exciting, so women must have grown them so that the men could be sexually excited?

DESMOND

Now you get it! Yes!

YOU

Isn't that what they call a circular argument?

DESMOND shrugs and runs back to the 1970s. He doesn't need a sports bra.

Because of their non-essential nature, the obvious conclusion is that breasts are a sexually selected trait, like peacocks' tails. But it's an unsatisfactory answer and it feels unfeminist to accept it. There are other theories, like the claim that changes in the shape of our faces millions of years ago meant that babies found it too difficult to latch on to a flat chest. Other apes and most mammals have snouty faces that can feed easily from fatless nipples – maybe as our faces got flatter our breasts had to get pointier? The aquatic ape theory (the little-credited claim that we lived in water for part of our evolution) argued that breasts needed to dangle down a bit so that a mother could feed a babe in arms while standing up in water or crouching on a rock.

Remember that every other mammal's young can suckle

---

* Heterosexual men, obvs.

while the mother lies about or gets on with her business. Not so human babies, who need their heads supported and cannot hold on like our ape cousins. So it's probably truest to say that breasts came to exist via a combination of natural and sexual selection. The fat deposits on a chest enable survival in lean times just as they do elsewhere on the body. Our ancestors may have looked to breast size for endurance, pertness for an honest indication of youth, and symmetry for an honest indication of health.

The most fascinating thing I found out is that when a woman breastfeeds her child, her brain releases oxytocin, that gorgeous hormone which promotes bonding. This makes perfect evolutionary sense – women need to be well loved up with their babies to put up with all the annoying stuff they do. Many women really enjoy breastfeeding and recognise it as an emotional communion between them and their child. And babies' brains also release oxytocin when their stomach is stretched by milk during feeds, so that love is building in both directions – it is so amazingly clever. But guess what? When a non-lactating woman has her breasts sucked, touched and stimulated her brain *also* releases oxytocin. The result is that she will feel lovely and warm towards the sex partner who is paying her boobs lots of attention; she will feel more attached to him or her. What this means is that something that evolved for better mother–child bonding has been hijacked to promote monogamy and pair bonding. So there's an argument that the males who were most fascinated or obsessed with breasts would have touched and caressed them more during mating, which would have resulted in stronger pair ties. More parental input via that cohesive partnership then increased the odds of the infant's survival and so strengthened the genetic propensity for breast fetishisation in future generations. A fun hundred thousand years later and we end up with boobs on every billboard – thanks nature!

For our pre-civilised ancestors, the exposed breasts of a woman would have been a quick and easy way of assessing exactly where she was in her life. Uncovered and unbra-ed they announce a history of our body, our nutrition and our fertility. Perhaps that's why we are so sensitive to what our breasts say about us. That's why we want them to fib, to tell a better story. We want them to tell everyone we're younger and fitter than we are. We want to be well represented – and that leads us to disguise and adapt our breasts, to lift them, pad them and alter the shape of our silhouette. Or have surgery and amend them permanently.

Obviously some women have breast surgery because they have suffered cancer or pain and some women need reconstruction to their breasts after illness or dysfunction. But other women, physically healthy women, choose to have their breasts operated on because they don't like the way they look. When these operations first became widely available, in the 1990s, over ninety per cent of the women who requested them were recorded as having 'psychological difficulties' or 'psychiatric issues'. That's because back then, wanting to be sliced open to have a globule of plastic or saline shoved inside was absolute madness. But the odd thing is that the statistic is now inverted, and over ninety per cent of people who want boob jobs are recorded as being entirely sane, because who *wouldn't* want to improve their rubbish tits when there are options available? When something's common enough it can't be mad any more; we just upgrade our definition of sanity to include unnecessary and painful surgical procedures. Except

I still think it is baffling and crazy – I think it's a terrifying sign of how toxic the world has become, and yet I feel incorrect and intolerant in my anger towards it. The lone troglodyte ruining the parade by refusing to admire the emperor's new boobs.

In Essex, where I'm from, breast enlargement is relatively common. I reckon one in five women I know have had a boob job. And people are super-relaxed about it. Like repainting a house or something, these operations are viewed as a decorative tweak. When a young lady from Basildon or Romford announces, 'I'm getting them done,' she is greeted with reactions ranging from nonchalance to congratulations. Her family and friends will giggle or check they'll be allowed a squeeze to test realism and they'll be accepting. Breast enlargements are discussed as a sensible corrective: 'Oops, did God forget to give you boobies? Let's have a whip round.' No one stands on a table and says, 'YOU WANT YOUR HEAD CHECKED, MATE, DON'T YOU DARE HURT YOURSELF LIKE THIS, I'M GOING TO SHOUT AND SHOUT UNTIL YOU REALISE THAT YOUR BODY DOES NOT DEFINE YOU,' except me. I'm no longer welcome in that fine county and it's my own fault for being judgey and preachy.

When I was sixteen one of my aunts had an appointment in Harley Street and I went too in an attempt to change her mind. I was exceptionally opinionated as a teenager, never afraid to rant and ruin a birthday party or cinema trip. I was moralistic and 'right on' and had very few friends. Growing older is helping me to become empathetic to other people and their reasons for making choices. I used to think there was a definitive right and wrong and that only I knew what they were and so I should be DICTATOR OF THE WORLD!

Now I realise that we all have our own subjective realities that affect our decisions and that it wouldn't be fair if I was in charge of everyone. Unless I was elected.

Harley Street is superficially attractive (ironically). It snakes off from the top end of Regent Street, so you walk along thinking you've run out of shops and only have houses to look at until you reach Regent's Park. But Harley Street is FULL of secret shops where you can buy cheeks, noses, lips, thinness and wrinklelessness, they just don't display that stuff in the window. But they *should* as it would probably put people off to see all the bits and pieces hanging up, pre-embodied. So we were in the waiting room and I was quiet. It was here that I'd planned to berate my aunt for what she was doing, using clever arguments about how she was an idiot and everyone at her work would notice. But the waiting room wasn't empty as I'd planned, but busy with everybody chatting, full of excitement and apprehension. I stared at wood-panelled walls as people began to cross-pollinate, introduce themselves and ask 'What you here for then?' and then 'HA HA HA,' they would laugh, because it sounded like they were in prison or something. People laugh at nothing to put each other at ease. It's a social sign of reassurance that everything is okay. This is very handy for a professional comedian because even at an awful gig you can probably get the audience to pity-laugh in some embarrassed, encouraging way. Then you come off stage and say 'NAILED THAT' really confidently and everyone believes you and you get to go on *Live at the Apollo*. Twice.

It must have been Implants Day at the clinic because all the women were there for the same operation in a variety of sizes. They were intoxicated by the proximity of their lumpy goal, and each shared her back story unguardedly, encouraging and praising each other, while I pretended I wasn't listening and judged them.

There was a woman who was getting hers 'done' on the NHS. Everyone said she was so lucky, getting freebies. People were asking how, wondering aloud if they should have tried that. Freeboobs said it wasn't luck but that she couldn't afford to pay, so she'd had to go to the doctor loads of times and cry and cry and say she was depressed. Then she'd gone to a psychiatrist and said that she would kill herself if she didn't get them. She had to get the doctors to agree she was mentally unstable and couldn't function until she got this operation; that was the only way to get the NHS to buy them for you. But of course she WASN'T REALLY CRAZY, she added, she'd just cheated the system. I would have argued that pretending to be crazy is pretty crazy and she should stop bragging about it. It seemed unfair to me that she would be getting the same surgeon as these other women who were paying thousands of pounds, although maybe her NHS implants would be shoddier? Crude and unsophisticated, like when you got NHS glasses in the olden days.

At the time I was still wearing a thickly padded bra every day, and when I went out at night I wore two, one on top of the other. I let boys feel them up when I was getting off with them, believing that the padding was passing for real body, trusting they couldn't tell the difference. This kind of amateur tryst would happen in classy nightclubs in Romford. I was sixteen, so would only go to over-twenty-ones nights because on over-eighteens nights everyone was about twelve. All the kids there were from local schools, and my pulling technique was to go up to a guy and accuse him of being gay until he got off with me. I'd let him pummel my cottony sponge boobs for about three minutes and then walk away, stealing his drink as I went. He'd assume it had been cleared by a bartender while we were snogging. I didn't feel anything sexual about these encounters, just the achievement of proving I wasn't repulsive plus getting a drink without having any money.

I wore a padded bra every single day and night from the age of fourteen until I was thirty-one. Giving up padding was my New Year's resolution. I had known for ages that wearing a stuffed bra was a form of hiding my real body. I realised I was walking around with two lies on my chest: 'Wanna squeeze my tits? They're in the washing basket.' And that's ages ago now, I should be used to my new honesty but I still feel insecure without padding, and I have to fight the urge to fake it. Especially if I am on TV or something; who would know? I'd just look like I had a slightly fuller bust, no harm would be done . . . except. I think that *is* where the harm is done. If all small-breasted women are wearing padded bras and look bigger, then the teenage girls with small breasts feel they are alone in their small-boobedness. They aren't offered a vista of unenhanced, bottom-heavy, perfectly contented three-dimensional women to combat the pneumatically proportioned two-dimensional ones in the media. The young women are duped and begin to pad and enhance and the cycle continues. It only stops if we accept ourselves. We are all responsible for a little slice, whether we want to be or not.

I used to be so outraged with friends and relatives who had enlargement surgery. I believed that when a woman felt her figure was insufficient or incorrect she should be FURIOUS with the culture that generated those feelings, not change her body. Sara *circa* 2010 would tell you that when a woman got implants she crossed over, she ceased to be a victim and became part of the problem: 'She walks around with her en-hanced measurements and increases the pressure on women around her to conform,' I would bellow. 'The more women who get breast enlargements the more difficult it becomes to be flat-chested!' I would rant at you and you'd notice how my nostrils flared and how inflexible I was and make a mental note not to take me to the cinema again. I am an idiot for my anger and I regret it, and I've had to learn that women telling other women what to do is not feminism.

For ages I was very anti the topless Page 3 girls in the *Sun*. Through my teens I was uncomfortable about it although I couldn't articulate why. I felt embarrassed when I saw pic-tures on the wall of the garage that fixed my mum's car, or left discarded on the District line. Boys at school would occa-sionally rip that page out and shove it in my face, a hilarious form of intimidation. You had to act very disgusted when this occurred as it was a homophobic version of the 'buttercup under the chin' test and anything less than nauseous horror proved you were a lesbian. When I was eighteen my boyfriend Mark had an obsession with glamour models. He thought my rage at him was down to jealousy of their curvy perfection but it was *more* than that, I didn't want them objectified. Not because *I* wasn't good enough but because all women are *too good*. If this was how some women were looked at, if we ac-cepted that, then *all* women were commercialised, compart-mentalised – for sale, you know. Mark would argue that these models were being well paid and were ambitious business women in control of their lives and then we'd sit silently, un-able to understand each other.

So I thought the 'No More Page 3' petition that started in 2013 was brilliant. It was a focused, targeted attack on one instance of objectification in our society, and getting rid of it seemed achievable and symbolic. But as the campaign gained momentum I became aware of criticisms, people saying that this was an example of feminists attempting to control and oppress other women. That we live in the *western world*, no one is coerced to become a Page 3 model, they do this by choice and feminism should be liberating women, not limiting their choices or taking away their livelihood. I agreed with this, of course, and sat silently once again, thinking that the whole issue was an unsolvable problem . . . until I did solve it in a dream. I dreamed that we made Page 3 like *jury duty*. So suddenly every woman over the age of eighteen became eligible, and all that happened was you got a letter one day and it said:

Dear _____ ,
Please come to the Sun offices at 9 tomorrow morning.
Bring some snazzy pants and a pithy quote about Syria.

So you would *have* to go, and you would *have* to do it. Because if Page 3 represented the whole spectrum of what it looks like to be a woman, it wouldn't be objectification any more, it would just be nudity. It wouldn't be dangerous any more as Page 3 would portray all the different kinds of breasts: there would be small ones, saggy ones, different-sized ones, hairy ones. And straight men would still like it, cos it's still boobies. And the other difference would be in the model's face. Currently the facial expression they all have is 'coquettish', an expression that says, 'Oh, you just found me in the garden, and I don't have a top on, and you shouldn't really be looking cos you're my BEST friend's dad!' It's permissive. But now with our new system the model would be a fifty-two-year-old dinner lady, aghast and horrified at what they're going to say at work the next day and staring straight down the lens knowing *exactly* what you're doing . . . so Page 3 might just die out on its own, people might just lose interest with no one having to oppress anyone. And we can still give the Page 3 ladies all their wages and anything else they want and make sure they know that it's not them or their beauty or their decisions we're attacking. Maybe we could keep them in a donkey sanctuary so they can run around with their breasts flowing in the wind, safe from prying eyes? Or not, if they don't like that idea. So if you know Rupert Murdoch or can hack his email, let me know as I would love to get the ball rolling on this ASAP. I saw how having a dream launched Martin Luther King's career and think this could be really big for me. And also for society and donkey sanctuaries etc., we'll all benefit!

Back in the waiting room, one of the women had a huge folder with her. She was very confident and assured as she talked through all the research she had done. 'It's vital, it's *vital*,' she kept repeating as people asked questions like she was Jeeves. Every plastic leaf of her folder contained a diagram or article she'd printed off the internet. She knew about incision areas, nipple placement, silicone versus vegetable oil,* round versus teardrop, under muscle versus over muscle, and everyone listened to her respectfully: 'You've got to research, ladies; it's your body here!' This was 1997, so cosmetic surgery was not yet as prevalent as it is now. Recently I worked at a fundraiser for a breast cancer charity** and I met a cosmetic surgeon and she*** was telling me stories of how flippantly

---

* Using vegetable oil in boobs is now illegal, fact fans.
** Because I'm a grown lady baby Jesus.
*** I've made this surgeon a woman even though in real life she was a man haha!

some people approach their operations. She gave me an example of getting a phone call on 20 December from a woman
wanting breast enlargements. The receptionist had explained
that they couldn't do the operation until January, because otherwise the appointment to check recovery would have to be
during the holidays when the clinic was closed. 'But I need it
now, I need it before then,' the woman kept saying, and so the
surgeon was brought to the phone to find out what the emer-
gency was, and it turned out the woman had bought a dress
for New Year's Eve which was 'too big up top' and she wanted
implants so it would fit her properly. I look back on Folder
Lady and her keen research more fondly now.

The spooky truth is how little is known about the dangers
of breast implants. A medicine would go through about twenty years of testing before getting official approval to show that
it's *probably* safe for humans. Implants were not studied until doctors were already performing operations. In fact, all
women who get their breasts enlarged are part of an ongoing
experiment that could be called 'What happens when you do
this to breasts?' It's been trial and error ever since the first op;
they've used substances that are poisonous and have migrated
around the body, like vegetable and soy oil, they've used sub-
standard and industrial-grade silicone, PIP implants were
found to have a one-in-six chance of exploding, all implants
make it more difficult to screen for breast cancer and can
interfere with breastfeeding and/or reduce breast sensitivity,
and that's only the success stories. That's without the awful
reports of operations gone wrong, the unqualified butchers,
the backstreet conmen and the deaths they've caused.

I read this horrible account of Japanese prostitutes after
the Second World War injecting military silicone directly

into their breasts before becoming, as you'd imagine, horrif-ically sick. Their story felt symbolic for me of the brutality of self-hatred and what we are willing to undertake because of it. Those women sought enlarged breasts because they could earn more money when selling sex. The white-coated, handsomely bricked facade of Harley Street disguises similar desperation in other women, normalises it. If breast enlarge-ment is advertised on the tube, talked about nonchalantly in newspaper columns and on chat shows, we are all complicit in making it an understandable response to body issues. We continue a culture where women who *don't* depend on men wanting sex with them for income behave as if they do.

Want to know a disturbing statistic? You know I said that all women who have boob jobs are unwittingly part of an on-going study; well, lots of studies are conducted using their data – health complications afterwards, further cosmetic pro-cedures, etc. And a meta-analysis of all these studies found that women who've had breast enlargements are two to three times more likely to commit suicide than women who haven't. We need to think about that. About why this is happening, about the vulnerabilities of the women who choose cosmet-ic surgery and the normalisation of such choices. When they asked cosmetic surgeons about this rise in suicides they didn't understand: 'they were happy with their operations,' they said; 'she didn't show signs of depression.' But someone who wants to have their body cut open, to pay for it, is already self-harming. Carving criticism on their body. The expense and clever doctors persuading us surgery is more reasonable than razor work in your own bathroom. Psychologists are now paying attention to this suicide increase, asking whether it could be a result of surgery or a predisposition in those who seek it. But the whole thing feels too casual to me. I wonder if a pill or tablet that made you three times more likely to kill yourself would get approval from government departments?

We know that our body *means* something, that we can never be invisible. We will naturally be concerned with our body shape. A little vanity is built in. But the way in which human beings communicate with each other has dramatically changed in the last century. For the bulk of our evolution female body fat was valued for health and aesthetics. Look at the Stone Age 'Venus' figurines, images of women with chunky drumstick limbs and round bulging bellies from twenty thousand years ago. Walk round any art gallery and notice that the women considered beautiful in all eras of human creation had dappled thighs and undulating stomachs. Skinniness is a new fashion. It reflects obsession with youth, a suggestion of pre-adolescence when a female's fertility can be dominated. It implies vulnerability, feebleness and fragility. The attractiveness of such traits is of no benefit to women's lives.

What I find most troubling is the recent expectation for sudden weight loss after pregnancy. It's perverse that the finest compliment given to a woman who has just made a person is that she looks like she hasn't. Magazines and websites and newspapers all trill about the speed with which famous women regain their figures, high-fiving anyone who has erased signs of the life they made and is ready to be found attractive again, to be prospective. The extra fat of post-pregnancy is not a fashion faux pas, it is stored energy for keeping a baby alive. We need to start congratulating the generously flabby for the healthy lives they are enabling rather than expecting them to burn it off on a treadmill. Here for me is our ironic position – women's bodies being scrutinised after making babies because our whole species is programmed to assess women's *potential* to make babies. Even though loads of us don't have children, or haven't yet, our reproductive capability underwrites every day of our post-adolescent lives. Let us think more about this as we jiggle on to wombs.

Blood and Babies

The day I found out, I was with my friend Hayley (laxative Hayley, not make-herself-sick Hayley) and we were walking from college to go and hang out in the Queen's Theatre foyer like *real* actors. As we went down the hill I continued to talk about how in love I was with Colin. 'Are you guys using condoms yet?' she asked. We were about to cross the road, the car that'd stopped was beeping, it was Aunty Sandra! 'Hello,' we said. 'Hello,' said Aunty Sandra. She asked if we were okay or needed a lift and we were and we didn't and she waved and drove off. 'Condoms?' Hayley repeated.

'Not very often.'

I could tell Hayley the truth. She was very sensible about those kinds of things, yet tolerant of my irresponsibility. She knew Colin and I had loads of condoms, a massive box full. At the beginning when we'd got together we couldn't afford any and Hayley had taken me to a clinic in Romford where they'd give you MILLIONS of extra-strong Durex in exchange for an hour of your life spent in the worst waiting room in the world. I explained to Hayley that we hardly ever used them, they were so stupid to put on and I couldn't be bothered. And then every month when my period was due I'd regret it and hate myself. 'What if this time I . . . ?' but I wouldn't even finish the thought, I would just resolve that I definitely wouldn't risk it next month, I wouldn't put myself through this worry again. I would tell Colin we had to use something. I would go on the pill. I had tried a pill before but it made me feel sick and I'd kept forgetting to take it and then had mini periods every few days when I'd missed two pills again. And so I had stopped and now we were supposed to be using condoms except we weren't. And I would count days in my diary and feel stupid and then TA-DA, it would arrive all over my underwear! Happy days, oh the relief of this womby pain, and it would be heavy and clotty and I would think, 'Is this clot a tiny baby?' 'Am I miscarrying quintuplets?' but I would be happy. I would swear to whatever god or ghost lives above the toilet bowl that I would not be so stupid again. I would be a wise and mature lady, in control of her fertility and destiny, not a pregnant teenager like my mother.

But when I had my period it was fine to have sex because I knew you couldn't get pregnant then. The magazines I read said that you should still use condoms just in case, but I knew you definitely couldn't conceive because the baby would fall out with all the blood. And the first couple of days after my period I'd think, 'I should probably introduce the ol' box of condoms sitting next to the bed,' but there never seemed to be a good time. And I knew that those days were safe really because women ovulate in the *middle* of the month. And when it had been a week, well, it was awkward to bring up 'We should probably put a condom on now' so I didn't. I always thought, 'We can use a condom tomorrow,' but then after a bit it is tomorrow, and it's weird – when *is* a good time to bring up putting a condom on? At bedtime? When you're kissing? When he's been in for a bit but he hasn't come yet? I would wonder all these thoughts, and those stages would pass me by and I would be mopping up with toilet paper and very in love and musing, 'This time will be fine, but we'll definitely use a condom next time.'

'So do a pregnancy test,' said Hayley. She says that stressing about your period being late makes your period late – 'Find out you're not and then you can relax!' Hayley is wise.

I have always had a late period, or what I thought of as late. If I had met you two weeks ago and you'd asked about my menstrual cycle, which would have been a bit odd for a first meeting but I wouldn't have minded, I would've answered, tutting, that I was always 'about a week late'. I have just found out – while researching for this chapter – that women have different-length cycles. How did I not know that? With the deluge of 'twenty-eight days' and 'four weeks' in the literature I had missed the fact that this is a composite average, and that healthy women range anywhere between twenty- and sixty-day cycles. So if I met you this week and you asked – and please feel free to enquire – I have a reliable-ish thirty-five-day cycle. What's yours?

Hayley and I went to a chemist in Hornchurch and looked at pregnancy tests for a bit. They were very expensive, I think £9 or £10. I currently earned £14 a week from my Saturday job at WHSmith. I told Hayley I would prefer to wait for my period to come or have a baby, it would be much cheaper. Hayley loaned me the money and I felt really grown up as we popped into a pub next door and Hayley bought a lemonade so they wouldn't bother us. In the toilets she did her mascara and I did a piss on a bit of plastic and then we chatted through the door about a bitch from drama club who had recently started being nice to Hayley, so Hayley was sticking up for her and saying she wasn't a bitch any more. But the bitch was still ignoring me so she was still a bitch, a bitch who looked like a combination of Bebop and Rocksteady from *Teenage Mutant Ninja Turtles*, and I was about to say so when— The box had said 'wait three minutes' but it only took twenty seconds and the stripes came up. So I said, 'Oh fuck,' instead and Hayley said, 'What?' and I said, 'Oh fuck' and then I read the box again and it repeated what it had told me earlier in the same 'not judging you, just giving you the information' tone. Two lines meant pregnant and I was pregnant and that meant— I laughed a jaded, been-around-the-world, seen-it-all-before cackle and opened the toilet door. 'I'm only fucking up the duff, babe,' I told Hayley. A woman who was washing her hands politely gave her congratulations and left.

At the time I didn't know how pregnancy tests worked, what element of my urine was sending up that second stripe. If I'd had a guess I would've plumped for 'extra oestrogen' or something. I now know (because I recently Asked Jeeves) that the wee-on pregnancy tests react to a chemical called human chorionic gonadotropin (hCG). But let's go back a bit and work out what had been going on inside me to get us there.

Ovulation begins in your brain, or just underneath, in the pituitary gland which releases a follicle-stimulating hormone (FSH). Follicle comes from a Latin word which means 'little bag' and in your ovaries there are tons of little bags with tiny clumps of cells we call ova or eggs inside them. The FSH travels from your brain to your ovaries in your bloodstream and causes your follicles to ripen and ripple, to ready themselves. Your ovaries are stimulated to produce and release oestrogen into your blood, and when that arrives at the pituitary gland, luteinising hormone (LH) is released. The luteinising hormone blocks the follicle-stimulating hormone; those follicles have been stimulated enough. When LH reaches the ovaries this prompts one follicle to open and release an ovum. It's a tag team of hormones flowing back and forth which results in a tiny ripe ovum travelling towards the Fallopian tube. This hormonal interplay means that your body understands which ovary has released an egg, and, incredibly, the nearby Fallopian tube will reach out to it, stretching towards the ovum and easing its trajectory.

Meanwhile, the follicle that has released the egg luteinises (turns yellow) and starts to act as a gland. It begins secreting progesterone into the bloodstream. This progesterone is shouting instructions to your body; your brain knows that an egg is released and on its journey, and your womb responds by beginning to build a thickened lining ready to receive it. There are two possible outcomes at this point, depending on whether your egg meets a sperm and is fertilised, or reaches the womb unencumbered and flying solo. Your emotional response to either state will depend very much on you, and what you are looking for in your life at the moment.

The night I found out, after Hayley and I had soberly left the pub and continued with our plans, I kept forgetting and remembering. It felt very exciting, I was hyper on it. 'This is really really properly it,' I thought, 'this is life, it has started.' I knew I was making a mess, that I was hurting myself. But I also needed to, I needed life to be interesting. The experience felt vital. Or it did at this dramatic 'oh my god I'm pregnant' point. I don't remember telling Colin, that bit can't have been important. I can't picture his face or whether I called him about it or told him face to face. But when I went home that night I was suddenly worried about telling my mum. The fun left. She was in the bath and I spoke through the door. 'I need to tell you something.' She let me in. I sat on the toilet seat as she lay back down in the water and said, 'You're pregnant' – not a question. The witch could read my mind.

My aunty Sandra had phoned up after she'd seen me. She'd told my mum she thought I was pregnant, that she could see it in my eyes. I hadn't done a test when she saw me so I hadn't even known. It's the oddest detail and I still think about it. What did she see? Softness? Fear? My mum had thought Sandra was being crazy until I knocked on the bathroom door and suddenly it was true. Mum said, 'Have a think about what you want to do.' I wanted a time machine. I went to sleep desperate to be undone.

Possible Outcome A) Fertilised

You'll know loads about this process already. Men make millions of sperm and can ejaculate them inside a woman via sexual intercourse. Sperm travel pretty slowly, it takes them about ten minutes to cross the distance of a full stop. Luckily there is not much punctuation inside a woman, instead there is mucus which is impenetrable if she has not ovulated but much clearer, stringier and perfect for the sperm to travel through if she has. Mucus is so necessary, vital, for conception it's *unbelievable* that it is not more respected and popular. Sperm can't reach ova without it – we all have mucus to thank for our brilliant lives, yet when you hand out fliers for your Mucus Appreciation Society no one wants to join. #ungrateful

If/when sperm reach the egg, they press their heads on the outer layer, trying to burrow in. You'll probably be familiar with this image. For ages I thought I could remember being in the womb. I would argue with people that I could recall *every* moment, the orangey light and the muffled sounds. I could even remember being a sperm racing towards the – and then I realised my 'memory' was the beginning of the film

Look Who's Talking, which you're probably too young to remember. Ask your grandpa – it was very popular.

If a sperm breaks through the outer layer of the ovum into the inner layer (zona pellucida), an enzyme is released which acts as a barrier preventing any other sperm from following.

Someone has begun.

My morning sickness started the next day, as if once I consciously knew I was pregnant my body could stop hiding it from me. My mum recommended crisps and dry toast. I went into college when I felt a bit better, although I now felt nauseous all the time. I told my teachers I was pregnant and might miss morning classes. I told my football team I was pregnant before we practised. I fainted in Law and told everyone in the class. I kept telling people until a girl came up and said she didn't believe me. I didn't know her very well. 'I just don't believe you' – she was shaking her head – 'if it was true you wouldn't be talking about it.' I felt no reservation about letting people know I was pregnant because it was just a fact of life, just this thing that could happen to you, like getting the flu or having feet. I didn't think people should keep these things secret. I was going to be open and unashamed. I was revolutionary. And a drama queen.

'It's a clump of cells,' I told my mum, 'like cancer. You wouldn't be annoyed with me if I was having a tumour removed.' She told me I wasn't allowed to think of it that way, she gave me this unbearable lecture about how those cells made a *person*, about how I had once been such a clump of cells myself. She insisted that I might regret this forever. She suggested I should have the baby – 'STOP CALLING IT A BABY' – she offered to bring it up for me, do all of the work, all of the getting up in the night and the arse-wiping. 'I'm

not cleaning up anyone else's bum,' I'd insisted early on in
our 'going through the options' talk. Mum explained that she
had got pregnant very young and that I was the best thing that
had ever happened to her. She told me of the love she felt as
I grew inside her, of the tears when she held me for the first
time. Mum said she'd been so happy when I was a tiny baby
and that I had given her a love she'd never felt from her family
or from a man and that it was complete and unconditional—

'Oh fuck off Mum.'

I'd heard various versions of this. A few years earlier, when I
was twelve or thirteen, the story of my creation had had some
details added. My mum explained how my dad 'didn't even
want you'. That when she'd told him she was pregnant he'd
insisted that she 'get rid of it'. The idea of my being aborted
was quite traumatic for me at the time. But I am a wise older
lady now and experience means I can make sense of that conversation. I understand the elements involved without feeling
it as an act of aggression towards myself. It's so common to
have doubts. Most people who find themselves unexpectedly
pregnant have a conversation along the lines of 'What shall
we do?' or 'I don't think I can do this,' but, and perhaps this
is obvious to you, I believe the rule should be DON'T TELL
YOUR ADOLESCENT CHILDREN ABOUT IT. The mere
sniff of rejection is magnified to unbearable proportions at
that age. It was metaphysical murder and I couldn't conceive
that it wasn't personal. I asked my dad about it recently; we
are very good friends and I'm sure he enjoys my foraging pain
truffles from the past. He said he couldn't really remember
and then he went quiet. I'm pretty confident he felt embarrassed about how he'd nearly denied planet Earth somebody
as brilliant and kind as me. 'Imagine if Mary had wanted Jesus

aborted?' I thought to myself. 'Now *that* was a surprise pregnancy!' Then I felt grateful that nobody could read my mind
and find out how often I compare myself to Jesus.

I begged my mum not to tell Dad I was pregnant so she rang
him straight away. I had an awkward conversation with him
on the phone. He'd recently moved to Australia, which I'd
accepted as abandonment. He was very relaxed and 'hey, do
what you gotta do' about me wanting an abortion. I thought
he didn't care and I preferred that to how much my mum
clearly did. She thought I should have it. So did Colin's mum,
so did Colin. I was very, very sure that I wasn't going to.

There were lots of things I didn't appreciate at the time,
or that I understand differently now. I really thought Mum's
sadness at my decision was an act of cruelty towards me rather
than a genuine response. I couldn't grasp that if you'd had
your own babies, if you had held them when they were really
tiny, if you had experienced the entire process of gestation
inside your body then maybe you couldn't help empathising
with them even as cellular embryos. When my sisters had children over the last few years, the affinity and attachment I felt
to their bumps and ultrasounds and the animal rush of holding my nieces revealed to me a sliver of what my mum might
have been feeling when I refused to contemplate continuing
with my pregnancy, when I stomped down the street referring
to her grandchild as a tumour.

There are so many cultural clichés about grandmothers
– pressurising their kids to procreate, embarrassing us with
questions, telling us to 'hurry up' and then being overly involved, bossy and controlling when babies come along. It's
another sweeping stereotype that appears to be based on universal instincts. We *evolved* to depend on grandparental care

in raising children. We are almost unique among mammals in that we undergo a menopause, a cut-off of fertility many years before we die. Lots of apes have a slowing down of fertility as they age, but never a complete cessation. Female animals usually retain their ability to create offspring as long as resources and environment support them. The evolutionary theory of human menopause is that it allows a woman to concentrate her efforts on caring for her children's children, foraging for their food supplies and assisting their mother in protecting and educating them without the distraction of having her own young children to care for. This input of effort has been proven to make a huge difference in children's survival rates in modern tribal cultures, and in fact a meta-study of developing and developed world nations found that the presence of a maternal grandmother was more beneficial for the survival and health of children than any other relative except a mother – that, statistically, kids are better off with a grandma around than a father.

Everything I read about the generosity of mothers and grandmothers makes me want to apologise to mine. I should send them some flowers and nice jackets. Then I remember how they were simply ensuring the survival of their own genes via me and I keep the flowers, jackets and sorrys all for myself. It's what they would want. Also, would you like to learn an incredible fact? Female children are born with their ova already in their ovaries, so a mother gives birth to half of each of her grandchildren with her daughter. Isn't that weird and great? A layer of Russian dolling in us flesh-and-blood women.

I had a doctor's appointment that I went to with Colin. They said I could wait for an NHS termination in a few weeks or organise one immediately if I went private. Going private meant paying £400. I needed it to be quick, I felt so sick and disgusting and my mum agreed to loan me the money. And I realised while writing that sentence that I never paid her back. I just emailed her – 'I still owe you for my abortion' – and she's written back: 'oh dear! X'. I've replied, 'Can you write something funnier so I can put it in my book?' and she has texted me her bank details with an aubergine emoticon.

The clinic was in a posh part of Essex I hadn't been to before. My mum drove us there early on the morning of my seventeenth birthday. Colin seemed like a child in the passenger seat and I felt like a child in the back. He'd bought me sweets for my birthday, Jelly Babies, and we laughed at the inappropriateness but I still ate them. When the car stopped, I got out and was sick in several colours onto the kerb. It was momentary, a few gags and gone, but when I stood up I was blurry-eyed and suddenly surrounded by people. They held placards with bloody, mangled pinkness, black-eyed, fish-looking, mashed innards and death. They asked me to look at the pictures and said they would help me and Colin shouted at them, 'Fuck off,' and my mum said, 'Don't swear,' and I was walking up towards the clinic and I felt embarrassed that they thought they knew something about me. No one asked my side of things. It was just a cluster of cells, a blastocyst six weeks into development, not a rabbit-looking baby thing like on the placards they were using to block my way. Late-term propaganda, split skulls and whisked-up limbs. As we turned towards the building they followed us and when we opened the door, they put their hands together as if to pray and a man said softly, 'There go the parents of another dead child.'

We're never all going to agree on when life starts. I don't think aborting foetuses will ever be an unemotive issue or occurrence. I don't think women will ever have abortions unthinkingly or unfeelingly. The upset, the rage of the pro-life people who stand outside clinics or send hate mail or shout on the internet, I get. Morality and the ego are connected. When we feel we are absolutely definitively correct about something, when we have no doubts or concessions, it is extremely physiologically powerful. When we live in a society that disagrees with us, it makes our will to be heard stronger. It makes us want to shout louder. To persuade more forcefully. You can try this with a thought exercise. Imagine something that you are completely, undeviatingly sure of – like 'paedophilia is wrong'. I use that as an emotive example. It's not an issue one could be on the fence about. If you woke up tomorrow morning and 'Newsflash, newsflash,' said the radio, 'Prime Minister David Cameron has repealed all paedophilia laws. Do what you like to kids now – have a nice day,' imagine how you would feel. The world would be crazy to you. How could something that was so obviously and utterly morally disgusting be permitted? Imagine how frustrating it would be to know something, deeper than an intellectual idea, to be *convinced* down to the foundations of your being and then be contradicted by those around you – it would feel like insanity. It would make a dictator of any of us; we all have a few beliefs which we're so sure are correct that we'd force other people to comply and not feel guilty about that. I can't imagine a person who didn't have some conceptions of rightness that they wouldn't budge on.

Happy Seventeenth Birthday Sara!

Let's have another look inside me. Sperm and egg collided around six weeks earlier. They travelled slowly, incrementally, through the fluid in my Fallopian tube, waved onwards by minuscule cilia towards my womb. Twenty-three chromosomes from the egg paired up with twenty-three chromosomes from the head of the sperm (its tail had been discarded) to create the DNA of a brand new organism. The DNA was replicated, so that there were forty-six chromosomes, and the original cell bulged and divided until it was two. These two cells replicated DNA and doubled. The four cells doubled. And so on, doubling and replicating and arriving in my womb. On attaching to the uterine wall, the building of placental cells produced human chorionic gonadotropin (hCG), an analogue of the luteinising hormone we met earlier, which signalled that an embryo was present. That was why the pregnancy test looked for it – it is a hormone that appears only when there is an embryo, and any trace of it is a sure sign of fertilisation. Hour by hour, week by week the embryo increased very gradually in size until at week six it was tadpole-like. It had transparent skin, organs forming in the correct positions and a heart the size of a poppy seed that was already beating.

When we discuss the rights of the unborn, we're thinking about non-conscious, non-sentient beings. But that doesn't mean they don't have rights. I do believe that unborn foetuses have rights, and they should not have to wait until birth to be accorded the respect we endow on the living; believing a woman is entitled to choose to abort a pregnancy doesn't mean the rights of foetuses are dismissed and disregarded. It means there is a hierarchy. It means that I believe the rights of the woman who is pregnant take precedence. It doesn't mean that I don't think that it is sad, it doesn't mean you are not allowed to be outraged and upset by it. Sometimes in pro-choice arguments we can get stuck in defending what seem to be morally stronger arguments: pregnancies that have resulted from rape, children who are impregnated by their abusers, women who may die if their pregnancies continue. These examples may help soften some pro-lifers, or help them empathise with the complexity of some women's experience and choices. But I am going to stand, hands on hips, and tell you that a woman like myself – healthy, wealthy and with love in my life – if I am pregnant and I don't want to be, it's top trumps and I win. It's harsh and horrible that a possible person can be unexisted and it might make you want to cry, but if you want fewer abortions then you should devote yourself to helping women who don't want to be pregnant not get pregnant, not terrifying and humiliating the ones who are.

I gave my name to reception. My mum left. Colin sat on a plastic chair where the Christians outside were still audible. I was called through for my 'counselling session'. I'd been told about it at the first appointment: everyone who wants a medical termination has to convince a doctor that they know what they're doing, persuade them they are making the right decision. I was really looking forward to it because I had seen counselling on TV and it looked great – you get to tell them how fucked up your parents made you and cry on free tissues – but this session was rubbish. A man said, 'Are you sure you want to terminate your pregnancy?' and I said, 'Yes,' and he said, 'Why?' and I thought, we'll start with the basics, 'Because I don't want a baby,' and a box on a form was crossed. He told me to jump on a couch – oh yes, here we go, this was far more Freudian, lie down, top up – the man put jelly on my lower belly and said, 'We just need to find out where it is,' and then I still hadn't realised what he was doing but I'd seen this on TV as well. Grown-up women with clear skin and happy faces, men gripping their hands, joyfully worried as they asked, 'Is it healthy?' and were told, 'It's a boy!' TV didn't show seventeen-year-old birthday girls with sick in their hair. 'Have a look,' the doctor said – I'd turned away, I didn't want to see, but I am obedient and looked back and there was a mess of static that meant nothing and the man pointed with a biro and said, 'It's very small,' and the counselling was over. Afterwards my mum said they don't have to do an ultrasound. She said that maybe they do it to check that you're sure, that maybe seeing it would change some people's minds.

I'd told my family that I was on the contraceptive injection but that I'd forgotten to go back for the next one after three months. I told the nurses and doctors that we'd had a split condom and that the morning-after pill hadn't worked. I did not admit to anyone that I was a really, really stupid person. And now I waited with my naked bum on a chair, in a cold corridor, queueing for an abortion. I realised I must really hate myself to have done this to me. I hadn't visualised this bit, I didn't know they would make me take my knickers off, put me in an operation gown, tell me where to wait and not look me in the eye. This bit was too hard and I would have liked to say 'Stop'. Very politely and firmly. 'Stop all this. Can I get dressed and go home now please? This is a mistake, I don't want to have an abortion. But also, I also don't want to be pregnant so can we all agree that I have made a terrible mistake, whizz me back to the past and undo this?'

That's the bit I would describe to my fifteen-year-old self. The moment when the realisation hit and I was alone and frightened with a cold bum. I always wonder what might have made me take better precautions. What I could say to my nieces, not to scare them, but so they could visualise the connection – hey guys, I hope you're enjoying this *Peppa Pig*

episode. Did you know that twenty seconds of awkward condom conversation can save you an hour of corridor purgatory
waiting to have your womb vacuumed?

Are you gonna call Aunt of the Year Awards or shall I?

I was taken in to lie on a bed in an operating room. I was
incredibly, incredibly embarrassed to see the two stirrups in
the air and putting my feet into them was an out-of-body experience. My mum had warned me about stirrups, she said
they make abortions as horrible as possible so that you don't
go back. There was an anaesthetist and a nurse and a doctor
and they could all see up me and I wanted to die. I had a rash
on my bikini line from shaving. I wanted to apologise for it.
A woman put an injection into the tube in my hand and said
count to ten, and while I counted I thought, 'Oh no – the
sleep stuff isn't working, I'll have to tell them,' and then I
woke up sobbing. I was in a different bed, on a ward. There
was a curtain around me and I was alive again and it was done.
A nurse came and was nice, and she explained the sanitary
pad in the knickers they had given me, to expect pain and
treat it like a normal period. She said no sex for an amount
of time I intended to ignore. And she got me a cup of sweet-
ened tea that tasted like freedom. While I drank it a bed went
past transporting a sleeping body. Curtains went round. She
woke up sobbing, got the same speech and tea, and when the
curtains were opened we chatted. She was from Dublin and
had come on a boat because abortions weren't allowed in her
country. I told her about my boyfriend and she told me about
her boyfriend and I had to ask again: 'Are you sure it's illegal
in Ireland?' I thought she must be unintelligent or mistaken.
Because she was just like me, from a country just like my country and right next door.

What if abortion was illegal in England, what would I have done? People who are anti-abortion and want it to become more restricted, less available, might say, 'You wouldn't have got pregnant, you'd have taken better precautions if there was no escape route.' I can tell you honestly, having *been* me, that I don't think I *would* have made more effort with contraception. I took risks, not with silent awareness of an undoing process available for £400, but because I believed pregnancy was something that happened to other people. It was their disaster, their bad luck. I have always felt immortal and that's been reinforced by years of undeath. I smoked secure that I would never get cancer. I cycled drunk certain that cars would bounce right off me. Having unprotected sex I knew I was dancing with something, that there was danger nearby, but I didn't think it would dare touch me. Until it did. And if legal termination hadn't been an option I would have done something else. I would have starved myself and tried to kill it, I would have got really drunk and taken boiling hot baths. Maybe pushed something inside me and done my best. Maybe visited some non-legal doctor. It must be difficult to imagine if you've never had some alien growing in your body against your will, but wanting rid of it is not a mild desire. And it is not a modern affliction. Techniques for ending pregnancy have existed for as long as medicine; Hippocrates himself recommended an abortion method of 'kicking yourself on the buttocks until the seed fell out'. If only that worked – any Irish girl in trouble could Riverdance herself out of it. I hope the law in Ireland has changed by the time this book is published so it's me that seems outdated rather than their legal system.

My mum picked me up after work. Colin was very quiet, I was exuberant with relief. The nausea had gone, I already felt better, even internally bruised with a bloody fat sanitary towel in my knickers. In the weeks afterwards, my feelings about sex changed. It was now connected to something painful. I had lived its consequences, I knew the damage it could wreak and so it wasn't sexy any more. I began to silently resent Colin and he resented me back. If he loved me, why had he let this happen? Why hadn't he protected me? He hadn't put his legs in stirrups, he was unscathed. It became clear that I was still in charge of whether we used contraception or not: if I didn't mention condoms then he wouldn't. In reverse, he hated me because I'd made a decision without him. I hadn't known enough to make a pretence of including him. When we broke up months later, when he was suddenly with someone else, someone unsullied by this operation, I was angry. I was glad I hadn't listened to him, but I wondered if he'd have stayed with me if I had. Would I be pregnant and with him or would he have abandoned me pregnant?

The male experience of a partner's abortion is interesting. Thinking about it now, I realise that none of my boyfriends have talked to me about whether it has happened to them. (I must write and ask on their Facebook walls immediately!) There is an obvious separation – the embryo is not growing inside the man, the father does not undergo the procedure – but I am sure, if a man wants children and his partner is aborting one, there must be an out-of-control and existential suffering that deserves compassion and consideration. I always think it's noteworthy that the ancient Greeks did not believe a woman was related to her children. Guys like Aristotle told how women and their wombs were just vessels that grew the male seed, like the soil grew plants. To me this seems more than a pre-science misunderstanding; it's an undermining of female power, it's a firm insistence of male ownership and responsibility. Fighting their terrified disconnection from their growing children by reducing women to flower pots.

People told me how I'd feel about my abortion. I was to expect regrets and tears and guilt and bad dreams, and perhaps I'm an awful person, but I was not sorry. I only felt relief and buoyancy as if cured from a sickness. I have been haunted since but the ghost is gentle and suggestive. Every year on my birthday, I do a little sum in my head to work out the unborn's age. Enjoy a flicker of imagining height and hair colour, and how different my life might be. The ghost child is now the age I was when I had the abortion and that is odd to consider. But it is nothing stronger than odd. I am not racked with sobs. I am not shaking my fist at the past. I did not make a mistake. Or I did, but I was not wrong to abort my mistake.

There's been some discussion amongst people who care about my professional life as to whether I should be writing about my teenage abortion. My agent Dawn, my brilliant career mum, warned me that once it was 'out there' it could be brought up in any interview, mentioned in any review. I don't care. I stand by it and I will talk about it every day if people want me to. Sex education in schools should involve women who've had terminations talking about them and answering questions. No shame and more prevention, that's my motto.

Let's forget the undone now. Instead we shall consider the terrifying business of babies that are actually born. The history of childbirth is a horror show. Our evolutionary combination of walking upright (producing slim hips) and massive brain development (necessitating huge heads) has made the natural process of birth dangerous, potentially fatal for the women undertaking it. Until very recently all women would have considered pregnancy and birth like a disease – something that you might not come back from. In developed countries maternity wards now have excellent facilities, antibiotics, anaesthesia and sterilisation that help make the process less deadly. But the majority of the world's women do not have access to this kind of medical care and around 350,000 women die giving birth every year.

Someone needs to write a book on the topic of patriarchy and childbirth. For swathes of recorded history the delivery room was all women taking care of women. The word 'gossip' apparently originated from 'God's siblings'. These were close family friends (think godparents and godchildren) but over time the term became used for the women attending local births and helping out. It conjures such a great image of a room full of bossy ladies, nattering away and sharing local news while mopping brows and cutting cords. It seems male involvement was a relatively recent response to the number of deaths and infections caused by childbirth; male doctors began to mistrust inherited female wisdom and local midwives, and wanted to invent forceps and get involved That is my very biased and abridged view of the matter – but here are a couple of examples of men interfering that are . . . perturbing.

First meet Dr Marion Sims, don't be fooled by his girly name, this man is a man. He lived in the US in the nineteenth century and was fascinated by the fistulas that some women are left with after giving birth. You don't know what a fistula is? Well, let me tell you: the skin around a woman's vagina can often rip while pushing her baby's head out. In some cases the tearing is deeper and can create an opening between the vagina and the bladder or colon. This alone indicates how *almost* unfit for purpose evolution has left our bodies. If women were a product you would take them back to the shop.

CUSTOMER

Oh yes, excuse me, I bought this 'woman' for the purpose of making people, but whenever it makes one, it breaks.

SHOPKEEPER

Ah yes, it's a very clever design. Despite great agonies and physical risks these 'women' are continuing to make people even though it rips and stretches them.

CUSTOMER

Can I have one that doesn't break?

SHOPKEEPER

They have to break to make people—

CUSTOMER

Could the people be smaller?

SHOPKEEPER

With smaller brains this whole product line would've died out.

CUSTOMER

Wow! You mean the sacrifice 'woman' makes in childbirth has enabled the continuance of human life on the planet?

SHOPKEEPER

I surely do!

SHOPKEEPER and CUSTOMER turn to camera and do a thumbs up.

CUSTOMER and SHOPKEEPER
Thanks, 'woman'!

So this vagina–bladder/colon rip is called a fistula. It is incredibly painful and it's an injury that ruins lives. With a fistula urine or faecal matter may leak constantly out of the poor woman's genitals. This incontinence leads to infection and smelliness and embarrassment. Nineteenth-century women were becoming disabled and housebound; their husbands were leaving them. Forget what you know of medicine in your lifetime – there were no tablets that killed viruses for these women to take, no creams to kill germs and no painkillers. Just hundreds of thousands of suffering women. I can only slightly imagine how upsetting that must be, not just the grossness and pain of it all but the constancy of focus. When I have cystitis it's all I can think about; a continual nagging, unsettling ache as my body throbs and reminds me 'something is wrong, everything is wrong'. And that's only stupid cystitis and I have a cure in my bathroom cabinet . . . those poor women – anyway. There was no cure and Dr Marion Sims decided to find one, hooray! So he decided to buy a load of slave women – oh no, hang on – and experiment on them until he found one.

I want it noted that I have taken my hooray back.

Reading different accounts of Dr Sims's work, you'll find a variety of opinions ranging from 'He was a despicable disgrace' to 'He was a product of his culture'. Are we expected to forgive people's atrocities if they lived in an atrocious time? The women used in Sims's experiments were young slaves. They were stripped naked, told to hold each other's legs open and then had their vaginas cut and stitched repeatedly with no pain relief while student doctors or medical voyeurs craned and watched. This continued for months and years and many operations. Sims's peers started to consider him obsessed and crazy, but eventually he worked out how to repair fistulas. He became very famous, and very rich now that he could use what he'd learned on the young slaves to cure wealthy white women. There are no records of what happened to the slaves afterwards, and some historians wonder if they were probably happy to have been cured or whatever. I find that notion really creepy, this modern-day defensiveness: 'Well, they got something out of it too.' In one description I read, the women were described as 'brave' and I don't like that either. If we assume these women sacrificed themselves for a greater good we are inserting a choice they were not given. Sacrifice is something related to will, something that can only be given willingly – not bought or taken. They are closer to martyrs.

It's so tempting to make what he did okay on some level because, you know, now women in many countries can have their fistulas repaired, but. It doesn't feel okay. It's an unhappy seesaw where the great medical breakthrough cannot obliterate the abuses that enabled it. And enabled it only for rich, fortunate women, still. Between fifty thousand and one hundred thousand women in developing countries get fistulas each year, and the World Health Organisation estimates about two million women worldwide are currently living with untreated obstetric tearing. There are charities trying to help as many women as possible with this, and I have listed a few at the end of the book. Along with a pattern for a knit-your-own Dr Marion Sims voodoo doll.

Now let's meet Dr Grantly Dick-Read. No, that's not a name I've invented to cheer you up, but a real-life man from the 1950s who wrote books telling women how to give birth. His main observation was that other animals didn't seem to make a huge fuss when delivering their young; a weird look in their eye, a grunt or a moo, and out the little one slipped. So, Dr Dick-Read wondered, how come human women are doing all this screaming and going bright red and everything? His conclusion was that they must be *imagining* the pain. Everyone had been telling women to expect pain during childbirth, so their fear made them *think* that they felt it. Lovely bit of logic from a medical man there, and all built entirely on nonsense. On the one hand you had the subjective experience of women who'd actually given birth; all the variety of things that they'd felt and undergone. On the other hand you had Dr Dick-Read shouting, 'WRONG! All Wrong! I am the only one who understands – ignore your sufferings and read my books!' And many people listened and agreed and did their best to believe their pain was psychological and HOW WAS THIS ALLOWED?

We understand that the danger and pain of giving birth are caused by those big-skulled babies we've evolved to have, but in the olden days people didn't realise that. They constructed myths of explanation and considered the female body cursed and mysterious. Those myths still linger even in our post-Darwinian, all-information-available-on-the-internet times, resulting in so much babble and rubbish. Remember Eve from the Bible? You know the one, always with Adam, big fan of fruit – when God was doling out punishments after the tree of knowledge debacle he told Eve that he'd 'multiply her pain in childbirth'. The explicit message here is that birth does not *have* to be painful but it is because women deserve it, because of . . . apples? I am not a biblical scholar.

I guess this combination of 'birth is the most natural thing in the world' and 'birth is agonising and dangerous and can kill everyone involved' is difficult for us to absorb. Consequently pregnant women are bombarded with contradictory and impassioned instructions on how and where to have their children. Our vulnerable physiology is still widely misunderstood. Of all the stuff I've read, the most consistent piece of advice is that stress is very unhelpful to childbirth as it tenses the body, and that relaxation will lead to less trauma for mother and her baby, but it's paradoxical that pregnant women are having that information *shouted* at them: STAY AT HOME! GO TO HOSPITAL! GET A BIRTHING POOL! NIPPLE MASSAGE! PUT MUSIC ON! CANDLES! ORGASMIC BIRTH! RELAX! HAVE A NICE PERINEUM RUB! GET HYNOTISED! Plus all the conflicting advice about pain relief versus 'natural' birth. There's an insinuation of nobility in denying anaesthesia when available. Some sense that the pain is *supposed* to be felt, which seems medieval to me. How can 'natural' birth be sanctified in any way, when according to nature, at least one in every hundred women would die from it?

Don't answer that, it was a rhetorical question.

We've been thinking a lot about what happens when the ovum meets a sperm but I'd like to talk now about something I have much more experience of. My monthly *non*-fertilisation and the madness it brings with it.

No Babies Just Blood

Possible Outcome B) Unfertilised

Please delete as appropriate: Hooray/Boo hoo.

I am a complete expert about the menstrual cycle. My mum bought me a book called *Have You Started Yet?* when I was about ten. It gave me all the information I needed, I knew exactly what to expect from my first period. It would be like a gushing wee, but made of blood and it would mean I could have children. And so for a couple of years, every time I went to the toilet, if the wee felt particularly smooth I would have a look in the toilet and check what colour it was. Sometimes I pressed very, very hard into my belly button to see if that might get everything started up, but so far, nothing. I wasn't desperate for it to start or anything – just curious. And one day, after having stomach aches all morning, when I went to the toilet and found a smear of brown blood on my under-pants I put two and two together – tummy pain, blood – I knew exactly what was happening and shouted downstairs to my mum, 'I'M PREGNANT'.

Good old Mummikins ran up to find me in the bathroom. I wouldn't let her in as I needed my privacy, but I described my dirtied knickers in detail and she told me I was now a woman. Which I was not, I was twelve. My mum said some spiritual, beautiful things about cycles, magic and the moon while I sat quietly waiting for her to finish talking about rubbish that had no relevance to me.

Mum then took me to our local Tesco, where she proceeded to put every single sanitary item available into our trolley, and there was a lot because this was a megastore, and when we got to the till and my mum was loading up the conveyor belt with cotton in different shapes, sizes and absorbencies the lady behind the till gave us a questioning look. My mum answered that look by explaining, 'Sara's just started her period,' which was true. She continued, 'She's a woman now,' which had already become my most hated phrase. 'We didn't have anything in the house,' my mum told the complete stranger; 'she's only got toilet paper in her pants!'

Embarrassment doesn't cover it. I was flooded with adrenaline, my face bright red, what's called a 'fight or flight response', except neither of those responses was appropriate – I couldn't hit my mum, could I? And I couldn't run away, she was driving me home. So my body reacted in the noblest way it could, by having a nose bleed, while I stood there, frozen and ashamed. And the lady on the till, clearly a bit of a wit, said, 'Oh look, she's bleeding from both ends now,' and then she laughed and my mum smiled politely and I wished I was dead and wondered how adults could be so insensitive and so cruel. I already loathed my period, not because of anything physical but because it encouraged other people's input and judgement. It didn't feel like it was mine, rather something external, taking me over. I begged my mum not to tell my dad; it was nothing to do with him. But she rang him when we got home – I heard 'She's a woman now' echoing through our little house. I couldn't bear that people were talking about a thing that was taking place in my underwear. And that my mum was trying to make it mean something that it didn't, trying to make it special when it was actually gross. My sister Cheryl learned from my horrible experience and never told my mum that she'd started her period, and thanks to that shopping trip she didn't have to – we had a lifetime's supply of pads and wads under the stairs.

After my first period (five days, medium heavy, medium pain) I didn't have another one for a year. I thought that was it, I'd tried it out, decided it wasn't for me and gone back to girlhood, great stuff. Some time in between we had a special assembly at school, after regular assembly had finished. All the girls were asked to stay where they were and all the boys to get up in their rows and follow their teacher back to their classrooms. We watched them leaving and wondered why we couldn't and they stared at us as they left, wondering which group of us was being punished. What strikes me now is why did they send the boys away? Why don't boys get educated about menstruation? Is it because the teachers think girls will be embarrassed? I feel like the secrecy of it, the action of seg-regating us, sends the message that we *should* be ashamed. That our periods are something to hide from the opposite sex. I still – and I am thirty-four flipping years old – when I take a couple of Nurofen in front of someone, and this usual-ly gets a comment because I can't swallow pills, I poke them down my throat with my fingers – YES, I am cool, I'll show you some time – well, this could be at a gig or a meeting or with someone I don't know and they'll say, 'Headache?' and I'll say, 'I've got period pain,' and then there is this awkward beat like I've said something gross and personal when I'm not supposed to. I'll wish I'd lied, 'Yes, headache,' instead. I've got male friends who say 'urgh' and 'yuk' about periods, I had a boyfriend who didn't want me to ever talk about being on because it made him not fancy me and I've had boyfriends who liked to use code words and silly phrases about painters and decorators or Arsenal's playing arrangements and surely, *surely*, if boys had been included in those assemblies with their female classmates they wouldn't be such idiots about it. They would have been given their chance to ask questions about bodies that were different from theirs. They'd have been taught that the menstruation that affects fifty-one per cent of the world's population for one quarter of most of their lives also concerns the non-menstruating forty-nine per cent. Little boys grow up to have female co-workers, female friends and maybe female lovers and female children. Isn't it dangerous to have given them this early indication that female bodies are mysterious and unknowable? Doesn't their exclusion suggest dirtiness and shame? Surely it's this lack of information that creates a taboo? Boys may not physically experience menses but they still owe their very existence to it.

When the last of the boys were banished, a nice woman stood at the front and she told us about eggs and tubes and monthly bleeding and cramps. We were told about hot-water bottles for the pain, and sit-ups and hot baths. And then we were shown tampons and towels and that old belt thing that female dinosaurs used and asked if we had any questions.

'Why are these sanitary products taxed as "luxury items" with VAT payable, despite being considered a necessity by those who have no choice but to use them?' I could have asked if I had known or cared about that then.

'What about girls my age in other countries, those who have to be sent out of villages – is there anything I can do to help?' would've been a good question if I hadn't been a privileged western chick who didn't yet realise how fortunate she was.

'Is there any truth to the rumour that chemicals in tampons make you bleed more and thus need more tampons?' is the kind of thing I would ask now, because that's what I worry about and I have looked up about on the internet but am distrustful of every source, so – I don't know. I *have* found a charity that helps refugees make their own sanitary products though. It's listed with the others at the end of the book.

The first question came from Jordanna, who asked, 'Could the string come out of tampons?' The lady called her to come up on stage and have a go, and Jordanna tugged and tugged at the blue thread but she couldn't pull it out and we all laughed and clapped. The atmosphere was relaxed and convivial now and I felt safe and excited and so I asked, because they hadn't mentioned this and I couldn't work out the logistics: 'Can you have sex with a tampon in?' I knew that people had sex in their vaginas and, apparently, vaginas were where you inserted these max-flow Tampax and whatever. 'Can you have sex with a tampon in?' I repeated in the quiet. The lady looked around at everyone and laughed. A couple of teachers laughed too. Like it was obvious or unimportant. It bugged me for years, this conundrum. It didn't even say on a tampon leaflet that I read. The vagina was such an unreal place to me, a portal to another galaxy, the sandpit the Psammead lived in, Mary Poppins's never-ending bag. I apparently had this space inside myself that things would go inside and where people could grow and I didn't know what shelves there were, how many compartments and doorways. But I now knew not to ask questions, because some were right and about strings, and some were wrong and left you exposed as a pervert or something.

My mum criticised the sex education we got at school. 'They don't teach you about love. They just tell you the mechanics,' she used to say. But I didn't really understand the mechanics either. I was a child without internet access, I don't think I even used a computer until I was at college. I had to look up sexual words in the dictionary. If I'd been born fifteen years later, I probably would have left that assembly, typed 'period sex' into a free porn site and known much more than I needed to. I was obsessed with collecting as much information about sex as possible and trying to piece it all together so I could visualise it. I shoplifted magazines from the 7/11 near school; *More, Minx, Just Seventeen*. I absorbed details about positions and fantasies and 'tricks' to make boys like you and I filled out quizzes pretending I'd done it all already with nameless guys outside nightclubs and I left the completed pages around school to impress girls like Jordanna, who saw through me. She'd had her period for ages, and boobs since she was about nine.

SFX: RING RING RING RING

Hello?

Oh hi ovum, what you up to? Just been released by the ovary? Cool. You want us to come and see you? Why of course!

The sliding doors moment for an egg is after it has been released and before it reaches the womb. I call it sliding doors because this is when its fate could be massively changed by the arrival of a sperm, but it's more accurate to say 'sliding window of a few days'. For our hypothetical ovum no sperm is on the way, but she doesn't know that and floats towards the Fallopian tubes, tiny and determined. During this time the luteinising follicle is producing progesterone and the womb gets busy creating a thickened lining of cells called endometrium. After around two weeks, if the brain detects no hormones indicating foetal development in your bloodstream, progesterone production stops. Oestrogen drops. This sudden reduction of hormones signals to the womb that the sumptuous lining is unnecessary and can be evacuated from the body. It's like a landlord putting down carpet in case she gets a new tenant, but by the end of the month she realises no one is moving in and so she tugs the carpets off the floor and chucks them wastefully out of the window. She's listening to Alanis Morissette and crying for no reason while she does it.

The ~~landlord~~ womb undulates gently to slough off the endometrial cells (think of the wiggling motions of peristalsis in your intestines to get an idea) while local capillaries restrict their blood supply and oxygen, causing them to drop off. This process is what causes that painful, cramping feeling. The activity of clearing the unneeded tissue takes several days, and the cells gradually leave the body via the vagina along with fresh blood caused by broken capillaries, and some cervical mucus and vaginal secretion. A typical amount of menstrual fluid is between five and twelve teaspoonfuls. It doesn't actually travel out on spoons although sometimes it can feel like that.

There it is then, menstruation, a basic bodily function integral to the process of making people. It's simple physical mechanics, an external signal of cyclical fertility. So why has everyone always been so weird about it? From the earliest human records people have been chatting crap about periods. In ancient Rome, Pliny the Elder said that if a menstruating woman took her clothes off she could scare away hailstorms and lightning and cause all the caterpillars to fall off the trees. Even with her clothes on she would turn wine sour, rust metals and cause 'a horrible smell to fill the air'. Aristotle in ancient Greece told everyone menstrual blood was women's semen

and that it stopped us from going bald. This was shortly after Hippocrates had spread the word that menstrual bleeding was a healthy way to get rid of poisons and cool down,
and that it helpfully turned into breast milk when a woman
had a baby. In the thirteenth century a book called *The Secrets
of Women* revealed the previously classified information that
menstruating women would poison the eyes of any baby that
looked at them and that children conceived during menstruation would have epilepsy and leprosy because of all the ven-
om. AND THAT'S JUST THE SCIENCE BOOKS LADS.

When you look into the world's religions you find that virtually all have taboos around menstruating women. In the
Hindu faith they are considered 'ritually impure', not allowed
to enter kitchens or temples, to have naps in the daytime or
touch anyone or drive a car. The Torah dictates, in the book
of Leviticus, that anyone who touches a menstruating woman
will be 'unclean until evening', and Orthodox Judaism forbids all sexual contact between husbands and their menstruating wives. In Japanese Buddhism menstruating women are
banned from attending temples and in Orthodox Christianity
women are supposed to abstain from Holy Communion while
on their period. The common theme through all is 'dirtiness': a woman's menstruating body is considered sullying,
contaminating the objects and people around her.

Nowadays many faiths have softened in their attitudes and
don't take ancient writing about menstrual impurity literally,
but there are still villages and towns where women on their
period are banished, sent away to separate dwellings for days
at a time. In Nepal apparently ninety-five per cent of girls have
restricted lives during their periods, having to stay off school
or sleep outside. Twenty per cent of girls in Sierra Leone

have to skip school when menstruating and thirty per cent in Afghanistan. In India twenty-three per cent of girls stop attending school altogether after their first period. When we're considering menstrual stigma we have a spectrum of consequences: at one end, the erosive effects of embarrassment and shame; at the other, actual physical restriction and oppression based on a bodily function. Missing one fifth of their education or having to quit school at eleven or twelve has a massive knock-on effect on a girl's later life – her work opportunities, her income and thus her independence and autonomy.

There is residual, old wives' tale misinformation about women's wombs and their business everywhere. Throughout my teens I was given a range of advice I was *nearly* certain was rubbish: don't go swimming/don't wash your hair/don't bake cakes when you're on your period, but never a proper explanation as to *why*. In 1920 Professor Bela Schick attempted to support age-old taboos with scientific evidence. He proposed that 'menotoxins' were emitted by menstruating women; that they were present in their sweat and on their skin and were poisonous. He then conducted a lot of not very reliable studies which proved that if a menstruating woman held a flower it eventually wilted. Whereas flowers in water, well, they don't wilt. Da da da da da da, SCIENCE! That was less than a century ago and we continue to live with the consequences of 'periods are disgusting' indoctrination.

While I was in my early teens, coming to terms with my own menses, all the slang terms were so negative. 'The curse', old people called it; boys at school accused teachers of being 'on the blob' and then laughed; my dad called it 'women's troubles'. WOMEN'S TROUBLES. Something we brought on ourselves when we ate that blooming apple without permission. Something that was none of men's business. Mine to experience, mine to deal with. And 'troubles' is such a belittling word. I have been in agony for nearly a quarter of my life. AGONY. Can't leave the house, can't get off the toilet sometimes – it's not a trifling trouble, it's been a monthly apocalypse. Sorry for shouting, Daddy, it's not you I'm angry with.

I am relieved to be talking about this actually.

I am a modern lady, a cutting-edge, very recent woman. And yet the only menstrual blood I have ever seen is my own. Is that weird? I can see sex on all the movies and TV programmes, I can watch murders being enacted and people pretending to shit themselves in the street, yet no periods. All the advertisements inviting me to select sanitary products prove absorbency with a clear blue fluid, the exact opposite of the mushy muck that ruins my underwear. The absence of public dialogue about periods is implicitly instructing us to shut up. The scandal and shock of a used sanitary towel explicitly tells us we're gross. When I started stand-up comedy I occasionally fielded questions like 'Do you just do jokes about your period?' 'No,' I'd reply defensively, 'no, I don't do any,' and I thought I'd passed some kind of test. Well done me. Women aren't allowed to talk about their periods because some people don't like to hear about periods. When I started comedy I thought I was being ever so clever avoiding topics that were seen as 'things women talk about' and it took me a while to realise that I had been coerced into not expressing my experience as a human because I happen to be the kind of human that is not male. If you are repulsed by periods that is completely fine but you have to understand that the problem lies with you, and not in a bit of blood and cells escaping the vagina. Menstruation is not going away (or it will, but it'll be back in a few weeks). People's responses are the only thing that can change.

To be disgusted by periods is illogical – we know from science that women aren't more germy or polluting around this time. The cells being sloughed are the purest imaginable, suitable for a tiny vulnerable foetus. Yet the prohibitions and stigma are almost universal, so where have they come from? Do they have a communal origin?

It's quite easy to imagine that before knickers, showers and mooncups women were a bit smelly on their periods. The oldest evidence of tampons is from the time of the ancient Egyptians, who made them from softened papyrus, and most civilisations have had versions ever since, made out of lint or grass or whatever. But even then, without access to running water I'll concede that women probably did find it difficult to manage their menstrual blood. Hence all the banishments and 'don't touch my food' stuff. I mean, it's awful but I can see *some* logic to it. Another thought I had was that as women are unlikely to conceive during their period and religions are always insisting that sex be for procreation rather than pleasure, maybe that's the root of all those religious proscriptions? No better way to ensure marital sex occurs during fertile times than spreading rumours about menstruating women being toxic. But then I found out that periods weren't even linked to ovulation until 1831, when Charles Négrier worked it out and told everyone. So the ancient cultures that produced these taboos hadn't even connected periods and the fertility window yet.

My new theory is that without education and comprehension, menstruation does seem magic. It ignores the rules of nature; women feel pain, they bleed, they exhibit the symp-toms of illness or disease and then suddenly recover their health and appear unharmed. It's so at odds with the rest of human experience – no wonder early people didn't trust it. We are the first humans to ever understand it properly. By meas-uring hormones and watching the body on ultrasounds and MRIs, scientists and doctors can now witness the womb at work. Our physiological processes are common knowledge and so we can make sense of our internal manoeuvres while our poor an-cestors had to make up stories and whisper at the moon.

Most animals don't menstruate. Monkeys and apes do, and some bats and the elephant shrew,* but none as much as we do. All other mammals have 'triggered decidualisation', which is when the body waits for the hormonal trigger of an embryo before building up those uterine walls, which seems sensible. Their landlords wait until someone is moving in be-fore laying the red carpet. We lucky *Homo sapiens* bitches have 'spontaneous decidualisation', which means we build it up first, ask questions about embryos later. Why don't we wait? Because:

a) We enjoy it.
b) The ironing's finished and there's nothing else to do.
c) We think it burns calories.
d) We need more endometrial lining than any other animal.

CORRECT, we have to build up more of a womb recep-tion than other animals, and why might that be? It's because human embryos are incredibly needy, very hungry, greedy, they attach deep on to the uterine wall, as deep as they can,

---

* You need to image search this cutie pie right now – you won't regret it! Now imagine her all moody and on her period.

and if there was less endometrium, mothers would become vulnerable to the vampirism of their unborn children. In what scientists refer to as an 'evolutionary arms race' (one side improves and adapts slightly, and the opposition adapts and responds accordingly), human mothers and their tiny cellular pre-babies have been evolving together so that each gets enough and neither destroys the other. Can you guess why even at a few days old humans are so desperate for nutrients? Sing it with me: because we have massive brains!

Toot toot on the 'we all knew the answer' trumpet!

When a woman is pregnant, and usually while she's lactating, she will stop having periods. Scientists who study women's bodies and understand our evolution say that tens of thousands of years ago, when we foraged for food and lived outdoors, the average woman would've had about fifty periods in her lifetime because she would have been reproducing and breastfeeding so much. Nowtimes, a woman might have between 460 and 500 periods in her life. Our great fatty diets mean we start our menses earlier, and our quality of life and lower infant mortality mean we average a lot fewer children. I have had absolutely no children. None. I don't know if I will ever have them and I am not sure how I feel about that. It changes.

I have a special kind of jewellery called ovarian cysts. They are super-common, one in fifteen women have them, and they're caused by insulin resistance, which makes your pancreas release more insulin and then all that extra insulin confuses your ovaries, lowers your oestrogen and results in a too-high testosterone level. This interferes with the follicle-ripening egg stuff we talked about earlier, so instead of an ovum floating off towards your tubes you get a cyst and Madame Ovary ends up looking like a cloud covered with grapes. I saw mine cos I went to the hospital. A nurse put a camera wand inside my vagina – she put a condom and lube on it first and explained that the condom was 'for hygiene, not because you could get pregnant'. It was very kind of her to assume I'd be confused and be expecting a baby wand in nine months. The camera sent a grainy video to a small telly and I saw the mess of my grape clouds and the nurse said, 'Oh yes, sorry dear,' in a sad voice like I was going to cry. But it was a relief for me.

I had suspected something was wrong because of my up-and-down ~~women's troubles~~ moods. Books and articles aimed at helping women understand pre-menstrual tension (PMT) describe emotiveness and 'feeling crabby'. Crabby sounds so sweet. I imagine an American woman apologising to a super-market worker she forgot to smile at while she packed her groceries – 'Forgive me, Mary-Sue, and have this $5 tip, I'm in ever such a crabby mood.' My menstrual moods are monsters, not crabs. I am hit by the pointlessness of everything. The futility. I think of death and I am filled with hate. And I've done nothing about it except taking evening primrose oil and fantasising about the menopause.

I have blamed my 'hormones' for all my negative behaviour since I was about seventeen. But when I met John, he didn't believe me. He said I had some much more serious mental disorder. 'Surely all your girlfriends were like this while on their periods?' I asked, head spinning round like that bit in *The Exorcist.* Apparently not; he has had a sheltered life. John told me to go to the doctor so I did. I explained all my symptoms and she told me I was depressed and I said, 'I'm not,' while tears fell onto my lap. She agreed they would test me for polycystic ovary syndrome (PCOS) because I had all of the hairy/weight gain/irrational mood symptoms.

I insist I am not depressed because I shouldn't be. I have a stimulating life and neither of my parents is dead and I'm really enjoying series 3 of *The Bridge*, yet for a few days every month everything is turned inside out and terrible. I think of it as reverse alchemy; my menstrual hormones touch my life and turn it to sludge and slurry. Knowing it's my hormones, that it's episodic and will pass, does not help me. That was John's advice: 'If you know it's hormones just ignore it, it's not really you,' but when the monster arrives it doesn't feel 'not real'. Instead it seems it's the rest of the month that's a fiction and the true me with my true feelings has been waiting underneath, coping, repressing, and now here she is to CRY ABOUT IT.

I cry very regularly anyway, let us say on average one small cry a day in frustration or disappointment or whatever. But seven days before my period it goes into overdrive. My boyfriend jokes about how much I cry; sometimes he laughs when I start, because what I am crying at is so stupid. He has written a funny list of 'things my girlfriend has cried at' to do in his stand-up routine, and if you heard it you'd think he'd made them up but he didn't. I cry getting dressed, I cry thinking about how big space is, I cry at the thought of an animal being stuck in our bin, I cry if John can't hear me from the other room, I cry when I remember Amy Winehouse is dead, and Samuel Beckett and Nanny Babs, I cry at all television, advertising, music and some print media. And John doesn't even know about all the times I cry on my own. It's like I'm leaking something that I can't hold in. I am a TSUNAMI of tears for all the people in all the world and I am not separate from anything any more. I am misery, sadness and self-indulgence personified for seven days out of thirty-five. Come round some time, I'll show you.

I am interested in finding out what causes this pre-menstrual sadness and I am reading around on hormones and their effects but it has really surprised me how many books say 'We don't know why this happens' or 'This is another mystery of women'. Oestrogen and progesterone both completely plummet just before a period, so this hormonal drop must be something to do with it. Things like drinking and smoking make it worse – I had always known this but not understood why; your liver balances the hormones in your blood (or tries to) and when it's working on stored alcohol (which it has to if you drink more than one unit per hour) then the hormones can become more unbalanced. Interesting, huh? And annoying, because downing wine and hoping it will make everything better is one of my favourite nonsensical behaviours.

Apparently, with my polycystic ovaries, the extra testosterone can cause a higher sex drive, but it has also caused nobody to want to have sex with me because of the accompanying aggression and facial hair. When I am not crying at John, it's usually because I have taken a break to shout. Usually about wanting us to have more sex together – there is loads of stuff written about women having an increased interest in sex around their periods; apparently orgasms are really helpful with cramps and the heaviness of the engorged womb imitates arousal. But what no one acknowledges is how difficult it is to seduce someone by raging at them with snot down your face.

The PCOS can also make it trickier to have children, because your eggs are tied up being cysty. And it's a strange thing; when I was sixteen and planning my abortion, I was so certain that I never wanted to have children. *Ever*. And people told me I would change my mind and I hated those people. And through my twenties even. People don't believe you when you say, 'No kids, not for me.' They act like you're not qualified to know what you want. And I didn't, and I never changed my mind – but something changed in my body. My body cleaves and clenches and saddens. Perhaps it's all these periods I shouldn't be having, but I'm thirty-four and the baby thing has confused me without my permission. I think I understand why people don't believe you when you say you don't want children, because they know it's a compulsion rather than a choice. That a woman's body changes with age – it begins as a beautiful, bouncy machine for her brilliant mind to travel about in and some time in her thirties it transforms into BabyWantingBot2000 with her rational 'the planet is so overpopulated already' mind trapped inside.

Or, I should say, that's my experience. I'm not saying it's true for all women, it's not even true for me all the time, I reckon for seventy-five per cent of my day it wouldn't cross my mind to worry about procreation. I am busy, excited by my varied life and the fun and chores and my excellent bicycle with a basket. Then for fifteen per cent of the time I am low-level thinking about it, I have long-game thoughts like 'Once I've bought a house I could register for adoption,'* or 'I could go to a sperm bank, no need to panic now, I could just buy some sperm when I'm forty.' So it's only the remaining ten

---

* For me to adopt a child, silly, not for a family to adopt me.

per cent of my day when I anxiously fret, 'WHAT WILL I DO WHEN I'M FIFTY?' I don't want to be still living this child's life, I want to be responsible, I want to care about people who aren't me. I don't want to be still talking about sex on stage and having to make jokes through my menopause and barrenness before going to bed with my stupid bicycle. I want to read stories or make them up. I want to complain about the school system, I want to go into assembly and insist that the boys are taught about periods and tell everyone how you can't have sex with a tampon in actually. Then I could show them a used sanitary towel and say, 'THAT'S LIFE, KIDS, DON'T LET ANYBODY SHAME YOU.' I want to share. I have been a daughter for thirty-four years and it's been great but I also want to try being a grown-up. I feel stupid when I worry about this, I'm not sad *now* but maybe I'll be sad later. But maybe when later happens I won't be sad at all, and then I'll regret the tenth of my time I wasted feeling like a cliché and not knowing what to do about it. Stupid stupid thoughts and thinking.

I've said it before but it bears repeating that without the very powerfully embedded drive to procreate any species would dwindle and disappear, ARE YOU LISTENING, PANDAS? We humans are the first species to consider procreation a choice – or to consider anything at all. Before science created artificial insemination, sex was the only way for our species to procreate. Thus the urge for sex IS the urge to procreate (although that might be the furthest thing from your mind at the time). It's unconscious, most sex isn't 'baby-making sex', but any kind of sexual behaviour has evolved because sex makes babies. Making children is also the most exhausting, demanding and dangerous thing a woman can do with her body.

Our evolution has had to counterbalance this. As our species's brains grew exponentially in size the difficulties of pregnancy and childbirth increased. This meant that women with certain attributes would be 'fitter', would be more successful in their child-producing. There are the body adaptations; wide hips, stored body fat, etc. But there were also behavioural traits that benefited our ancient female ancestors – for instance really wanting children and being able to love those children very deeply – which would result in better care and higher survival rates.

And sexiness. Women with no sex drives would have left no genes. Even with the widest hips and the hugest potential for bonding with offspring, if the human women of millions of years ago did not want to have plenty of sex, they did not get the ensuing plenty of children. We modern women have inherited the genes of the most sexual women through thousands of generations because they were the most reproductively successful. Yet our gender's sexuality has been repressed, ignored, misunderstood and outright denied by our civilised societies. Take your knickers off and follow me, it's time to find out why . . .

You Have Genitals!

We already know about the meeting and greeting of sperm and egg that makes a person. We've followed the pairing of chromosomes, the floaty swim ending with uterine embedding. We've thought about the six-week-old embryo, developing limbs, the beginnings of brain and lungs and the first heartbeats. We're paddling past that now to week eight, a mere two months old in human time but already past your first birthday in dog years.* Until now you'd enjoyed a warm, watery genderless existence. If there were a soiree for embryos all body shapes would be identical and all foetuses united in their similarities until the clock struck eight weeks, when those with XY chromosomes would glide off home before their penises appeared and embarrassed them in front of everyone.

Our chromosomes hold the instructions for our body's gendered development. XX = a female body and XY = a male body.** During this 'gonadal phase', male-bodied foetuses

---

* Not all families celebrate the seven birthdays a year as specified by dog time.
** It is worth reminding ourselves here that some people are female or male but born into a differently gendered body. This is something we are learning more about as it becomes more commonly discussed in public. If I slip up in my sweeping descriptions of women, in my use of broad strokes, I apologise. I intend to always include anyone who identifies as a woman even if her body is different to the one I am describing. I also should mention that there are a variety of chromosomal disorders that affect sex development in the womb, e.g. females who have testosterone flooding at eight weeks' gestation, males who do not receive *in utero* testosterone. It's a fact that some women have penises and some men don't. It's a long washing line of bodies we're all sitting on, our perceptions and experiences will all be disparate, and I am writing in such a subjective way that I'm sure I will occasionally appear ignorantly unaware and uncaring about many people.

are flooded with testosterone. This alters their genital development: their clitoris swells into a phallus, their ovaries descend to become testicles and their labial folds converge into a smooth crest between penis and anus. This unfurling development is pretty magical. There are websites with photographs of male and female foetuses day by day, so you could watch how we mirror and differ while you're at work tomorrow and see if that's enough to get you fired.

During the Middle Ages, when anything that happened inside a living body remained mysterious, they believed it was the other way around, that males were the prototype, the basic format for human, and that females were males who hadn't received enough warmth in the womb. That we were failed males. There was a common misunderstanding back then that if a woman got too excited and 'overheated' in adulthood she would spontaneously 'put forth' her penis – which, while factually inaccurate, would be a brilliant way to end an argument. We now know that a female body is the basic frame for all human beings and while it's tempting to spend a day shouting at boys, 'You're actually women that testosterone came along and mucked up!' we shouldn't place too much importance on this. Nature isn't making a powerful feminist point in our wombs, it's just growing cells in the most efficient way. One sex was always going to be the building block for the other, so let us accept our fundamental category with the composed grace of the vastly superior.[*]

Now, let's stop concerning ourselves with the other and concentrate on us. Here is a labelled diagram of the female genitals. Feel free to trace a copy for your wall. I have based

[*] Joking, obvs.

this on pictures and photographs in books, this is NOT a self-portrait and if you tell anyone it is I will TRACK YOU DOWN and ask you to stop.

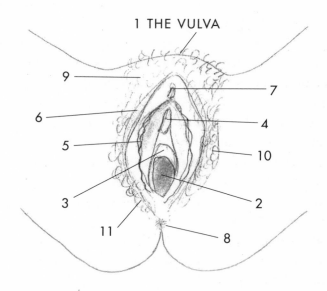

1 THE VULVA

1: The vulva. Sometimes people use 'vagina' to describe the whole shebang, but 'vulva' is the truthful name of our external genitalia and it is such a *beautiful* word, isn't it? Maybe I've been looking at pictures of genitals too much recently, but I love the plush and velvety sounds of 'vulva'. 'It's really quite a pretty name for a girl,' I told John as we travelled home last night and he looked out of the train window and didn't speak for twenty-five minutes. Reading between the lines, I've a feeling he didn't agree, with an added sense of 'please don't use words like that on public transport'.

2: This bit is the *actual* vagina. It is the interior passage, leading towards the cervix at the neck of the womb. The word originates in Latin and could be translated as 'sheath' or 'scabbard'. Somewhere to put your sword then. The vagina is an adapting, responsive organ. It lengthens during sexual arousal and widens in preparation for childbirth, and shrinks into a closed resting state in between. It is not a hole. Women do not walk around with an empty space inside them (unless they've been shot by a cannon ball in the film *Death Becomes Her*. If you haven't seen it, track it down online and watch immediately in order to get my dated nineties references).

When girls are born they have a small slip of skin partway inside the vagina called a hymen (3). There are usually some remnants of this skin inside the vagina years after it is broken.

The exterior of the vulva features the urethra – this little hole here (4). That's where urine from the bladder leaves the body, in case you haven't noticed.

Then we have the labia minora (5) and labia majora (6). They sound like constellations, stop looking upwards – these galaxies are in your underpants. 'Labia' means 'lips' in Latin, and 'minora' and 'majora' mean 'small' and 'large', so there's some factually accurate naming right there. There is a very wide range of appearances in these genital lips, just like with facial lips. The minora are sometimes packed inside the majora, while other women have minora that extrude. The labia majora swell up with blood during sexual arousal and are often unsymmetrical, with one being slightly lower than the other. I have tried to draw a vulva here that is less neat than the ones you might have seen in pornography. Pleased don't be offended if you have neat symmetrical genitals, you're normal too.

7: Here is the clitoris. There is a hood of skin that protects the organ a little bit in day-to-day non-sexual mode, but when aroused the hood retracts and the clitoris swells with blood and increases in size. For some women there is only a slight hardening, for others a more noticeable size shift. The word 'clitoris' is Latin although originating in Greek and it could mean 'to shut', or 'key', or 'little hill'. The etymologists don't really know for sure, so nor do we. To me it sounds godlike: 'Oh no, you have angered Clitoris, here she comes flying on her angry sheep to take revenge.'

8: This is your bum hole. Some people consider this a sexual organ and have great fun with it. Not me, I'm afraid, I probably won't mention it again, unless bum hole whitening comes up later. Who knows?

Around here (9) is where pubic hair grows from puberty onwards. And also here (10). And here (11). And sometimes the odd one halfway down your thigh that looks like he has had an argument with all the others and is making a break for freedom.

Before I had any pubic hair, I had read about it, probably in that *Have You Started Yet?* book. And it made sense of a picture Aunty Juliet had in her flat. It was a really big painting that a friend of hers had done. The lady in the painting had no clothes on and the lady was my aunty Juliet. And when I went upstairs to the toilet, I would often peek in to look at the naked painting, because she had something all over her botty. It was black and I wondered why she hadn't washed it off but was just sitting there. I asked my aunty Mickey once why Aunty Jools had a dirty botty but she just laughed and told everyone. But after I read the book I understood, I was mature and informed and a grown-up now. 'Don't worry,' I told Mickey next time I saw her, 'I know Juliet has got public hair.' Mickey laughed again and corrected me. 'Nope, I'm pretty sure it's public hair,' I assured her. It made sense to me; this hair provided protection from the gaze of the public when you were naked on a painting.

Nowadays the public gaze is very rarely interrupted by pubic hair because hardly anyone has got any. In pornography if you want to see a woman with pubes you have to search for a specialist category like 'unshaven' – the norm has become extraordinary. Before I start ranting on about this, let's consider the evolutionary theories of why these little tufts of genital hair exist in the first place. Two million years ago our ancient ancestors would have been hairy all over like other apes. Hair is an animal's way of regulating body temperature and is an absolute necessity when living outdoors without clothes or sleeping bags. And then, over thousands of years, our variety of *sapiens* became a lot less hairy. Persuasive theories argue that we needed to thermo-regulate in a different way, that we were overheating from all our running about and lost our hair in order to sweat more effectively. Others argue that we sexually selected less hairy partners as a sign of youth. Some say we lost hair in order to rid ourselves of the ticks and lice that would have lived in our fur, while the aquatic ape theory pops up again to insist that we evolved out of full body hair to be more streamlined when we lived in the water.

Whatever your favourite explanation, the result is that you are not as hairy as other mammals, though we still grow loads of hair on our heads (to protect us from the sun) and during puberty lush tough hair sprouts around our genitals. In sex education at school I was told that pubes had a hygienic role, keeping unhelpful particles away from sensitive areas, similar to how lashes function around the eye. Another theory is that the hairs trap odours and promote pheromones, adding to sexual attractiveness and aiding partner selection. Then there is the even simpler explanation that the arrival of pubic hair announces adulthood and is a clear visual signal that a female has reached an age where she could bear children.

It's difficult for me to accept that puberty = adulthood, because I was such a child when it happened to me. I have to remember that my city-bound, modern upbringing allowed and expected this childhood of mine. Had I grown up in a nomadic tribe on an island in the Pacific I might have felt more mature at twelve. I certainly would be more familiar with adult bodies if I had lived in a non-clothed culture. Apart from that painting, I hadn't seen any pubic hair before I grew it, my family kept the bathroom door closed. Indeed I was in a locked toilet when I first noticed the arrival of my 'publics'. They were blonde and soft and I stroked them proudly. Over several months they became dark, coarse and wiry and I wasted many bottles of conditioner trying to tame the tangle. I felt disgusting and horrific. Desmond Morris wrote that women dislike pubic hair because it reminds them of spiders. Or that they dislike spiders because they fear the sexuality which pubic hair signals. Either way this is a terrific bit of nonsense, although I like the idea that my screaming at a spider is because I'd thought a clump of pubes were making their way across the living room. Sadly in the modern world both spiders and pubic hair commonly end their lives down the plughole.

If some women/most women/western women/you [delete as appropriate] feel that pubic hair is unattractive, is that a *natural* aversion, a psychological rejection of adulthood, or is it because we've been subtly and explicitly advised that femininity = body baldness? Virtually all the women I know shave some part of their body. The unimaginative mockery of feminists refers to unshorn armpits and legs as often as smouldering bras,* and when I make the decision to go unshaved for a bit, it feels brave and political rather than lazy and unworthy of comment. So monstrous is female body hair that adverts for razors depict women running blades down pre-epilated legs. To show a woman's leg with hair, even if that hair was in the process of being removed, would be to signal that it's okay, natural, not a big deal, and that would subtly undermine the sale of such razor blades.

A couple of years ago, while promoting a show, I did a Q & A for a men's magazine. They said they were contacting 'real' women (lad mag speak for 'small-breasted') to be interviewed for a feature about how 'real' women (not those synthetic robot women usually featured in the media) felt about sex. 'Don't worry,' they said, 'we won't need a picture for the interview.' I was stupidly keen to do it – this type of ~~misogynist drivel~~ magazine is read by young men with unformed minds; I would be able to educate them, contradict the porn they consume and help them learn about female pleasure. I spent hours answering the stupid questions about penis size and how long he should last and then arrived at question 7: 'How can a guy politely ask his girlfriend to get a Brazilian wax?' Like it's the *politeness* that is the issue in that scenario. 'Oh, everyone else who's asked before has been *so rude*, I *do* appreciate your civility – yes. Yes I *will* have hair ripped from my genitals.'

Brazilian waxes became de rigueur as I was making my way into my twenties and remained popular, more than popular,

---

* HISTORICAL CORRECTION ALERT: there is no proof that any feminist ever burnt a bra. Protesters at the 1968 Miss America contest threw some underwear in a bin, but nothing was set fire to. It's a powerful image that stuck in the public consciousness without ever happening.

expected until relatively recently. I always felt I had to warn people before I went to bed with them, 'Just so you know, I have pubic hair – stop screaming, I promise it's not spiders.' Also why are they called Brazilians? I know it's probably where the style originated or something but wasn't it insensitive to name a near-total wax after a country suffering from wide-spread deforestation? SAVE THE RAINFOREST! Leave the Amazon alone.

I obsess about pubic hair because attitudes to it are typical of the pressure on us not to *be* like us. Something happened about a year ago, I was at the gym near my house. (You mustn't imagine a horrible place full of vain people looking in the mirror; this is a council-run gym so most people are there for free because the NHS thinks they're dying. We have a real carnival atmosphere. No one wears gym stuff, you can go in whatever you're wearing that day, high heels, sombrero – nobody cares.) For financial reasons we only have one working hairdryer in the ladies' changing room, and what I saw, just over a year ago, was an older lady using that hairdryer to dry her pubic hair. And she was taking her time over it, she was combing, doing a thorough job, and there was no embarrass-ment; if you looked over at her, she looked straight back at you. BUT because she was using the only working appliance, a queue had formed of other women waiting to use it, and one of them, she's had enough, she decides she's going to use the hand dryer, which is at waist height, to dry her head hair.

So older lady number two is now crouched down, drying her hair as best she can – and there is no problem with this whatsoever, it's an ingenious solution, except that because she's got no clothes on she is splayed to the room. Every-body else is okay about this, carrying on with their business in the changing room, and I am frozen to the spot. I am not prepared for such confidence, I am from a shy family. I wondered if perhaps I should go over and say something, in case she didn't realise she was so exposed? But then I reminded myself, 'No, this is just nudity, we are *animals*, bodies are just bodies, it's only civilisation that makes you think there's something wrong.'

And yet I did feel something was wrong, not physically, she was exactly as I depicted earlier, but you can't, can you? You can't go over to a stranger and say 'Sorry, *excuse me*, I can see in your womb' – but luckily the gym has a tannoy.

Since then, I think about those two women often. After I'd gone home I kept pondering what my problem was, why I'd felt so concerned with their behaviour, and I realised it was because they were accepting of themselves and relaxed with their bodies in a way that I am not. I don't even get undressed in the changing room because I'm so anxious about being judged. I wouldn't have a Brazilian wax and then wander around confidently because I would worry other women would look at me and think I was a bad feminist. That I had succumbed to social pressures; that I wasn't resisting as I should. But I also wouldn't go into the open showers with all of my pubic hair because I worry everyone will ~~think it's spiders~~ assume I haven't got a boyfriend. And it's frustrating because when you think about it, women's genitals are like men's faces. They grow hair because they're ADULT and they should only be fully shaved if you've got a court appearance or job interview.

Those naked ladies are my heroes. They prance around my memory, inappropriately using drying appliances and reminding me that it is always society that's wrong, never our bodies.

I have a number of friends* who have no pubic hair. I must stress that these are *adult* friends. They've chosen to have laser hair removal, which is permanent, and to hear them speak, it's like they have corrected something that was wrong with them. Erasing an unsightly blemish. And I hate it and they are bored of my lectures, but I feel like they are denying something animal about themselves, maybe even encouraging the fetishisation of the pre-pubescent, and – AND I think they are going to confuse future generations. When they're in their seventies and drying off after a swim some kid's gonna turn to their parent and ask, 'Mummy, why is that baby so old?'

I am BORED of being told pubic hair is unsightly. There is an advert on TV at the moment, not *right* at this moment, I am giving you my full attention, it's an advert that has been on for a few months and it's for a razor blade aimed at women. Pink, of course (the women and the razor), and the woman in the ad, she is talking to the camera, all relaxed and sharing her story of when she was at a BBQ and having a great time when everyone decided to jump into the swimming pool. And the lovely razor lady, she was worried, she points down her groin, reliving her pitiable plight, and asks, 'Am I beach ready?' Then she smiles to reassure us and we know it's going to be okay as she announces, 'Of *course* I was beach ready!' It was a happy ending and we were silly to doubt her and the moral of the story is, if you've got pubic hair, please don't come to parties. Just stay at home, there's food here, it wouldn't be hygienic. Also, when did we start using that stupid phrase 'beach ready'? Beaches are inanimate meetings of land and sea, why are we trying to impress them?

* Bragging.

I should tell you now that I spoke to my aunty Juliet, yes, the one from the painting, about this the other day, moaning about all my friends being pubeless, and she said, 'Maybe they're all having fun – experimenting, having a sexy time?' and she's right and I shouldn't be preaching to people. I am not telling you that you're not allowed to shear off as many pubes as you like, I just want to strongly assert that you should never feel like you have to.

Enough with physical appearance, let's move on to genital aroma. 'Is that the name of your celebrity fragrance, Sara?' You wish. I'll never release a perfume because I am pretty sure they're all tested on animals by bastards.

The female genital system, interior and exterior, is a self-cleansing organ. It has a delicate and specific pH level which alters incrementally throughout the menstrual cycle. This affects how the organ smells. Some women find that they smell more pungent or earthy at times, just before their period, for instance, or mid-cycle during ovulation. Recent sex can change the smell a bit, use of condoms or lube or vibrators, anything that introduces new bacteria; menstrual blood can have a tangy smell – but all this included, healthy vulvas smell like vulvas. And that smell only reaches as far as the people with their head in your crotch. In fact the guy who put forward the theory of sperm competition, Robin Baker, claims in his book *Sperm Wars* that oral sex may have evolved as a way of checking genital health pre-intercourse; that the instinct for a full face-to-genital meeting may have prevented mating with diseased, infected or weakened partners. I have no idea if that is true or how you could even prove it, but what I *am* certain of is the taboo/disgust/fear of smelly fannies.

At school it was a semi-common insult, the kind of thing boys shouted to embarrass you and girls bitchily commented on behind your back. With boys the theme was usually fish-related, whereas with girls it was either that they could smell when you were on your period or that your sexual promiscuity had to led to some kind of rotting or decay of the groinal area. Yes, you're right, I did go to a horrible school full of awful people but I'm free now, FREE. If you're still at school you too will be free one day, I promise. They're not allowed to keep you there.

Years after I'd finished school, a man approached me in a bar. He gave me a meaningful look and dribble-spoke into my ear: 'I could smell your cunt from over there' – he gestured to the far side of the room. What would have been a nasty playground taunt, his sleazy tone and demeanour meant me to receive as a compliment: the first line of an invitation for an evening of what would've certainly been the most inept love-making of all time. A few years later, on my first panel show,* one of the rounds was 'Worst Ever Chat-up Lines' and I tried to make this guy in the bar into a funny story. As soon as I said it I really wished I hadn't. It was too gross and personal, I should've said it happened to a friend, not to me. The other comics made a few jokes and I sat there brave and blushing and it felt like school again. No one meant to be mean to me, it was a topic I had introduced and they were just, you know, riffing on it. Wondering how far away my genitals could be smelled ha ha ha ha, maybe he was doing me a favour, sending me to the toilets with a wet wipe ha ha ha.

---

* If you are not familiar with the genre, a panel show is a long boring conversation between arrogant people edited down to look funny and interesting. I love doing them so much. I'm not being sarcastic, I love them.

Even in the complete jest and hyperbole of it I felt diminished and so, so ashamed of myself. To be reminded that one is the owner of female genitals is weird. It makes me feel vulnerable and repulsive. And belittled. Less respectable.

Despite all this, I am not paranoid about my genital smell. There I go, bragging again. And while I understand, you know, washing every day, changing underwear, a quick flannel wipe if you're about to have sex with someone you want to impress, I don't get the whole Femfresh thing. I name them although I know there is a whole load of speciality vulva cleaning products available; I'm guessing that Femfresh are the market leader. And I name them because their adverts made me want to – not hurt anyone, I don't condone violence – but their adverts made me want to shut down the whole department of advertising execs who created the campaigns and find them new and fulfilling jobs where they could put their understanding of female insecurity to good use. Counselling maybe? Writing self-esteem quizzes? Moulding the public persona of a boy band? Something they could be proud of when people asked at dinner parties.

I must have known that Femfresh existed as a concept – that there was a range of products (wash, wipes and deodorant) created specifically to prey on women's and girls' fears. There is no male equivalent of Femfresh; there is no market for specialised penis wash because it is an idiotic and unnecessary idea and no one would buy it. People only fall for that kind of rubbish when they've been brainwashed (and wiped and deodorised) into believing there could be perilous consequences otherwise. So – I was vaguely aware of Femfresh, though I had never bought any or spotted it in a friend's bathroom, and then in London near my house there was suddenly a huge poster: an ecstatic and beautiful woman frozen in celebration as a mega-font yelled across her body: 'WOOHOO for my FROOFROO'. Her happiness, according to the poster, was due to the effects of Femfresh. The subtextual message was that when your genitals were properly cleansed, you too could be happy and beautiful. The explicit message was that this grown woman called her vulva a 'froofroo'. Baby talk and flippancy and an assault on our natural odours all wrapped up in one billboard by the station.

I spent all day arguing with the poster in my head. I hated the infantilisation of the language, sure, but I hated the separation of genitals and body even more. The compartmentalisation of who we are and this extra (gross and idiotic) appendage. 'Whatever you call it make sure you love it' was the tagline. What is this IT? I wondered all day, some add-on? A parasite or mollusc that wasn't truly me but hung around in my underpants and needed caretaking? The billboard was not alone, it had siblings that used alternative words: 'mini', 'twinkle', 'hoo haa', 'fancy', 'lady garden', 'kitty', 'va jay jay', 'nooni', 'la la', 'privates' and 'down there'. And I know the advert was supposed to be a bit of fun, that all those silly slang terms were supposed to make us smile. Lots of people have childish names for their genitals and if this advert had been for something like, I don't know, a cancer charity I would've been less angry, just thought it sad and pathetic. Actually there is a poster campaign at the moment raising money/ awareness of cervical cancer. There are little posters all up the escalator on the underground and they show different kinds of pink shoes on a staircase and I tut at it daily because how could anyone who cares about women think we can be symbolised by, be reduced to, pink footwear? But their heart is in the right place (if not their advertising account) and I don't go on about it. But Femfresh can go f**k themselves,* they were double-damning us. 'You're not clean enough,' they targeted us from the streets, 'and and you don't own your body.'

Around the same time, maybe a couple of months later, Gwyneth Paltrow advocated a 'vaginal steam' on her website Goop.com. Before we go any further let me say that I respect and admire any woman who pursues health and happiness. I love Gwyneth and her incredible work as an actor and I am not criticising her personally. However, she does occasionally channel some BS. 'It is an energetic release – not just a steam douche,' she reassures us. She claims it 'balances female hormone levels', which it definitely doesn't, that is not how hormones work. Remember the interplay of oestrogen and progesterone communicating via your blood during your menstrual cycle? Imagine if their behaviour was altered every time you sat on something warm. Your 'female hormones' would be 'balanced' every time you had a bath or leaned on a radiator. 'If you're in LA, you have to do it,' says Gwyneth. Well we aren't, and we don't. This treatment (which involves sitting above some herb-flavoured steam with no knickers on) may be very relaxing, and being less stressed is certainly very good for your health (as proved by a little old evidence-validated practice called science). But the websites for V-steams claim to 'energise the uterus', which is meaningless nonsense, and to 'detoxify your vagina', which, by the way, isn't toxic. Any time you see the word 'detox' someone is trying to sell you absolute waste-of-time crap. Your liver detoxifies you, with help from your kidneys, lungs and skin. Face cream

---

* I have not disguised my swearing, I put two bum holes inside to make it worse.

doesn't detoxify you, nor do fad diets, or tablets or expensive spa treatments. Vaginal steam is just Femfresh for people with money, it's the same forces at work. Presumably even movie stars were sometimes called 'fishy flaps' at school.

I Asked Jeeves to see if he knew how much money is spent on genital cosmetics each year, but he kept sending me to pages with stats on regular cosmetics and finally to a website that sold little boys' foreskins, so I have stopped looking now. Let's just say that some money is spent by some women each year on just the most unbelievable, surreally weird stuff. I already knew about anus whitening creams, I'm not Amish – I'd learned about such potions from an article I read about Simon Cowell. But I was very surprised when (because of all the stuff I've been searching for lately) the sidebar on my homepage started offering me labia paints. YES, pastes for women to apply to their genitalia because they are – well, I guess they are not pink enough. Following the rabbit down the hole to its vendor I was invited to purchase labia lightening creams if my crotch was too dark, and tightening gels if my vagina was too wide. All the language seemed to be describing a scary walk home rather than human genitalia. If I was a women's magazine I would describe a 'growing trend' and a 'worrying increase' in women wanting to use such products on themselves, but more interesting, I think, is the *why?* Cos people take pictures of their vulvas more now so vanity is rising? Because of porn? Maybe women are more familiar with other women's vulvas and are thus more critical of their own? Do their partners demand prettier labia like men in the seventies expected their dinner on the table when they got home from work?

Let's just remember that cosmetics of all varieties – whether for your face or your fanny – are never providing a service you need. They are always, in their advertising and in their very existence, telling you that something is wrong with you. The entire 'beauty industry' is the financial exploitation of people's inbuilt, animal insecurity. Wanting to be attractive is not new, it's just that the fashions change. The Victorians had bustles and corsets, we have boob jobs and lighten our bald pudenda. We're all mad, but it's been this way for ages.

Not all of this genital embellishment remains superficial. Some women go to extreme lengths and have surgery. The operations have names like 'labiaplasty' or 'vaginoplasty' and involve cutting and reshaping the external genitals (for instance making the labia minora even minora-er) or cutting and stitching the vagina itself to make it feel smaller and tighter. I'm not going to sit on the fence with this one (impossible after this kind of op). I am sure a small percentage of the women undergoing such surgery do have medical conditions that need correcting. Perhaps their labia minora are so long they trail behind them and act as a parachute, slowing them down when they're running for the bus? Maybe their vagina is so wide their lungs and gall bladder fell out at Zumba? I'll stop being silly for a second – of course there will be women with injuries caused by difficult births. But having such an operation for aesthetic reasons is ridiculous. 'Designer vaginas', the women's magazines call it; their letters pages feature women who want to have a smoother contour in their gym gear, to look like the women in pornography or to be a 'virgin' again. We discuss female genital mutilation (FGM) as something that occurs in African nations or other faraway countries with exotic and unknowable cultures but all women are subject to the same pressures to be attractive, to be sexual *in the right way*. 'Designer vagina' is upbeat and rhymey but it's still a form of physical mutilation.

I would say that the stigma of having a loose vagina is worse than smell. It was another angle for the boys at school to terrify me. (Where the hell did they learn this? From their dads? Do they teach boys sexual bullying – is that where they went when we were learning about periods?) The idea of being baggy or having a massive fanny was an easy insult in the nineties, and is something I still hear male friends say occasionally about women they have slept with or wouldn't want to. And of course it's denigrating because tight vaginas = youth and sexual inexperience, and not tight enough = the opposite. This idealised, vice-like grip of the vagina is for the penetrating male's pleasure and reassurance. Olden-day sex guide the Kama Sutra (look out for it on a friend's parent's bedside table some time) is matter-of-fact about males and females having a variety of genital sizes. It suggests that it is sensible to match up with someone who is a similar size to you; women range through deer, mare and elephant and would well suit men with small, medium and large penises accordingly. This information is given without judgement or scorn, it's a genetic reality that our bodies are built differently. Sexual experience is not implied.

Despite what we start off with, our bodies *are* affected by childbirth. The sexual openness in our culture has allowed pop stars to talk about elective C-sections to protect their sex life, and male comedians (not all of course, but a few) to do funny routines about the state of their wife's genitals after giving birth. The oldest joke, recently recycled by Robbie Williams, is that watching your partner give birth is like 'watching your favourite pub burn down'. Implicit in this quip and others like it, is that the vagina exists for ~~men to have a beer in~~ male penetration. That it is his place, and it is he who is suffering from its transformation. OH LOOK!

ROBBIE WILLIAMS walks in and tells me to chill out in a Northern accent.

ROBBIE

Don't take it so seriously, don't analyse it, it's a gag to make you laugh!

SARA

I'm not laughing, jokes like that make me paranoid.

ROBBIE

You've not even had a baby—

SARA

But the implicit ownership—

ROBBIE

I never heard of that kind of ship.

ROBBIE turns to imaginary laughing crowd and winks and waves.

SARA

Our vaginas are ours. Not our partners'.

ROBBIE

Yes, you're the brewery, you own the pub—

SARA

We are the brewery *and* the patron and the landlord and you, you are just someone who walks past the pub and are lucky that you're even allowed on the same street actually, you aren't even a shareholder, you don't own even one share, you—

ROBBIE

I'm leaving. It was just a joke.

SARA

Okay. It was nice to meet you! I'd like to write a sitcom for you one day I think you're very— He's gone.

Rich people sometimes have cosmetic procedures at the same time they're in hospital having their baby. Liposuction to reduce their weight, a boob job while they're swollen and people won't notice and maybe a vaginoplasty while their genitals are being stitched anyway. If a woman who's literally just given birth feels compelled to rapidly return to her pre-pregnancy state that's because she believes that appearing fertile and sexually available is her cultural duty. Of course such women are a minority, but they are symbolic. They are the women who have bowed furthest to the pressures of their culture. Similarly, some women who have been infibulated as young girls (infibulation is a form of FGM where the labia majora are cut and stitched so that scar tissue forms and the vagina is virtually sealed), some of them ask to have their labia resewn again after giving birth. When I read about this I was so baffled. The vagina would be resealed, scar tissue would form, and before she could have sex her husband would have to break through that skin again, maybe even with a knife, causing much pain and discomfort – and it was the women asking for this and women sewing them up. This wasn't explicit patriarchy, it wasn't male demands. It was something the women assumed (rightly or wrongly) was attractive. It denied their own sexual pleasure, their experience of sex, in order to reclaim virginity, or rather to imitate it.

But why would sexual inexperience be attractive in a conscious mammal?

a) You can teach them how you like it.
b) You can tell them you're the best and they won't know otherwise.
c) Paternity certainty.

That's right, we've evolved to value virginity (well, straight men have) because it is the only way of being definitely sure that your partner isn't already pregnant by somebody else. Dominating a young, virginal partner would have been an evolutionary tactic for males to avoid bringing up children they weren't related to. Women can be pretty certain they're related to their babies so we haven't evolved to fetishise youth and sexual innocence in our partners. Instead we carry the burden of our experience, and if we can trick our way into appearing younger, we will often do so.

I could quote that Madonna song, but I've decided instead to tell you about when I was in either Scunthorpe, Blackpool or Hartlepool (I can't remember which because I am so jet-lagged from all my great travelling). Waiting for my gig to start, I was wandering along the seafront towards a huge black building, and as I got nearer the sign clarified that it was 'Fallen Angels'. For some reason I assumed it was a bakery and sped up, only to arrive a minute later and be disappointed by the truth: it was a strip club. Fallen Angels made sense for a cake vendor because the suggestion is all like, 'Who can resist our delicious cakes; even though you're a good girl on a diet you'll still want one.' And I guess there's sort of the same thing going on with the strip-club brand. 'Fallen' offers 'flirty, dirty, up-for-anything birds' while 'Angels' reassures patrons, 'These birds are clean and shiny new, don't worry, you won't catch anything.' They are wholesome women who have very recently decided to filth up for your pleasure. Sexual inexperience = good; sexually available = good, and so illustrated is the restrictive sliver of women at their sexiest: virginal but willing. Look like a porn star but have cellophane-wrapped, unused genitals. The hymen: nature's cellophane.*

Many women in the world are still expected to be virgins when they marry, usually because they or their family have strict religious beliefs. An intact maidenhead is often necessary for securing a dowry or bride price. In very extreme examples it can affect a woman's role in a restrictive society, for instance there are countries where women have to undergo 'virginity inspections': Egypt forced them on female protesters in 2013 and Indonesian students are given them yearly in order to remain in education. Up until 1979 a woman entering Britain for marriage purposes could be subjected to one, which is like, WHAT???? In lovely present-day Britain we have a wide range of cultures and subcultures ranging from the sexually relaxed to the very exacting. For some British women shame, dishonour or punishment remain the price for engaging in pre-marital sex, consenting or otherwise. This prevents me from making a generalised statement about how we aren't virginity-obsessed any more and us ladies can go out and get some whenever we want – that's not true for all of us. It's better for me to say that we are emerging together gradually from a history that was

---

* This is a great advertising slogan if you are planning on selling some hymens. You can buy it off me for £65.

unbelievably controlling of women, but we are gaining our liberty at different speeds.

The very oldest record of lawmaking, going back to 9000 BC, is indicative of the male fear of paternity uncertainty and aggressive attempts at ownership of women. It's called the Code of Ur-Nammu and it states that a woman who cheats on her husband should be killed. Thanks a lot, Ur-Nammu, whatever you are. Records from all ancient societies seem to have had variants on this; Assyrian women were killed if they were seen talking to a man in private, Hebrew brides were stoned to death if discovered (or suspected of) not being virgins on their wedding night. Ancient Rome is interesting: records show that all women were officially and explicitly owned by father or husband – a woman who didn't have either was given a guardian by the state. The only exception were the Vestal Virgins, who were owned by everyone – their magical virginity was believed to protect Rome and make sure they won all their wars and stuff. If things started going badly, if they lost a few battles or someone nice got struck by lightning, they would blame the virgins: 'One of you must have done it with a guy,' they would shout, and if it was proved, the lady would be buried alive in a hole. People believed in this. They kept the Vestal Virgin system going for five hundred years or so. The virgins' only job was to keep the fire of Rome going and not have sex, and if they failed at either of those things, everyone would cry and line the streets as the girl was taken to her hole to suffocate. Even if she had been raped – didn't matter, into the hole.

Whenever I find out about things like this I realise olden-day people were *insane*. Before there was science and evidence anyone could just say anything and use it as an excuse to kill someone. Even now when we have lots of medical knowledge available, myths endure and are detrimental. There's this commonly accepted connection between hymens and virginity – an intact hymen can be expected as 'proof' that a woman has not had penetrative intercourse, while in fact hymens are very unreliable indicators of that kind of thing. At birth the thin sliver of skin seals the entrance of a girl's vagina, and as she grows it splits. During puberty it becomes more elastic and remains in a crescent shape around the edge of the vagina But many things apart from sex can diminish a hymen further, such as tampons, exercise and masturbation; also some rare women are born without one. So any kind of hymen-based virginity test can only ever be a guess. Yet some women are choosing to undertake 'hymenoplasty',* an operation where the hymen is reinstated for the purpose of bleeding during sexual intercourse. The frequency of this operation is rising in the UK, although it is still very rare (less than a hundred a year). And while my aunty Juliet could pop up and say 'Maybe people are just having a fun and sexy time?' I don't think the people choosing to do this are spicing up their sex lives, I think they're fearful of the consequences of not seeming virginal enough for new husbands within prescriptive religions.

Why do we have hymens at all? It's another lady mystery, although we are not the only animal with one; horses, elephants, manatees, whales and hyenas have them too. Good old Desmond 'spider pubes' Morris reckoned hymens were naturally selected so that first-time sex would be painful for girls and we wouldn't be flippant about it and put out too easily. We would wait for a great guy who would stick around and help with the kids and thus ensure evolutionary success.

---

* Obviously I'm completely anti these kind of operations, but to the surgeons involved: remember I do have that advertising slogan if you fancy it? Only £65.

Presumably our ancestors without hymens were a lot free and easier with their first shag and just died out from being such slags? Everyone's favourite crazy conjecture, the aquatic ape theory, says that maybe we developed the hymen while we were in the water to stop sand and small shells from going up into our vaginas. Some scientists say that the hymen might be an important part of genital development while we are in the womb and that what remains during puberty is just a by-product of that phase, not worth thinking too much about. Try telling that to the guys over at 'virginity hypothesis', who reckon that hymens were sexually selected because our ancient male ancestors preferred sex with women who had hymens. I mean, come on – how did they check? At what point did they bring this up on dates? Did prehistoric women have labels stating 'Do not consume if seal is broken'? Guys, seriously, so many of these ideas are ridiculous.

People generally accept that a woman's first experience of sexual intercourse will be painful, which is perturbing. Speaking as a lay person with my own personal theories, most of the pain during losing of virginity (or any sex after that) comes from being tense or not aroused enough. Yet girls growing up are taught to expect this pain rather than being told to spend more time in foreplay to prevent it. Girls should be informed: 'First-time sex can cause a bit of pain unless you wait until you're so aroused that it doesn't.' I will tell them that, GET ME ALL THE GIRLS ON THE PHONE, I'VE GOT SOME IMPORTANT INFORMATION. With first-time sex we expect men to enjoy themselves, but not women. It sets a terrible precedent, but is easily shifted if we can make an effort to teach young people more about a woman's body and how to give and receive pleasure. When I say 'we' I mean society, not you and me with diagrams and pointy sticks in a blue tent outside the shopping centre.

For a long time, pleasure and sex were supposed to be unconnected. The Christian Church has spent two millennia bossing everyone about and telling us not to enjoy sex. The urges of our loins were the inherited punishment of Eve's sin, and marriage was perceived as a sensible way to contain this disgusting behaviour. 'Sex is for making babies, so you probably have to do it but you absolutely mustn't like it,' they told people. Pope Gregory the Great (his words not mine) claimed that marital intercourse was blameless only when there was no pleasure involved (blameless = you won't go to hell for it). All this suppression of sexuality worked, you know, and the population of Europe declined between ad 500 and 1050 because there were so few days when a married couple were permitted to have sex – it was banned on Sundays. And Wednesdays, Fridays, Saturdays, saints' days, festivals, the whole of Lent and for ages around a woman's menstruation. If you weren't married you were permitted to have sex never. And of course the Church also banned homosexuality and masturbation and punished and terrified those who were caught or accused of doing either. Most modern branches of Christianity have become more tolerant and accepting but still have a focus on procreation when it comes to sex. Fundamentalist churches remain as dictatorial as anyone adhering to a two-thousand-year-old rule book tends to be. But whether we are religious or not, the ramifications emanate through our culture, and none of our lives are free from ancient attempts to quell and control sexuality.

Another form of sexuality control is genital cutting, which is thought to have originated in Africa over five thousand years ago. Certainly the ancient Egyptians practised it; there's a rumour going round that Cleopatra herself was probably 'circumcised'. Nearly a hundred million women in the world are currently living with some form of FGM, 137,000 of those in the UK. If you have never been sure what FGM is, there are three main types: 1) clitoridectomy, where the hood of the clitoris is removed; 2) excision, where the clitoris is completely removed, sometimes with the labia minora; 3) infibulation, I mentioned this earlier, which is when the clitoris and the labia are removed and the vulva is sutured together, leaving just a very small hole for urine and menstrual blood to escape.

So why?

Well, the first type, clitoridectomy, sometimes referred to as sunna circumcision, is thought to be the female equivalent to male circumcision, with the hood of the clitoris acting like the foreskin of a penis. Trauma aside, if the operation is undertaken very carefully and without damaging the rest of the clitoris, it does not necessarily harm a woman's ability to enjoy sex. The clitoral exposure may even enhance sexual sensation. With excision and infibulation, the intention and result is to reduce or destroy a woman's pleasure. To cause pain, to diminish sex drive and to subjugate women. The cultures who practise these forms of FGM have many strong beliefs in support of these operations (don't imagine white coats and anaesthesia, imagine women with razors or scissors while girls are held down by family members). Girls are told that the procedure will make them healthier, folklore tells them it will make them more fertile or prevent them having stillborn children. In societies where FGM is the custom, girls who don't undergo it are considered 'dirty' and unmarriageable. Some cultures consider all uncircumcised women prostitutes. In such circumstances, despite the agony, the risk of infection and death, many girls would much rather face these operations than not. Their mothers, who have survived the practice themselves, often consider these mutilations to be a part of growing up as a woman. For millions of female children there is no choice; girls who refuse are forced. Families succumb to social pressures, just like all families everywhere. Generations are moulded, boys are taught to be aroused by compliance and distrustful of passion, women are taught that sex is for a husband's gratification or to make children.

For huge swathes of the modern world, female sexual enjoyment is considered dangerous because if a woman likes sex, she might have it with people that she wants to, rather than being made to endure it by the person that owns her. The clitoris is feared as the headquarters of female pleasure, so let's get to know it a little better.

Here is a diagram of the clitoris:

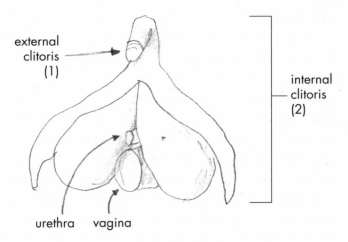

You can see the external nubbin (1) is connected to a much bigger internal organ (2) composed of connective tissue, erectile tissue and a dense network of nerves and sensory receptors. The position and size of the external part of the clitoris varies from woman to woman – all the books say 'pea-sized' but it is often much smaller. Or bigger. I read about a tribe where they call the women with large clitorises 'chickpeas' but when I tried searching for it online just now I only found delicious recipes.

If you have a clitoris, you are probably already aware of how sensitive it is. Despite its small size it is completely packed full of nerve endings and is by far the most responsive organ on your body. The dorsal nerve connects your clitoris to your spinal cord, meaning that for most women the clitoris is the centre of their sexual response, arousal, pleasure and orgasms. However, the way that women's bodies are composed means that penetrative sexual intercourse is possible without the clitoris being stimulated at all – and this *is* confusing, it doesn't seem to make sense. How can it be a sexual organ if, for women, sex seems possible without it? The clitoris has suffered a history of misunderstanding and mistreatment as a result.

Like I only recently realised how SEXUAL the witch hunts of the fifteenth to seventeenth centuries were. The claims against women were often variants of: 'She had sex with the devil,' 'She lets the devil do her,' 'The devil takes the form of an animal and shags her proper.' After accusation (usually from another innocent woman being tortured) a 'witch' was stripped naked, her pubic hair shaved and her body examined for 'marks of the devil'. As her relationship with Satan was presumed to be sexual, her genitals were closely scrutinised and often a little bump was found between the labia – 'the witch's teat', they called it. One is described as 'a preternaturall Excrescence of flesh between the pudendum and Anus much like to tetts & not usuall in women'. It was claimed that this bump was incredibly sensitive and sexy and that the devil could suckle from it and use it to manipulate the woman. During torture, they might prod and poke this blameless clitoris as the woman writhed and screamed in agony. When these poor women were taken to 'trial' (usually saying whatever they'd been told to in order to get the torture to stop) the men questioning them were *obsessed* with the size of Beelzebub's penis, how hard it was, what it was made of, etc. This historical phase epitomises   societal fear of a woman's sexuality. Through prudish culture and religious puritanism, sex and bodies had become mysterious. Genitals that throughout our evolution had been functional and knowable were now alien, and this strangeness became dangerous. In the thousands of years when humans were post-animal yet pre-science, the bodies we should have taken for granted became unfamiliar to us. Women make children, and female desire is (in nature) a prerequisite to this, but the hundreds of years when sexuality was repressed by religion meant that we only half understood things. We knew that women had blissful potential in their loins, but Christianity taught that this was temptation. That it was ungodly. Women's potential for pleasure became potential for evil instead. The male imagination transferred a subconscious fear of cuckoldry into symbolism, a large-phallused enemy of God who seduced anyone he wanted. And women's bodies were punished to assuage his fear.

Ignorance about female sensuality has continued until the present day and still exists right now this second while you're reading this book. We live in a world where penetration is considered as the main aspect of sex, the very definition of it, and because most women do not climax via this process, and men do, our entire gender is considered broken in some way. We are maladapted. We are taught that something is wrong with us if the conventional penis-inside-vagina sex does not get us going. The fact that this kind of sex makes babies is proof, PROOF, that it is the correct, best kind. The sort we've all evolved to want and enjoy for thousands of years. If the majority of modern women are not enjoying it as much as men, well, they must need therapy, say some psychologists. 'Women get their enjoyment from the pregnancy that follows sex, not the act itself,' the olden-day scientists used to say. 'They need to work harder, try different positions, buy sexier underwear and take more toys into the bedroom,' rant the women's magazines.

If you can bear another of my younger self's sexual tales: I went out with a guy called Dan in my second year of college. I had liked him for ages because he was a bit older and always had very smart clothes; his navy jumper and neat trousers stood out in the crowd of Kappa tracksuits in the canteen. Dan was the third person I'd ever slept with and it was – fine, it was fine. It wasn't *really* fine, but it was fine, it was just very thrusty. I felt very thrusted upon. I kept thinking I would have to ask him to change what he was doing, to calm down a bit, but it was too embarrassing so I broke up with him instead. He didn't care very much and we remained friends. At the pub months later, he was telling everyone at our table how great he was in bed. 'Tell them, Sara,' he insisted. 'I've got a system,' he was telling everyone, 'I worked out how you can *guarantee* that a woman comes.' Everyone was very intrigued, no one more than me who'd never managed to get anywhere close to orgasm in his vicinity. 'I worked it out with my first girlfriend,' he boasted calmly. 'All you have to do is hit the cervix thirty-five to forty times with the tip of your knob and it starts to tremble and that's an orgasm.' So there you have it, a perfect example of how a little bit of information and a dose of ignorant presumption create a terrible sex partner.

In Dan's defence, many anatomists and biologists have proposed equally baffling theories perfectly illustrating how the female orgasm is half known. We can be certain of *some* things, like the names of body parts and that it's nice when it happens, but the mechanics don't make any sense compared to the male framework – there *must* be a system to it, we just haven't figured it out yet.

Sigmund Freud had a good go at ruining women's sex lives for ever. He knew that some women could orgasm from penetrative sex while other women needed clitoral stimulation to climax (people told him everything) and he decided that the difference between these two types of women was psychological. The clitoral types were 'immature'; they were stunted in a pre-adolescent 'girl' state and needed years of psychoanalysis to move through to a 'mature', appropriate state of womanhood when they'd be able to come via the poking of a penis. To clarify, Freud believed that there was a right and a wrong way for a woman to orgasm, and that the wrong way should not be encouraged. Women and girls should not masturbate, as that would increase their difficulty in reaching a vaginal orgasm. There was a brief Victorian trend of removing the clitorises of female children who masturbated. There are documented cases in the UK and the US, and Freud was very supportive of the practice and recommended it. It's impossible to stress here how much the Victorians feared masturbation.

They thought it 'moral leprosy', blamed it for epilepsy and insanity and ugly children and anything else you can think of. Consider the difficulty for our gender, who mostly require clitoral stimulation to enjoy sex, during a time where desiring such stimulation was considered indicative of nymphomania and perversion. At least one woman responded by having her clitoris moved. DON'T WORRY, I am obviously going to give you more information, that's not the kind of fact you can drop, shrug and walk away . . .

Marie Bonaparte was one of Sigmund Freud's patients. She was Napoleon's great-grandniece and a brilliantly bright woman who enjoyed freedom in a restrictive society thanks to being very rich. Marie had clitoral orgasms, which she knew from therapy were 'wrong', and she became obsessed with 'fixing' herself. She had a theory that rather than being purely psychological, perhaps the position of a woman's clitoris made a difference to whether she could orgasm from penetration. She conducted a study – YES, she measured the distance between the clitoris and the vagina (C–V) on around 240 women, asked them how they orgasmed and published the results under a male pseudonym. What she found out should be common knowledge, but it isn't because everyone apart from you and me is an idiot.

Marie B. found out that if a woman's C–V distance was 1 cm or less, then she could have these vaginal orgasms. If the C–V was between 1 and 2.5 cm then the woman was on the cusp; she might sometimes be able to reach orgasm this way but it was unreliable. And if a woman's C–V* was over 2.5 cm

---

* I know you're waiting for me to make a joke about sending out your C–V when you're looking for work but I'm not going to – this orgasm stuff is vital information and you need to concentrate.

then she would always need extra clitoral stimulation, penetration would never be enough. Maybe it is not in our minds but in our measurements? Over fifty per cent of women are unlikely to experience orgasm without some excellent clitoral work. Including Marie: her C–V was 3 cm, so she decided to have an operation to move her clitoris closer to the entrance of her vagina. It didn't work, she still couldn't orgasm from penetration (I'm amazed she could walk afterwards, let alone screw), so she had another operation that moved her clitoris back again. That's how powerful the hetero-penetro norm was, Marie Bonaparte decided her *body* was wrong rather than the type of sex she was having. Just like modern women who have their labia trimmed and vaginas tightened, blaming their bodies when it is the cultural ideals that are wrong.

Orgasms are difficult to describe. In fiction they are depicted as explosive and satiating; in movies/porn women make gasping, animal sounds as they convulse and writhe about. There is a broad definition of orgasm being a 'climax of sexual feelings' or 'release of tension'. More scientifically it is a series of muscle contractions or spasms which induces a pleasurable feeling. Even more scientifically, stimulation of erogenous zones (usually including genitalia) activates the pudendal and vagus nerves, which send pleasure signals to the brain. More and more of the woman's brain becomes activated, including the amygdala, ventral tegmental area, cerebellum and pituitary gland. Blood floods to the genitals and engorges the clitoris and labia. Heavy breathing oxygenates the blood and thus the brain. As orgasm nears, the lateral orbitofrontal cortex appears to shut down – this part of the brain controls behaviour, civilises us. This shutdown results in a loss of inhibitions and a visceral, animal response to sensations for a number of seconds until climax ensues. Vaginal and cervical muscles contract and release. Then the hypothalamus sends out oxytocin, which promotes loving feelings and relaxation. If I worked on a sex line this is the kind of shit I would be saying to guys who called: 'Ooooh, my amygdala is so activated right now, uh yeah, I can feel my cervix contracting . . . Hello? Where's he gone?'

You will no doubt be familiar with the idea that men get sleepy post-orgasm whereas women don't. It's a bit of a cli- ché that men roll over afterwards while women want to cud- dle. There is a theory that this reaction evolved so that men wouldn't stop women leaving after sex, they'd be all curled up in dreamy land, leaving our lady free to pursue her next sex partner and benefit from some excellent sperm selection. Scientific tests have proved that men and women do have different patterns of sexual response. Masters and Johnson (sexologists working in the 1960s and 70s) created a model which outlines the four stages of sexual response in humans: excitement, plateau, orgasm and resolution. The difference between the genders is that women may be re-excited after orgasm rather than quickly returning to a pre-excitement state like men do. This seems to support theories that a woman could go off and enjoy more sex partners after ex- hausting one guy – go sister! Literally, go, he's snoring and won't notice. Studies have also discovered that women always make more noise during sex than men – that our gender is more vocal. It has been argued that this could have been a way for our ancient female ancestor to allow future suitors to locate her while she was in the mating mood, all her gasps and grunts letting someone in a nearby tree know: 'Hang on, mate, he'll be asleep in a minute.' This is just one theory, of course, and not a proven validated thing, but I most enjoy the explanations that keep female choice and action in mind when understanding our sexual responses. To contrast, another theory claims women make more noise during sex because it arouses their male partners. Studies prove that male orgasm is quicker when the female partner is vocal, but then that's another circular argument – 'it turns men on so women do it to turn men on'. And surely that could be flipped on its head? A circular argument driven by female activity: if sex noises are a signal of female arousal then men get turned on by it because aroused women are sexy. Perhaps I'm quibbling – anyone turned on by that?

Unfortunately for us, the female scope for pleasure and multiple orgasms has not resulted in widespread sexual satisfaction for women. And that is because our difference from men, our need for stimulation other than penetration, has been interpreted as dysfunction. Freud was not alone in considering orgasms achieved through penetrative sex as the only viable type. Many other doctors and therapists agreed. In the 1950s psychoanalysts Edmund Bergler and William Kroger stated that they believed between eighty and ninety per cent of women were abnormal in not being able to orgasm from sex, which has me LOL-ing out loud over here. The majority *is* the norm; that is the very definition. These men's subjectivity is similar to that seen by the Victorian anthropologists. Their idea of 'normal' and 'right' and 'female' blinds them to the evidence in front of their eyes.

I'm also laughing at a doctor called Alexander Lowen. He was writing later, in the 1960s, when more was known and clitoral stimulation was becoming more accepted as a reasonable part of heterosexual foreplay and intercourse – but not for

Lowen. He couldn't imagine at what point during intercourse men were supposed to be doing this stimulating. It couldn't be beforehand or the man would lose out on 'intimacy' and his erection would wilt. He couldn't possibly rub a clitoris *during* sex or it would put the poor man off his 'genital thrusts' and deny him his pleasure. And he couldn't be expected to do it afterwards as that would interrupt his relaxation time, which was his reward for exertion. This for me sums up perfectly the inequality in sexual approach – *his* pleasure, *his* exertion and *his* reward. If a woman didn't come, well, that was her fault for being so fiddly. Two decades later and a *Playgirl* survey found that three in four women believed their male partner's pleasure was more important than their own. So it's not just men that have disregarded female satisfaction – we have too. And that means that no one has ever got round to understanding it properly. There is no agreement about vaginal and clitoral orgasms or whether they are the same thing, or blended orgasms, which are apparently a mix of both except some scientists say they don't exist. Some women ejaculate when orgasming and no one is sure why or how and evolutionary theories of the female orgasm are a tangled mess.

Some claim that an orgasm is a vital part of pair bonding because it produces a large amount of oxytocin. It could've been naturally selected because, as we already know, bonded parents = better offspring survival rate. A further take on this is that it affected mate choice; women stuck with partners who could make them come. Others claim that the female orgasm promotes conception but there is a lot of disagreement about how. Perhaps the waves of the womb's contraction help move sperm towards the Fallopian tubes? Maybe orgasm makes a woman more likely to lie flat and exhausted after sex and that helps her retain sperm? There does seem to be some evidence that if a woman orgasms within a few minutes of a man coming inside her, she retains more of the ejaculate. But all of these theories are undermined because female orgasm is not imperative for conception and doesn't improve conception chances enough to be a genetically selected trait. A woman who has never had an orgasm could have the same number of children as a woman who has, which supports the arguments of those who believe that the female orgasm is an accident, a by-product. Not important. That it's a mere consequence of the way our genitals develop in the womb, that the mechanisms that went into making men orgasm champions have been left as an awry afterthought in women. So we have this tricksy, unreliable machinery that we don't need. 'It has no relation to baby-making so no useful function,' they say; 'let's just stop thinking about it and put it in a drawer with all the other bodily disjecta.'

There is an interesting theory that our genitals had to adapt a lot during the millions of years when babies' heads were getting larger and childbirth was getting more difficult and dangerous. It could be that to prevent a mother's urethra tearing every time a baby was born, we gradually evolved to its current placement, slightly further away from our vaginal opening than it was for our prehistoric ancestors. This in turn edged the clitoris higher. Perhaps our ancient ancestors had much more pleasurable penetrative sex than we do? So we evolved to have orgasms as an enjoyable sex incentive, but now the system doesn't work as well as it used to?

Whether that is true or not, my hypothesis (not scientist – amateur lady) is that the female orgasm does have a function, that it *was* sexually selected, but that scientists get confused in only considering completed orgasms as important. Orgasms are potential. Female arousal, the early stages of engorgement and lubrication have a sense of direction, of purpose, *because* the orgasm exists as an end point, whether it is reached or not. Anyone who has grown up with a female body will understand the urge to touch yourself, wanting more of the things that feel nice – our vulvas have a hunger. I believe that the unreliable nature of our orgasms was an evolutionary strength. Rather than being irrelevant, our ancestors who were sexually frustrated, who got close but not quite there – maybe they had more sex than the women who came easily? They might have demanded more sex from a regular partner, or they might have multi-partnered more and then had more genetically successful children via sperm selection? That would explain why women display such a wide range of orgasmic responses.

Women are not complicated, we're just not the same as men and we're not the same as each other. That's why I can't tell you what will sexually satisfy you, you'll have to find out for yourself. What I CAN tell you, what I wish was common knowledge, is that we have a dual-response method of sexual arousal, what sexologists call 'accelerator and brake'. So some things turn you on (accelerator) and other stimuli might make arousal impossible (brake). Understanding your body and its responses in this way will help you remove 'brakes' (bright lighting, living with parents, overly energetic thrusting) as much as exploring and exploiting your accelerators. There is a great example of this: after some MRI experiments, scientists found that women wearing socks orgasmed more easily than those who weren't and they were like, 'EVIDENCE, women find wearing socks super-sexy,' but it was actually that the women with cold feet couldn't get aroused.

Cold feet *are* really distracting – or maybe you're into that? We're all different.

And we're ACTIVE, that's the main thing to remember. The impractical, almost impossible difficulty of pushing out a baby and keeping it alive has been combated by the development of two powerful forces in women: the potential for deep love and a filthy hot sexual instinct. If women were passive and unsexual, human beings wouldn't be here any more – giving birth got too deadly and childrearing too costly, who would've bothered with it? Our gender's around-the-clock, any-day-of-our-menstrual-cycle lust ensured that no matter how ill-adapted our species to every single type of terrain and weather, there were always humans on this planet. Probably there's too many now, we've ruined the place because we're too damn sexy. But we're often treated as passive, expected to be compliant and available and that is wrong. My aunty Juliet corrected me once when I was a teenager; I was telling her about how one of my friends had fucked some guy and she was like, 'No, she was fucked. Women can't do the fucking.' She wasn't making a political point, she was correcting my grammar but I always believed she was wrong. At sixth form I remember someone telling me that all the difficulties between genders were based on this – men oppress because they are the penetrators and women succumb because they are penetrated – and I just don't recognise that. We are not penetrated, we consume, we engulf, we devour. We do not permit, we DEMAND; we are not gatekeepers, we are diners, yes, diners eating penises with our ravenous sopping wet vaginas, I've gone too far.

At university I was lectured in a more sophisticated version of this theory, I was told that 'all penetrative sex is rape'. I could see their point, and I had some very enjoyable debates ending in angry crying, but for me, my very definition of sex is a meeting of equals. When it is not that, it is something else. And that is something we have to think more about now. I have so far spoken as if all of the mating undertaken by our ancestors would have been consensual and that is not the case, it would be wrong to assume that our evolution has only been moulded by willing sex.

There is a really famous experiment where the psychologist Meredith Chivers measured men and women's arousal when watching different sex videos: homosexual, straight and bonobo. The results showed that men were aroused by the videos you'd expect (gay porn if they were gay, straight porn if they were straight) but women were more surprising. They lubricated to all of the videos. Even the bonobos. This is confusing, right? If lubrication is a sign of being turned on then women get turned on by watching apes mating. When the women were asked, they might say that they were not aroused by any of the films, or maybe that they enjoyed the lesbian porn or the straight porn – but their vaginas suggested otherwise; they had responded to ALL. At first the media and social commentators were like, 'Women's bodies know what they like more than they do.' People started saying it was only repression or civilised expectation that stopped women having sex with everyone all the time. People discussed the plasticity of female arousal, said it was proof that we could get turned on by *anything*. Perhaps this was our evolutionary strength? It enabled us to fancy whoever was around.

Then along came much more astute scientists and sexologists and they said that this lubrication, rather than being a lady-boner, was probably a protective measure. That women's bodies respond to all kinds of sexual stimuli not always because they want to have sex, but because sex might ensue anyway. That lubrication is not an 'I'm turned on' signal so much as an 'I don't want to be damaged' response. And we evolved it because we had to. Our bodies are clever enough to do what they can to protect us from sex that is not consensual, to stop us tearing or ripping as much as we might. This is an unconscious response, no more a sign of wanting sex than blinking or sweating, and it is the result of our gender's exposure to forced intercourse.

Rape is part of women's history and part of our present and it is the last section of this book. I want to say 'I have tried to make it fun' but that would be misleading. I've tried to make it bearable – readable, an exploration of ideas and grey areas. Stop dawdling, come on!

Musings on Fear

While I was at university, a girl I knew had her house raided by the police. Someone living there (not her) had been selling drugs and they'd arrested him and searched the whole house. And then my friend got arrested too because in her room they had found loads and loads of books about Hitler. She was in the second year of a history degree, and guess who she was studying? So she had to sit in an interrogation room and answer questions about how much she 'liked' the Führer and which of his ideas was her 'favourite', until the police were convinced she wasn't planning something awful.

While I have been researching this book, I have occasionally imagined a similar situation happening to myself. If I was assaulted, by someone I knew or didn't know, I would go to the police. I would undergo physical examinations and scrapings and I would provide as much detail and evidence as I could. And if I was one of the 'lucky' few, if the Crown Prosecution Service thought they might have enough for a conviction, I would go to court.

I play different versions of this trial in my head all the time. I am always practising it. This could be my pedestal to correct notions of female sexuality, how I could confront the routine terrorising of the victim, if the victim was me. Point out how inappropriate they are – but I couldn't be too calm, too collected, or the jury wouldn't believe me. No, I'd still have to be broken and weepy, just composed enough. I go through the things in my life that would be brought up to sully my reputation. Most of them were pre-twenty; I prepare arguments in explanation that are not ashamed or apologetic but that point out the irrelevance of my sexual history to the night of the attack. But I always get caught on how I would explain all my books:

DEFENCE COUNSEL
You were obsessed with rape—

I worry about it every day, I have done ever since I was a child and found out what it was. And now I worry about writing about it and possibly upsetting people who have personal experience that they do not find reflected, or who just plain disagree with me. I worry that writing on this topic might encourage a twisted psychopath to come and get me. And then in the trial that I have been preparing for all my life, this chapter will be judged and inspected for clues that my obsession was based on desire rather than fear, or that I had engineered this situation for research or point-making.

DEFENCE COUNSEL rises and walks towards the victim.

DEFENCE
Isn't it true that you like sex?

SARA
Yes.

DEFENCE
That you have stood on stage in front of hundreds of people proclaiming yourself to be horny—

SARA
That's a *joke* I do—

DEFENCE

Done long routines about being sexually unsatisfied with your partner?

SARA

I'm a comedian—

DEFENCE

Advertising your willingness and availability—

SARA

No I didn't—

DEFENCE

You yourself told this court that you have slept with over twenty people—

SARA

Yes. And I didn't accuse any of them of raping me, suggesting that I can tell the difference between when I wanted it and when I didn't—

DEFENCE

Your flat is full of books about rape, case studies and textbooks. Your web history is all sex-related. You've been planning this, and now you're *enjoying* it.

I worry about not being believed. I worry about the people who are hurt twice – once by their assailant and then further by the way our legal system treats victims. I worry that rape is being accepted as part of life, something that happens to people. I worry that many of us do not agree on definitions or that we can't empathise with each other's experience. And the only solution I can think of is that we have to talk about it, as upsetting and stressful as that may be, we have to talk about it more.

Fantasy Versus Fiction

In my first year at university we studied an eighteenth-century novel called *Pamela: Or Virtue Rewarded* by Samuel Richardson. The story is told from the point of view of a fifteen-year-old servant girl who finds herself repeatedly harassed and assaulted by the young Squire who has inherited the house where she works and lives. She is trapped with no escape. Pamela writes long letters to her parents, who advise her to keep avoiding the attentions of the Squire, in order to protect her honour and maidenhead. Pamela always faints from fear when he attempts to touch or undress her, and luckily he finds that a turn-off. The Squire becomes increasingly frustrated and imprisons Pamela, steals her letters and stops her communications with her parents, all the while pressuring her to have sex with him. She fights and fights and swoons and swoons and eventually, just when she thinks he is about to kill her, she earns his respect, nay, his love. The Squire decides to *marry* Pamela because she is so good and chaste and fainty. Everyone is thrilled, including Pamela's parents – she has proved herself *worthy* of his love by not succumbing to his molestations. And it's NOT EVEN FINISHED! Post-wedding, Pamela finds out the Squire has a daughter with a woman who didn't manage to fight him off as successfully as our heroine. Pamela decides to adopt the daughter and teach her to be virtuous, unlike her brazen birth mother who was clearly well up for it if she couldn't even be bothered to faint. The end.

I HATE SQUIRES!

The explicit message of this book was that not wanting to have sex isn't enough, saying no is insufficient. Men bear no responsibility for their actions, their urges and instincts are completely understandable and it's up to women to control them and keep everybody virtuous. This is a world where the girl is blamed if she can't defend herself, if she's *allowed* herself to be overpowered. Because that's how *overpowering* works, right guys?

The term before this we had read *Don Quixote* by Miguel de Cervantes. It's a really bloody long book, and somewhere within it there is a trial scene, Sancho Panza is sitting as a judge and hearing the town's cases and solving them, and then this woman accuses a rich man of raping her and the man claims that it was consensual, and then Sancho orders the rich man to give the woman a purse full of money. She leaves, then Sancho tells the guy to go and get his money back. The pair return to court after a couple of minutes, struggling over this purse, and the victim is told by Sancho that if she had cared as much about her honour as she did about cash then she wouldn't have got raped in the first place.

After reading the books, we were required to discuss them in seminars. In both cases the tutor (separate but indistinguishable old men) tried to lead a debate about the literary merit of the text, but we were TOO FURIOUS. *Pamela* was a book about RAPE, both books perpetuated rape myths and victim blaming, THEY SHOULD NOT BE ON OUR SYLLABUS. My fellow students and I had a wonderfully passionate row about what would be left in the canon if we chucked all the misogynistic rubbish in the bin. The teachers countered with good arguments about cultural materialism and historical context, but they could not swerve the EMOTION that these stories produced in us, and we quarrelled over their heads about modern issues. These two literary cases of rape apology were hideous to us, not because contemporary beliefs had changed so much but because they hadn't changed enough. We were familiar with modern judges berating victims for their choice of outfit or being out alone. Blaming them for not screaming or fighting hard enough. Telling them they were 'looking for trouble' if they hitchhiked or went to a house party. Or drank alcohol or had nice hair. Or had ever had sex before, especially if it was WITH THE DEFENDANT. These 'historical' texts made us angry because they didn't feel like a reflection of some other time, but of our own.

Pamela was incredibly popular. From publication in 1740 it became a bestseller throughout Europe, provoking a 'frenzy' of discussion and inspiring a flurry of other works. Paintings, waxworks, murals and operas were created to depict the story and its heroine. Journalists wrote articles warning against the 'lasciviousness' of the text and how it would lead the youth astray. Merchandise was produced and sold, and then came the parody novels. Henry Fielding wrote *An Apology for the Life of Mrs Shamela Andrews* under a pseudonym. As the 'sham' might suggest, his version portrayed a servant girl tricking her master into marriage. Further critiques were proffered by the anonymous *Pamela Censured* and the particularly bitchy *Anti-Pamela, Feigned Innocence Detected*. Society was split between 'Pamelists' and 'Antipamelists' as the worth of the book was debated. Much of the outcry was due to the class implications of the text, with a squire marrying so far beneath him. And the rest was due to the book's pornographic content and – sorry, WHAT NOW?

Oh yes, this story depicting the abuse of power and the

assault and exploitation of a pubescent girl was sexually arousing to many women. But this was in the olden times, remember, when everyone was all repressed and stoic about sex, it probably had an unsheathed ankle in it somewhere so they all went crazy. Nowadays we'd never have a . . . HANG ON, who's that writhing over there trying to get my attention?

It's *FIFTY SHADES OF GREY*!

Two hundred and seventy-one years after Pamela married a rich bloke who treated her terribly, Anastasia Steele did the same. And there was no ambiguity this time around: the book was written with the express purpose of arousing women, although I once overheard a woman at Dublin airport meekly complaining, 'How come no one mentions the story? It's a real cliffhanger.'

How come indeed; the story is that Ms Steele is a twenty-one-year-old virgin. (Yes, it's a book about a virgin who weds the bloke she loses it to, because even erotic literature cannot escape dated ideology.*) The bloke's called Christian Grey, and he's all messed up because he lost *his* virginity to an older lady who bondaged him all the time. Now he would like to do the same to Anastasia, please, if she would just sign this special contract that is very long and legal-sounding. It sets out that she is to be the 'submissive' in a sado-masochistic relationship with him as the 'dominant'. The contract takes ownership of her body and sexuality; she must not masturbate or get pregnant and she must agree to all the sex stuff he wants 'without hesitation or argument'.

The crazy logic of this document exhibits the separation of fantasy and reality. You cannot give somebody *permission* to

---

* Sing it with me, 'Paternity certainty'. ♩♪♫♩

force you to do things, any more than you can *allow* yourself to be *overpowered*. There is an inherent contradiction in the contract, though it would be wonderful to see someone try to legally enforce it:

CHRISTIAN GREY (*whining*)
But she hesitated when I proffered the bum dragon,[*]
your Lordship, I want £25 in damages.

But sexiness doesn't need to make sense. E. L. James originally self-published the book in 2011; people could pay to download a copy or print on demand. By 2012 it had become so popular that Vintage bought the rights to publish, and it subsequently became the fastest-selling paperback ever in the UK and shifted over a hundred million copies worldwide. What's most exhilarating is that it created its own audience. Women sought out the book because it was something they *wanted*; its success was not the result of a huge marketing campaign telling us all how hideously fat and old we are, but down to women recommending something they enjoyed to each other. Something that they had liked and thought their friends might too . . . something that had brought them pleasure. Not 'woman eating yogurt in an advert doing come face' pleasure, but real actual pleasure in their bodies and desires, which seems so incredibly vital and . . . then you remember what it's about and feel confused again.

We've found a contradiction. On the one hand:

Pornography has always been an industry dominated by male consumption, and the vast majority of pornography is created to stimulate men. Women's bodies are present and

---

[*] I am working in the library today and don't want to ask the nice lady if there are any books about sex toys.

are utilised in a variety of ways, but the male orgasms are real and the women's are faked. I am not saying that male porn actors enjoy their job any more or less than their female peers, I am pointing out that ninety-nine per cent of the sex shown is far more indicative of male sexuality than female. And E. L. James, a WOMAN, creates some porn for women, and suddenly there is a step towards balance. A commercial and public acknowledgement that women get horny and masturbate and have a sex life with themselves as well as with their partner(s). The book's popularity showed true democracy at work, and it generated vital discussion about female sexual satisfaction: on daytime television, in comedy routines, on the radio and on the bus.

But on the other hand:

The book describes a woman allowing a man to control her life and body, relinquishing the autonomy women have fought for centuries to gain. It could have been written by the Taliban.

And an abundance of women were really into it, so why? *Because what we fantasise about has nothing to do with what we want in real life.* Maybe fantasy is a reaction to circumstances? For instance, if you are a busy working woman with a hectic home life, the idea of being tied up while someone else organises the whips and bum dragons and then cleans up afterwards might seem very attractive. Perhaps women who DO feel in control of their own lives and bodies are exactly the people who can enjoy a fairy tale about the opposite?

The only danger resides with those who do not understand the nature of fantasy, who confuse the fictional and literal – those who think that if a woman enjoys the *idea* of something, surely she would *really* enjoy the reality. 'If women fantasise about rape all the time, why do they complain when it happens?' says someone somewhere every second. Rather than shutting that down as an idiotic question from an awful person, let's attempt to answer it.

Fantasy as a concept, or even as a word, can refer to different things. Sometimes it might be something you would like to literally happen. Maybe you would be up for a threesome, perhaps you're desperate to play in the World Cup? Some women who read *Fifty Shades* went out and bought the accompanying S & M merchandise, so the fiction did bleed into their reality. But fantasy can also exist in an imaginary space. Not a wish to be fulfilled. Not goal-setting with some hope of future achievement. What I think about during sex, and I presume this is true for every woman in a long-term relationship, is wide-ranging, disgusting and almost the literal opposite of what attracts me in real life. I imagine gross fat old men. People with bad hygiene and clumsy hands. And what they're doing feels so good that I can't stop them even though I hate them.

I have a Rolodex in my head of every person I have ever met[*] and I scroll through while my boyfriend is going down on me. Hundreds of men and women that I can use to get me off, but who I would never allow to lay a finger on me in actuality. These fantastical imaginings are not an exaggerated version of the truth; they're a separate dimension with no gateway to this one. They don't shape or influence any of my decisions. They do not in any sense feel 'real'.

So let's understand fantasy on a spectrum, from 'I wish this would happen to me' at one end and 'Only in my imagination' at the other.

[*] Yeah, if I've met you, then you're in there. And I am not even weird with you when I see you afterwards.

Now it's well known that whenever there's a study of women's sexual fantasies, "'rape'" (and I can't put enough quote marks around it) usually comes near the top. There are varying statistics from a variety of studies, claiming that between seventeen and sixty-two per cent of women fantasise about forced sex. This 'evidence' has supported the myth that 'no means yes' and that women can 'really enjoy' sex they say they don't want. It baffles even really intelligent men, because it seems to be a paradox. A brilliant stand-up once had a routine about how 'rape has been proved to be the number one female fantasy, so how come women always run away when I try?!' Another comic, a woman, told him he had to stop doing it and they had a row outside a gig, with the audience streaming past. Both of them were so upset that the other couldn't understand their point of view. He thought his joke was funny because he believed it was so clear that what people mean by a 'rape fantasy' is far removed from the reality of a man attacking them. She felt that the distinction was not clear and that his comedy was excusing predatory behaviour and violence.

Comedians argue amongst themselves about rape jokes a lot. People are always very defensive of their own material and consider themselves to be 'promoting conversation' or 'stimulating debate' by venturing into 'don't even go there' areas. But comedy is a form of cowardice. Its very definition is a refusal to deal with things seriously; the comic is flippant, laughing is cathartic. Some argue that comedy can be used to promote good social conscience or political ideas but I've never been convinced of that. Maybe that means it can't do much harm either? I don't want comedians to be censored, and I have never told anyone what they should or shouldn't say on stage. But I've also noticed that when a comic's joke has upset someone, they only ever get really defensive about what they meant or what they were trying to do. They never apologise. I'm in Melbourne as I write this and early in the festival, a male comedian began his routine with this:

'So you know how gay people can make jokes about being gay, and black people can make jokes about being black? Well, I can make jokes about rape.'

And at the gig, a woman made a silent protest, she slid under a table and lay there. The comic was frustrated with her and eventually told her to 'fuck off and die'. And then in all the furore that's been following it, with newspapers asking if comedians should agree not to do rape jokes, if they should be banned, and comedians writing tweets and opinion pieces in defence of the joke or the comic – 'He wasn't condoning rape, he was saying he looked like a rapist' or 'Chris Rock said he thought that joke was one of the cleverest he's ever heard' – even within all this discussion there is no space to absorb and acknowledge how joking about rape affects its victims. There is no empathy.

Every defence of 'offensive' material should begin with a brief description of how it affects those upset:

'I the comedian understand that sometimes when a person who has experienced rape or sexual assault hears that word used in a joke her body physiologically reacts in fear. Her heartbeat will speed up, she may feel nauseous, lose her hearing, feel suddenly faint or claustrophobic. Her[*] body may be flooded with adrenaline and she might want to escape the room as quickly as possible although she is trapped, aware that if she moves the comedian will make fun of her,

---

[*] This says 'her' but men get raped too and male victims suffer similar societal insensitivity.

or that she will be drawing attention to herself as a victim. The laughter of those around her can feel malicious and personal. However I still think my joke is worth doing because _____.'

The existence and misunderstanding of '"rape"' fantasy has warped common understanding of the crime and has allowed many people, juries and judges included, to mistrust victims. Using the same word for the fantasy and the assault has, consciously or unconsciously, led people to believe there is possibility of pleasure in the latter. That it can be craved or enjoyed by some women. The distinction is simple:

A classic *fantasy* scenario, whether in Mills and Boon-type literature* or the stories women themselves have told researchers, involves a very good-looking man being so overcome with passion and attraction for a female protagonist that despite her protestations he expertly arouses and stimulates her to climax. This is *seduction*. Whether acted out or imagined, the sex is anticipated and enjoyed. It's not the handsomeness of the aggressor nor the woman's orgasm that signifies no crime has taken place, but the desire and thus consent. The fantasy of being 'forced' hides it, but it is there. This sex is something wanted and agreed to. Yes, she may have said 'no' out loud, she may have resisted because she is married/does not know the guy/is a virgin, but within this fantasy scenario the very fact of denying something she physically desires enhances her arousal. It could be called a 'rough sex fantasy', 'stranger sex fantasy', 'unfriendly banging fantasy' or anything else you can think of, but it needs to be understood completely separately from rape. This fantasy

---

* A study found that 54 per cent of narratives in such books involve a central character being 'raped'.

occurs in a safe place, whether alone during masturbation or acted out as role play with a partner; the woman is imitating submission whilst being completely in control.

Sex is possible when you are unsafe or scared, but arousal isn't.

So why does this fantasy persist? Why would something horrifying in actuality be sexy in pretend? There is a variety of theories, all equally interesting and unverifiable. 'Sexual blame avoidance' suggests that because women are socialised to suppress their desires, hide their sexuality, NOT WANT SEX, the idea of being sexed up against their will alleviates all of the guilt they might feel at enjoying it so much. This is undermined slightly by the 'Openness to sexual experience' theory, which has found that more sexually adventurous women are likely to experience more fantasies in general, including those involving forced sex. Other psychologists have speculated that the fantasy is a result of being conditioned by male rape culture, or a reaction to trauma, or simply masochistic tendencies.

And then there is the very problematic 'Biological predisposition to surrender' theory, which argues that male animals often subdue females and mate with them in situations which can look to us as if the female is resisting and the sex is 'unwanted'. Thus such forced intercourse has played a part in every species's evolution . . . rape is a 'natural' part of sexual selection and so modern women's fantasies about it are an echo of a successful mating strategy. This is an exceptionally dangerous idea because it justifies the crime of assault in human beings; the act of heterosexual *sex* and the act of heterosexual *rape* are the same: penetration by a penis. In the same way that giving someone a present is the same action as theft: a movement of property between two people.

But giving someone your television is very different from having your television stolen; regardless of whether you were home or whether there was violence during the robbery, the distinction is intention, or consent. Yet someone who has their wallet stolen is not doubted because they may have given money away before or didn't hide their property properly or were walking around in a dark street late at night looking like they might be up for sharing cash. They are not disbelieved when they say their wallet was taken against their will. And we don't have politicians and intellectuals explaining that animals take each other's stuff all the time, that it's part of healthy competition and survival, thus excusing a thief's behaviour while undermining a victim's reaction. No one claims that there is secret enjoyment in having your wallet stolen because you are usually a generous person.

Sex is how people are made but sometimes rape is too. And this is too confusing for pro-lifers. Like Todd Akin. In 2012 this Republican Senate candidate and anti-abortion activist[*] was asked if victims of rape who get pregnant should be allowed to have a termination. He responded:

TODD AKIN
From what I understand from doctors, that's really rare. If it's legitimate rape, the female body has ways to try to shut that whole thing down.

Playing loudly to drown out stupidity trumpet:

---

[*] Please, old man, tell me what *you* think I should do with my body.

I'll let you get cracking on your Todd Akin voodoo doll while I unpack that sentence . . . great use of 'legitimate' before the word 'rape' to stress how much '*illegitimate* rape' there is in the world. Just fake old 'we made it up, it was actually fantastic, that's why we're so pregnant' rape that you hear about all the time. It's such a sweeping way of undermining and doubting women. It's a dispassionate tsunami that destroys our credibility and allows him to ignore our experiences so that he can continue educating us about how our bodies work. Which is to 'shut that whole thing down'. Refuse to be fertilised. CLANG CLANG CLANG ring our ovaries, cranking everything into action as our womb spins upside down and our Fallopian tubes tie around the cervix while we curtsey and our labia give us a lovely round of applause.

It is mostly pro-life Christians who use arguments such as the above. They have to be dismissive because a rape victim's rights are contradictory to an anti-abortion stance. It's a very human trait; all of us, even excellent fellows like you and me, collect the evidence which supports our pre-existing theories and opinions and dismiss those which challenge us. Todd Akin is not completely wrong: stress or anxiety *can* cause a fertilised egg to pass through a woman without bedding into the womb to divide and become a baby. This also occurs in women who have not been attacked, by the way, and more importantly, CAN YOU READ THIS BIT SLOWLY, TODD AND FRIENDS, BECAUSE IT IS IMPORTANT IF YOU WANT TO DISCUSS THIS KIND OF THING THAT YOU HAVE ALL OF THE INFORMATION, it only occurs in some women who have been raped. Not all. Just some.

Statistics collected from Rape Crisis centres over the last few decades show that thirteen per cent of women reporting a rape became pregnant from it. These results might be skewed, of course, if women who've found themselves pregnant are more likely to seek help and support. Other studies place the likelihood of pregnancy occurring from rape at between one and five per cent. There is vast discrepancy and unreliability in the statistics and I don't feel confident that any number is definitively correct, as so many women do not report what has happened to them. However, there does seem to be some evidence that women are slightly *more* likely to become pregnant from rape than from consensual intercourse.

Emotionally, this is too horrible to contemplate. Morally it shouldn't be true. Morally it would be preferable if our bodies *could* stop such an upsetting and confusing thing happening, if we could eject or reject, if we had some control over our biology.

Unemotionally, our bodies are amazing. We are the descendants of only the finest breeders of our species. In *Sperm Wars* Robin Baker claims that rough sex (consensual or forced) can stimulate ovulation, which suggests that we evolved to reap the biological benefit of unwanted mating. However, I can't find a proper scientific study to back this up, it could be BS. There is so little certainty in this area. Much more research would be necessary, but I'm sure it's very difficult to find victims of sexual assault who want you checking what their eggs are up to or counting the sperm inside them, so maybe we will never know. This might be an area of science that remains mysterious. And perhaps, actually, irrelevant.

I think people who point out that rape is part of nature are UNHELPFUL. They are sometimes very persuasive and interesting people, it's not that they condone the crime, it's that they know some really fascinating things about ducks' vaginas and how dolphins have gang bangs and penguins have been seen to practise necrophilia. But they are technically incorrect. Let me show you my working:

I used to do gymnastics in the garden to impress my cat. His name was Roly and I'd show him cartwheels and he would do a really long blink at me if he thought I'd done a good one. During one of my exhibitions he ran off and started vigorously vibrating on a black cat in next door's garden.

SARA, 6, wears pink-and-black leotard, shouts towards the house.

SARA
WHAT ARE THEY DOING?

DEREK, 28, not yet absent father, enters the garden.

DEREK (*slowly*)
Roly is a *boy* cat and he is hugging the *girl* cat—

GAIL, 24, shouts from an upstairs window.

GAIL
Don't lie, Derek, he's raping her.

Window slams. SARA's confusing childhood continues.

My mum claims not to remember this incident, so maybe my subconscious made it up, but even so it's very consistent with the kind of thing she would say. If we understand animals via a human framework, then of course Mr Cat's fast and furious approach to love-making with no foreplay or sensitivity looks self-pleasing, perhaps even causing Mrs Cat pain and suffering. We cannot help but anthropomorphise, we project our emotional perceptions onto animals. As discussed earlier, sex in humans evolved to be highly enjoyable to support our societal structure (or rather, only those highly sexed early human-types socialised successfully enough to pass on their genes). Each animal's approach to mating is fine-tuned for the most effective replication of DNA. If it involves bonding and pleasure, as it does in our species, that's mere lubrication for the machine. We kiss and exchange saliva to check genetic compatibility, giraffes wee in each other's mouth and hippos flick poo around with their tails because that's how we each best make healthy babies. And the same is true for animals that pierce, maim, bruise or kill each other while mating. It's not bad sex, it's effective life-making.

Last night I had a row with my friend about ducks. The problem with writing this book is that when I switch my pencil off and go out, my mind is really full of what I've been thinking and researching and I either lecture someone too polite to wriggle away or I get argumentative. So last night my friend is telling me and some others that she has written a show about sex, I haven't seen it but I will, she is telling us about it and it sounds gross and exciting and boundary-pushing and then she says, 'I have this whole section about *duck rape.*' And so all the other comedians are saying 'WHAT?' or going 'Don't they have weird vaginas?' and everyone is just having a nice evening and enjoying themselves and I am furious with her and yell, 'You're INCREDIBLY irresponsible.'

But she's not. And I'm sober now, so let me explain my emotions with more clarity.

This duck thing, mallards actually, was mentioned a lot alongside the Todd Akin comments, because the female mallard has a way of protecting her eggs from the sperm of unwanted mating. Some mallards pair-bond, form little male–female double acts who drift around lakes and ponds, nest together and share bread. The males who do not manage to find a partner form a brutish little gang who often try to separate bonded pairs and, working as a group, mate with the female. You can see videos on this online, and if you do, you'll realise how exceptionally difficult it is not to project, to emote. What they are doing does seem morally wrong. Our empathetic brains cannot help but imagine how we would feel were we one of that feathery couple, having their day at the lake ruined.

A female mallard (like all birds) possesses what is called a 'labyrinthine' vagina that has false openings and tunnels, and she can move its position to alter the route that semen will take, and thus, in many cases, prevent unwanted sperm from fertilising her eggs. This is usually interpreted as a 'defence' against forced mating: 'How swell, the lady duck has protected herself from rearing the ducklings of those awful gang members!' But her twisty genitals are much better understood as a *challenge*. She has chosen her mate based on genetic and parental qualities which are superior to those of the non-bonded drakes that have been unable to attract or keep a lady duck. So her twisty vagina will always direct her partner's sperm towards her eggs, and any other males' away from them. Her children will be healthier/stronger/better dancers if they share her partner's genes. She doesn't practise multi-partnering like humans do. She has made her choice.

With one exception.

Having been misdirected and sent down a blind alley, if one of these marauders' sperm manages to achieve the almost impossible and fertilise her this is GREAT NEWS. Because not all of her offspring will pair-bond. Some of her sons will be awful bachelors. The one trait that trumps all of her husband's is super-strength swimmy sperm that her sons will inherit. You see, the labyrinthine vagina is a TEST to find the male mallards whose offspring will be able to pass it. Clever sex, well done.

This defence/test confusion occurs a lot. I've been reading up on animal sex and sentences are often worded with intentions implicit: 'The male giraffe follows the female until she eventually gives up and lets him mount her,' or 'The female hare fights off the male until he subdues her,' and this framing is incorrect. Our culture has trained us all to interpret males as active and females as passive, but in almost every species I have read about it is the female that initiates sex. They do this with pheromones and scents and behaviours and they get males excited and then yes, sometimes she'll have him follow her around for hours or kick and bite him, but that's to ensure that he is fit for purpose. Female animals do not get 'worn down' or 'subdued', it is the males that have to exhibit traits that their offspring will need if they are to survive. What we interpret as unwillingness or aggression, from another perspective, is flirting.

Although of course it isn't actually, because flirting is a human concept that requires conscious thought, awareness of self and of other beings outside the self. And so does consent. We're the only creatures on the planet that have the capability to conceive of bodily autonomy, birth control, age . . . do you see? Animals behave automatically, they can't conceive that it was your hat they did a poop on or that it's impolite to lick your bum afterwards. They don't interpret the world with an understanding of others' emotions, like we do.

It should be obvious that if ducks cannot consent, they cannot rape. It is a crime performed purely by human beings. To lend it to the animal world subtly defends it as something instinctual or procreative. It undermines what is criminal about it. And you should be grateful I've not been shouting all this at you while spilling wine on your shoes like I did to my poor friend Katerina.

KNOCK KNOCK

Hang on, there's someone at my door, I'll just go and see who it is . . . Oh look, it's a person who still believes the issue of consent is a confusing one. He says, 'Sometimes you just can't tell if someone wants to have sex with you or not.' Please come in, sit down, this might help you.

We must learn from the BDSMers. Yes, the form of sexual fun that was showcased (and misrepresented) by the *Fifty Shades of Grey* franchise has a comprehensive and clear framework of consent that can assist even 'vanillas'* in our sexual communication. Bondage, Domination and Sado-Masochism involves all kinds of kinky tools and power play and does so with an understanding of 'rolling consent'. Taking part in one activity does not mean you will agree to another. Having enjoyed a certain pressure one day does not signify that you will tolerate it the next. Yesterday you loved the bum dragon, but today you want it left in the drawer. Most of us are familiar with the idea of the 'safe word', which is a prearranged code that signals DISCONTINUE IMMEDIATELY, and its very existence proves that saying 'no' and 'stop' can be part of the fun, can facilitate pleasure. And that equally, at any point during sex, you might stop enjoying yourself and want to break or rest or have something to eat or discuss buttons. This is also

---

* This means sexually bland people (not white people, as I once thought).

true of the most banal intercourse, yet in our culture there is this pervading idea that once you get a guy started he has to finish. I have had so much sex that I didn't enjoy. That I would have liked to pause, to explain my feelings. To slow down. Or reconnect. Or get dressed and go and cry in the bathroom. I have had kisses I loved lead into sex I hated. I'm ashamed of how much sex I have not enjoyed, and I have never known how to communicate this to my partners, because I have never understood it properly myself.

Rolling consent, my friend. The perverts invented it, and now we can all have happier, healthier sex lives, no matter how moderate the acts undertaken.

DING DONG

Gosh it's busy in here today, you stay where you are, I'll go . . . Oh hi there, Peter, what's that? You're still confused?

PETER

If a lady moans 'no' while we are getting off with each other, how do I ascertain if it's a sexy no, rather than a scared serious no?

SARA

Why the hell wouldn't you just ask her?

PETER

It's embarrassing . . . I might ruin the moment.

SARA

Just ask. Say 'Are we playing?' or 'Do you want me to persuade you?' Even if it is uncomfortable for a second, it will be super-sexy afterwards. Or it won't, because she meant no. Any moment that can be 'ruined' that easily was not a moment at all.

PETER

Thanks Sara, bye!

SARA

You're welcome, I'll see you at volleyball practice.

Sara waves goodbye and puts on wellington boots.

SARA

I'll see the rest of you over the page . . . it's going to get
even messier.

The Dangers of Assumption

I had a best friend at drama club, and when she was about fourteen she found an old diary of her mum's. She got very upset, and snuck it out of the house for me to read. It was terribly written but I admired the handwriting and – oh, I'd missed the point. Several of the entries were written during her mother's pregnancy. My friend was INSIDE HER and not born yet, this was so WEIRD, imagine a world where you don't really exist but people can write diaries about you being inside them and – oh, I'd missed the point again. Her mum was very sad about being pregnant. Shit. And she said that the baby was 'the result of a rape'. Oh really shit.

My friend had always felt like her mum didn't love her. They always rowed, but we were fourteen, so that was normal. We'd previously theorised that all mums were really jealous of their teenage daughters because of our youth and talent and vivacity and that's why they behaved like such unreasonable bitches. Except now we were holding some other explanation in our hands. It was very dramatic. We sat in the park and read bits out to each other. Like we were emotional detectives, putting her mother's behaviour together retrospectively. Then I suddenly realised:

'That means your dad is not your real dad—'

Oh my god, she wasn't even related to her own father. This was even more serious than we'd realised. We decided to start smoking, because of stress, but didn't have any cigarettes. We looked for butts on the floor for a while and thought about setting fire to the diary as a symbolic gesture. My friend got quieter and quieter as I attempted to rub sticks together and spark a flint. Then she wanted to go home and then she went.

When we next saw each other, she passed me a note. 'He is my dad. It was him.'

I don't know what my friend's life would have been like had she not learned this information. It could have been exactly the same, unfocused and self-destructive. But it makes more sense for her to blame her horrible beginnings. Her mum told her what had happened: she'd been asleep, said no, he'd forced her. She had no proof that it was *that* time she conceived, she just really believed it was. But she loved her daughter, and it wasn't her fault.

After about two weeks it rarely came up again. My friend still sees her dad. I never asked if she talked to him about it. I was teeming with questions I knew it was inappropriate to ask.

HOW can a man force a woman? Did he get a weapon? Did he hit her? Did she call the police? Did she bleed? Who cleaned it up? How did it feel? I always imagined like razor blades or a rat biting. Did it happen again? Did he say sorry? Was it like a werewolf on a full moon, and then he went normal again afterwards? Is that why she divorced him? Why was he still allowed round for dinner and Christmas and things? Did he even go to prison?

I asked my mum a loose, general question about what happened when wives said 'no' to their husbands. She proceeded to tell me a lot of stuff I never wanted to know about times she'd let my father have sex when she didn't want it, great, and then told me that rape within marriage had only been possible for the last four years. I misunderstood what she meant.

SARA

Men were nicer in the old days?

MUM

It was legal.

SARA

How was that?

MUM

Husbands were allowed to do whatever they wanted to their wives. They owned them.

Then she pulled a facial expression which combined 'See what an awful world we live in?' 'See what bastards men are?' and 'Interesting, isn't it?' (I have inherited that facial expression and pull it when reading 'Everyday Sexism' tweets out to my boyfriend.)

If you thought the 'contract' in *Fifty Shades of Grey* was offensively restrictive, you're not going to get on with his more binding and less respectful older brother, 'marriage'. Getting married is culturally universal. It's where the powerful urges of pair bonding led us. Falling in love, as we have seen, changes our brain chemistry and affects our bodies. Strong emotions and high sex drives ensured the reproductive success of our very early ancestors and continued to aid sexual selection during the millions of years when we were developing a conscious mind. So we became an animal that could communicate in a complex way, in order to better satisfy our animal instincts and intuitions. As explored in the 'Love' chapters, we know that lots of human relationship behaviours stem from protecting our genetic lineage or resources for our offspring. And the story of our evolution ends, like most stories, with a wedding. Marriage: the male attempt to own and restrict female sexuality, written down.

I've only been to two weddings. That's *weird*, isn't it? What with my loud opinions about it being outdated and patriarchal, you'd think I'd get invited more. The first wedding I went to was my best friend Katie's. I love her. I love Ben, her husband. There were about thirty of us in a registry office in Marylebone and they'd asked me and Vanessa to say something, but we decided to sing instead. We wrote a song about their first date from the perspective of the taxi driver who had taken them home that night. He had stopped the car and taken a photo of them, because he said he knew they'd be together forever. How romantic is that? And so Vanessa sang about this taxi guy and the picture he took, and I tried to join in but I was crying too much. Katie's mum had to bring me tissues after snot fell onto my guitar. Everyone was laughing at me and I was pleased, because I am a comedian. I'd kept it together as they said their vows, but when I stood up at the front and saw Katie sitting holding Ben's hand, newly married, their hopeful faces liquefied me. They were shiny with happiness and I was due on my period and I couldn't deal with how beautiful and good it was.

I'm telling you this so you don't think I'm a heartless, unfeeling bitch as I dismember this 'marriage' thing so many of you venerate. Most modern people choose marrying as an expression of love towards someone they consider their equal – lovely stuff. But historically, apart for a couple of rare matriarchal tribes, the basic of format of wedding ceremonies goes like this: male relative takes woman who belongs to him and 'gives her away' to a man who is buying her in exchange for a dowry. Of course the whole thing is livened up with organ

music and pretty dresses so that's probably why you didn't notice all the 'women as property' stuff. Traditionally, in western
religions, the new wife will take her husband's surname as
she is now part of his family. She is under his charge, he has
sworn to provide for her (hence why divorcing people often
get some of their spouse's money) and she has vowed her own
body in exchange. It is now his. The transaction is very similar
to buying a donkey, but with more dancing afterwards.

Don't start getting defensive, thinking 'That's not what my
wedding was like.' Obviously people write their own vows now,
and keep their surnames or give themselves away. I'm talking
loosely about the inherited framework. I'm afraid of upsetting you because I know how marriage-geared many people's
ideals of happiness are. STOP CRYING, YOU ARE STILL
ALLOWED TO LOVE WEDDINGS IF YOU WANT TO.

The second wedding I went to was with John. We had only
been together for a couple of months and I really didn't want
to go, but I did because I'm nice and I couldn't get out of
it. John and I had already had a conversation about how I
didn't want to ever get married and he agreed with me. (I
always like to impress boys at the beginning with how relaxed
and non-committal I am. The intense jealousy and whiplash
PMT is a nice surprise for six months in.) This ceremony was
Christian where Katie's had been humanist, and so I could
see the historical origins a lot more clearly. Like bridesmaids:
maids, as in virgins. A wedding was a useful time to show off
all the unmarried (thus un-sexed-up) women of the family in
case some guy in the congregation fancied one of them and
another wedding could be arranged. Even more surprising,
to me, was that after the ceremony the groom did a speech
and the father of the bride did a speech and the best man did

a speech, and the bride herself just sat there listening to men speak about her and on her behalf.

I kept thinking about this afterwards. I can completely understand that women might not want to speak at their weddings nowadays, that it's choice rather than expectation. Katie did a tight ten at her reception and even improvised a great joke about how I'd tried to upstage her by crying too much. HA HA HA, she was joking, we are best friends. But what struck me was that until very recently, for the majority of all the women who have ever lived and married, that day was not a happy one. Or at least not for them. Most women did not sit next to a man they had chosen and fallen in love with while he made their closest friends and family roll about with jokes about how drunk she was when they met. Instead she sat beside a husband chosen FOR her, by her parents or elders, who that night was going to take her virginity whether she protested or not. Might be best not to allow her a speech then, bit of a downer:

BRIDE

Thank you all for coming, it's great to see so many of you here to celebrate a world in which girls cannot survive without male protection and income. Please charge your glasses and toast my new husband, who'll attempt to make me bleed during sex later as proof of my maidenhood. Cheers!

I tried to do stand-up about this, and about how maybe that's where the idea that women weren't funny came from. But it was tonally very upsetting and that's a bit of a no-no in the comedy game. And also at John's friend's wedding.

From the age of fourteen up until I was thirty-two I was vehemently anti-marriage, because of where it came from and what it represented. And then good old homosexual people came along and changed my mind. In 2014, England, Scotland and Wales all made same-sex marriage legal. And you know what is so great about that? They reinvented the ceremony. Same-sex marriage is untarnished by history and archaic institution. Sure, people can still pick elements of tradition and spectacle to include, but they are building their commitments on fresh ground rather than the blood-speckled lino of heterosexuals. A same-sex relationship is not burdened with the expectations of stereotypes or outdated gender roles. There are no preconceived ideas about who will earn the most money or who will bear the children, who will clean the kitchen and who will fix the car. They decide for themselves. And so I think it's only fair that gay marriage be opened up to straight people. You and your beloved could simply decide whether you wish to become husband and husband or wife and wife, and make a lifelong commitment. HOORAY! A union of true equals. THANKS, GAY RIGHTS ACTIVISTS, you are teaching all people who love each other how to do it better.

But that's the future. Back to the past: in England, until 1991, wedding vows were considered unlimited, never-ending, can't-take-it-back consent. And a woman's body was something her husband used to procreate and she could not refuse him. He had 'conjugal rights'. This had been written in law since 1736, when a guy called Sir Matthew Hale claimed: 'The husband cannot be guilty of a rape committed by himself upon his lawful wife, for by their mutual matrimonial consent and contract the wife hath given herself up in this kind unto her husband which she cannot retract.'

When I picture Matthew Hale saying this, he has beady eyes and an awful moustache and does evil laughs at the end of his sentences. I try to be compassionate and think 'Maybe he wasn't a *bad* man, perhaps he rode his horse carefully when passing children and always gave great Christmas presents?' He was a product of his culture and its expectations, as we all are. But then I remember his words were used against women abused by their husbands for over 250 years and the moustache stays on.

In 1976 the Sexual Offences (Amendment) Act created a statutory definition of rape as forced sex *outside of marriage.* Outside. The wording itself protected husbands from being accused. In 1984 the suggestion that wives should also be protected was rejected by the Criminal Law Revision Committee. They said that rape was not just 'sexual intercourse without consent', the circumstances must be 'peculiarly grave', and that in the case of wives who will have had consenting sex with their husband previously, they never could be. If he was violent during the assault that was an offence with which he could be charged, but 'the gravamen of the husband's conduct is the injury he has caused not the sexual intercourse he has forced'.

Written down. In the law. You can't steal something that's already yours.

Over the next seven years, the law was contested by brave wives accusing their husbands and fighting all the way up to the high courts for their right to say 'no'. There were exemptions made for wives who no longer lived with their husbands (*R* v. *Clarke*) and for forced sex that was non-vaginal (*R* v. *Kowalski*) and finally, in 1991, the House of Lords finally ruled against Hale in a marital rape case (*R* v. *R*). No more evil laughing for him.

What's so brilliant about the British legal system is that because statutes can be altered or overturned by lawyers fighting individual cases the law can, in theory, evolve to reflect the fluid morality of society, to adapt with culture and new ideas. But isn't it galling that it took so long to protect married women? This very basic human right was created within my lifetime and is still not extended to all the world's women. Below is a list of countries where rape within marriage is currently not a criminal offence. Feel free to check up on this and tick them off as planet Earth gradually becomes a more bearable place to be female.

Country	Can wives say 'no' to sex yet?	Country	Can wives say 'no' to sex yet?
Afghanistan		Malawi	
Algeria		Mali	
Bahrain		Mongolia	
Bangladesh		Morocco	
Botswana		Myanmar	
Brunei Darussalam		Nigeria	
Central African Republic		Oman	
China		Pakistan	
Dem. Republic of Congo		Saudi Arabia	
Egypt		Senegal	
Ethiopia		Singapore	
Haiti		South Sudan	
India		Sudan	
Iran		Syria	
Ivory Coast		Tajikistan	
Kuwait		Tonga	
Laos		Uganda	
Lebanon		Yemen	
Libya		Zambia	

The *recentness* of these changes reminds me that we are at the beginning of a process, rather than the end. I believe bodily autonomy is an obvious and basic human right but our country and courts are governed by people older than me, who grew up in a culture where men did effectively own women, and this has ramifications. Shifts in attitudes percolate through the populace slowly, at glacial speed, and the result is that many of us hold different beliefs all at the same time. Of course we all think we're objectively correct too. There was a man outside Lewisham shopping centre the other day, he had pamphlets and a loud hailer and I was avoiding eye contact like everyone else but I was listening, and as I passed he said, 'If we don't follow the Bible and what was written down, then everyone is just making morality up for themselves.'

And I thought, 'Yes, duh,* that is *exactly* what morality is. We all invent it for ourselves depending on our experiences.' The problems begin when we believe our personal moral code can be applied to all other people. We judge and we subjugate and we become wrong because we can only ever see our own little slice of the picture. And the dangerous result, in this context, is that you and the person you're having sex with may have very different conceptions of what rape is.

In Great Britain, the law no longer sanctions men controlling women's bodies but there is residual misunderstanding about 'intimate rape'. The first fallacy is that it is much more bearable than stranger rape. That if you've had sex with someone before, then being raped by them isn't as bad. This is empathy failure. Or perhaps the difficulty of envisaging

---

* My inner monologue is late nineties.

a situation that you haven't experienced. I think if anybody tried to imagine, really literally imagine what it is like to have someone you trusted, someone that you love, or have loved, someone who knows your vulnerabilities, who is supposed to care about you – when it is that person who brutalises you, who ignores your protests, who knows that he is hurting you and doesn't care, then there is a whole other emotional level to the physical trauma. Do you think it is better to be punched in the face by someone you like? Do you stand there as they thump you, thinking, 'Well at least it wasn't my enemy'? It's a different kind of ordeal to an attack from a stranger, not a lesser one.

The difficulty with gradients and comparisons is that victims on either side of the spectrum have their experiences misunderstood and undermined. With marital rape, and the unwillingness to prosecute it, there's a similar failure of comprehension. Marriage does not mean the rape is less painful, cruel or abusive. It is not a more tender experience. It often means that you're trapped with your rapist afterwards. You may be economically dependent on him, with no chance of escape. No door to close to keep yourself safe from future attacks.

What keeps surprising me is how *relaxed* some people seem about men using women's bodies. Like there's something 'natural' or understandable about it. I'll give you an example. In 2010, a warrant was issued by Swedish police for the arrest of Julian Assange. The case gained a lot of publicity because of Assange's pre-existing notoriety as the co-founder of the WikiLeaks website. He was accused of rape by one woman and of molestation by another. In both cases the alleged assault took place AFTER consensual sex. In the first account, a woman who willingly had sex with Assange one night, at her apartment, awoke the next morning to find that he was having penetrative intercourse with her against her will.

There is no way that this isn't an incredibly complicated moral issue, right? Some couples find it very sexy for one to begin foreplay while the other is asleep. I am pretty sure that almost everyone has had sex that began with one or other of you asleep, OR BOTH? Would that be possible? Somno-sex? I tried to find out online but I'm in a Costa coffee and their wi-fi filter just told me off for being filthy. I can *imagine* two scenarios: I can imagine a one-night stand where in the morning, I am awoken by the guy getting sexy with me again and I'm fine and I like it. And I can imagine the exact same thing occurring and it being deeply wrong. This would have nothing to do with what he looked like or how great his moves were, it would depend merely on whether I wanted it. It's so dangerous.

There is no possible way someone can consent while they're asleep. Even if you wrote a note and left it on your chest – 'shag me awake please' – you might have changed your mind by the morning. You can't give consent in advance, you can't predict how you will feel in the future.

I spoke to John about this, because I can't stop thinking about it, and he was like, 'If you were asleep and I started sex with you it would be okay,' but would it? If I woke up and wanted him to stop and he didn't, if I tried to push him off, if I said I wasn't interested and he still carried on, then it would be – I don't have the right words.

I've only experienced something similar to this once. I'm embarrassed to tell you, I only ever told one person and they didn't react well, and I never spoke about it again. I'd been on a few dates with a guy, he wasn't my 'boyfriend' yet, but we had slept together about three times and all was going very well. He was super-clever and liked walking around London and I was very impressed with him. At his house, we did not have a condom and I was almost due on my period and said we could sleep together if he pulled out. I KNOW THIS IS TERRIBLE AND WRONG AND I DESERVE MY MILLIONS OF STDs AND WARTS. Very irresponsible and I hate myself. Anyway, towards the end of the completely consensual and enjoyable sex, I realised he was about to come and said something sexy and adamant like 'MAKE SURE YOU PULL OUT OF ME', which he ignored, and I panicked. I realised he was going to do it anyway, and I tried to get out from underneath him and he pressed me down and smothered me while he ejaculated.

From realisation to panic was a very short amount of time, probably four seconds. And then being physically restrained by him while he finished was probably fifteen. Less than twenty seconds in total. And it was deeply emotional. I was so upset and furious. I left his house, it was very late and I was the opposite side of London from home and I had no money for a taxi and I was scared and all I knew was that I never wanted to see him again. It was only twenty seconds of unwanted sex. It wasn't a stranger jumping out from a bush, he didn't beat me around the head. What right did I have to become hysterical? To shout at a guy, to feel betrayed and used by him? Two weeks later he wrote me an email saying sorry and could he take me on holiday to make it up to me? And I knew that he didn't know what he'd done wrong.

I am remembering this now because the fear my body felt at the time was so extreme and devastating. I was full of hatred and I was powerless, when moments before I had been sexual and willing. I was disgusted by what had happened to me and I felt separated from my body. Meat-like. So I can easily envisage how consensual sex in the evening can be followed by rape in the morning. Unwanted sex does not become tolerable with the memory of a previous session. Drowning isn't easier because you're usually a strong swimmer. That flailing loss of control, desperate for air, is a good analogy for this, because the panic is similar. Or at least that's how I'd describe it.

But many people of both genders find it impossible to empathise with intimate rape. Our personal experiences limit what we can predict feeling in a given situation. We patch together projections of imagined emotions based on what we have seen and felt in our lives already. We all know that knives are scary, so if I tell you I was mugged by someone holding a machete, you can understand my terror. But if I tell you I was mugged by someone with no weapon but I still gave him all my money and was scared for my life . . . then maybe you fail to sympathise. I was stupid or weak, I did something wrong. You might walk away muttering, 'Wasn't really a mugging at all, I dunno why she's so upset about it.'

Which was how George Galloway reacted to the claims against Julian Assange. In a podcast the politician went on record to say: 'Even taken at its worst, if the allegations made by these two women were true, one hundred per cent true, and even if a camera in the room captured them, they don't constitute rape. At least not rape as anyone with any sense can possibly recognise it. And somebody has to say this.'

It is clear that Galloway really believes this. He is not trying to be incendiary or hurtful or offensive, he feels he is bringing common sense and objectivity to the matter. 'Somebody has to say this,' he claims. Well, now *somebody* has to listen carefully to the definition of rape as a criminal offence.

In Sweden, where the allegations arose, a rapist is defined as a person who 'forces another person to have sexual intercourse or to undertake or endure another sexual act that, in view of the seriousness of the violation, is comparable to sexual intercourse'. In 2005 the Swedish penal code was extended and clarified so that 'this also applies if a person engages with another person in sexual intercourse or in a sexual act by improperly exploiting that person, due to unconsciousness, sleep, serious fear, intoxication or other drug influence, illness, physical injury or mental disturbance, or otherwise in view of the circumstances, is in a particularly vulnerable situation'. George Galloway may not recognise the allegations against Julian Assange as rape but the Swedish legal system most certainly does.

'Sleep', it says. In between 'unconsciousness' and 'serious fear', recognised as a state in which someone cannot properly give their consent. Oh but that's in liberal old *Sweden*,* maybe the confusion has arisen because our British legal system has a different definition and putting your erect penis in sleeping folk is okay here . . . let me check . . . okay, so looking at statutory law, since 1956 rape is 'unlawful sexual intercourse with a woman who at the time of the intercourse does not consent to it', when either the rapist 'knows that she does not consent to the intercourse or he is reckless as to whether she consents to it'.

IS RECKLESS AS TO WHETHER SHE CONSENTS TO IT. Having sex with somebody who is asleep, and who can in no way communicate assent, is reckless, isn't it?

Am I crazy?

---

* Sweden was one of the first countries to legislate against marital rape, in 1965.

If you'd had sex with someone who was asleep, and I asked, 'How do you know whether they wanted to have sex with you?' what could you possibly answer that would persuade me you cared whether they consented or not?

In his podcast, Galloway said that waking up with someone inside you is 'something which can happen, you know'. CAN IT, GEORGE? How many times has that happened to you exactly?

Our enemy here is the banality of unwanted sex. If it's common for one of the partners in a relationship to go along with sex they aren't into, if it's considered harmless for a woman to allow a man to have sex with her when she is not aroused, then the women who do complain, as in a case like Assange's, are seen as moving the goal posts. The boys get exasperated and whiney: 'You can't tell us off now, this is the way it's always been,' or 'Don't pick on me, everyone else is doing it!' The criminality is perceived as unfair or unreasonable because the act is something that some men consider their right. As is seen with Galloway; he believes that his own personal definition of rape is superior to the law. Of Assange's behaviour he said: 'It might be really sordid and bad sexual etiquette, but whatever else it is, it is not rape or you bankrupt the term "rape" of all meaning.'

'It is not rape,' he tells us. Despite the fact that, according to the legal definition I have quoted above, it clearly and really is. Galloway hears of an alleged assault and rather than realising that his preconceived notions of consent are wrong, he chooses to denigrate the women who accuse men in these circumstances. And in the most powerful way possible: they 'bankrupt the term "rape" of all meaning'. He proposes that these women are undermining the experience of 'real' rape victims.

This may seem like a personal attack on George Galloway and his opinions, but I'm using him as an example of how ALL OF US have a subjective definition of what we consider rape. And we ALL occasionally judge or dismiss cases that we hear of in the media or general gossip. We all victim-blame based on our own subjective moral values.

If you'd like to see this in action, bring up Ched Evans next time you are with a group of friends and be surprised and astonished at their reactions. You can read this bit out first if you want, so that everyone is dealing with the same information:

In May 2011, footballers Clayton McDonald and Ched Evans went out in Rhyl in north Wales. McDonald met a nineteen-year-old woman in a takeaway and she went in a cab with him to a hotel room, booked in Evans's name. McDonald sent a text to Evans saying 'got a bird', and he and the woman began having sex. When Evans returned to the hotel room, he also began having sex with the woman. Two friends outside the window attempted to film this on their phones. At some point McDonald left. Evans continued to have sex with the woman, but eventually left too. Neither man ejaculated. The woman woke up alone a few hours later. She did not have her phone or handbag. She contacted reception to call her mother, who came and picked her up. Later that day she returned to the hotel asking to view CCTV recordings, and staff told her the room she had slept in had been booked by footballers. That night she contacted police to claim that her drink had been spiked, as she had no memory of events. The police traced the room booking and arrested McDonald and Evans on a rape charge. (McDonald was found not guilty during the court case.)

Now discuss!

Honestly, you must. I had this case buzzing awfully around my head for months and every time I spoke about it to someone, they illuminated a new perspective. An angle I hadn't thought of, a fresh understanding of human behaviour. I heard alternative combinations of anger and compassion, and I found I could never predict what a person might say. Most importantly, I realised, none of us agree on what consent means. Some of my friends strongly empathised with the footballers because it *was* a situation they could imagine themselves getting into when they were very drunk or much younger. Two of my friends were very harsh towards the victim for a particular reason; one who'd been photographed naked after passing out on a one-night stand and the other who had been tricked into having sex with a man she thought was someone else after falling asleep. Both claimed the Evans/McDonald case 'wasn't rape' because theirs hadn't been. Their coping strategy was self-blame. Their thought process was 'I left myself vulnerable' rather than 'Someone took advantage of me.' Conversely, I have friends who think all sex offenders should be chemically castrated, and that includes the little shits filming outside the window and in fact maybe we should put all sportsmen in prison as soon as they turn professional since none of them seem very respectful of women. So there was a real range of impassioned responses.

There is a website, www.chedevans.com, which attempts to clear Evans's name while discrediting the victim. It refers to various aspects of the case. There is CCTV footage of the nineteen-year-old arriving at the hotel with McDonald; she is carrying a pizza box, which she forgets and then turns back to get. This was shown to the jury as evidence that she 'knew what she was doing' – that she was not unconscious and being dragged. Both McDonald and Evans claimed that the woman was asked if Evans could 'join in' but each said it was the other who asked. And because the victim has no memory of events, she could only testify as to what she can remember, which is her evening up to being in the takeaway, and then waking up in the morning. Further evidence was given by the hotel receptionist who listened outside the door while the sex took place and heard a man asking 'playfully' for oral sex.

It's all so gross and horrid, but how would you approach this case if you were a lawyer? How would you pronounce if you were on the jury?

This case illuminates how a man can rape without knowing it. Or rather, without considering his behaviour to be rape. There is a victim, whose life is deeply and irrevocably affected, and there is a man, Ched Evans, who, despite being found guilty by a jury of his peers, still shows no repentance. He absolutely and resolutely believes that he did nothing wrong. And so do his supporters, his family and his fiancée. They have all the same information as you and consider him an innocent man. On the website there is a tab labelled 'Feedback from a very brave lady', which contains a letter from a woman who was raped and failed to get a conviction in court. She says, '*This girl is the reason why me and plenty other girls who are VICTIMS don't get justice.*' In an echo of Galloway defending Assange, the website claims that this and other letters show '*a clear message that Ched's conviction and the complainant's actions demean and diminish the act of rape*'.

It is not a Welsh nineteen-year-old's fault that our legal system is not set up to try rape and sexual assault effectively. It's not her fault that other women are raped. It's not her fault that shame makes so many women hate themselves and each other instead of their transgressors. She is not 'lucky' that her rape was not violent and she is not 'lucky' that her case got a conviction where so many fail.

Why is it so difficult to understand that forced sex is a spectrum, with a wide-ranging variety of perpetrations? If you had your house burgled, would you feel affronted that someone else wanted to prosecute their pickpocket? Even if they'd been really drunk when it happened? We don't have these attitudes towards other crimes; we all agree that property is property and theft is theft. I would argue that lurking underneath sex crimes is the enduring, subconscious belief that women's bodies exist for male procreation and pleasure. That they are never really ours, despite what we're told. And we *are* told nowadays – it's a huge part of feminism. We tell each other. My mother told me, as did books and magazines and teen television. Like a mantra: My body is my own. MY genitals, MY reproductive rights and MY pleasure, all mine.

But did anyone tell the boys? Were they repeating '*their* bodies, *their* genitals, *their* reproductive rights and *their* pleasure' throughout *their* adolescence? As discussed earlier, throughout modern history male sexuality has been celebrated and accepted while female desire has been denied and suppressed. Consequently male sexuality is perceived as instinctual, natural, something outside of their control. Intimate rape can be dismissed as an automatic response or passion: 'He was too aroused to stop' or 'He was drunk and couldn't control himself.' We admit this slice of animal behaviour as unfortunate yet to be expected. But the conscious brain is always aware, no matter how aroused or drunk someone is. Defecation is as strong an urge as ejaculation, yet society has taught humans of all genders to be fiercely private and respectful about this and not plop it all about like horses. Sane men do not lose control and begin masturbating in front of everybody at the party; they remain aware of right and wrong, of embarrassment and propriety, even when intoxicated. Respect for women's bodies, whether they be asleep, or naked or drugged, should be learned like toilet training.

It has to be taught. It's too dangerous to presume consent is obvious and that anyone who gets it wrong is a bad person. This needs deep thought and conversations. And alcohol is a very complicating factor. There is a point of drunkenness where people are considered unable to give consent to various things, including sexual contact. There are multitudes of warnings aimed at young women, shouting about the dangers of being wasted and vulnerable, while there is virtually nothing aimed at educating young men. And so you get cases like Ched Evans's, where the defendant doesn't even know that he has done wrong.

KNOCK KNOCK

Sorry about this, I'll have to get that, I'm having a sofa delivered and—

SARA jumps up and opens the door.

SARA

Oh. Hi Jeremy, I thought you were my sofa!

JEREMY

No, it's me, Jeremy. Your next-door neighbour. I heard you through the wall saying that if someone is drunk, I mean, if a woman I'm with is really drunk, then maybe I shouldn't have sex with her—

SARA

Is this the first time that's occurred to you?

JEREMY

I'm not a bad guy, but what's the difference between
drunk and too drunk?

SARA

Listen up, Jez, I was going to outline it to everyone
anyway. Lucky I got that law A-level, hey?

JEREMY

I thought you failed law—

*SARA ignores stupid JEREMY and says the following with her
hand on her hip.*

SARA

Here is how it works. To be convicted of a crime under
British law, two things have to be proven beyond
reasonable doubt: *actus reus* and *mens rea*. *Actus reus* is
the action of the crime, the physical aspect. So in a rape
trial, proof that the sex (or penetration with an object
or some other forced sex act) occurred is required. In
R v. *Evans*, Evans admitted to the sex. This is common
in rape cases as the defence is not usually that the
intercourse or sex act didn't take place, rather that it
was consensual.

JEREMY takes notes and is nodding.

SARA

Mens rea is the mental element, the intention to commit
a crime. It's the difference between accidentally hitting

Tim while putting on your coat (the act is there but no intention) and Tim being bloody annoying today so while putting your coat on you gave him a smack in the mouth. Tim's face hurts exactly the same whether you meant it or not, but if you did it on purpose then it's a crime.

And now we see the whole twisted, tangled-up impossibility of trying rape. Victims are called liars by defence teams, told they wanted it, accused of being hypersexual, being fantasists, wanting to be beaten, turned on by knives, horny about gangs, etc., because this creates doubt in their testimony, and any doubt = no conviction. There are often only two witnesses (the victim and the rapist) and it is very very difficult to *prove* that either account is true. Our legal system is built to protect the innocent from wrongful conviction, and so instead the guilty go free.

But as we have seen, the statutory definition of rape includes more than *mens rea*. You don't have to have *intended* to rape someone; you can be convicted if you have been 'reckless as to whether she consents'. And it's here that all our assumptions and expectations diverge.

Here is an example from my life. I thought, drunk at a party, that if I got into a bed and fell asleep that I would be left alone, that I was safe and amongst friends. My friend assumed that my being passed out fully dressed in his bed was a sign of sexual interest and that he could remove my trousers and underwear and start going down on me. This was my friend, I don't think he is a nasty person, but I also don't understand how he walked into that room and – that's it, I can't comprehend what went through his mind, how he came to think that was appropriate behaviour, WHAT ON EARTH MADE HIM DO THAT? He was drunk. I was drunk. But we are the same age and have grown up in the same city, influenced by the same culture, yet we do not seem to agree on the rules.

And so with Ched Evans. He walked into a room where his friend was having sex and assumed he would be welcome too. Clayton McDonald expected him and had sent him that text. Men get aroused by watching each other have sex; this is animal behaviour. McDonald's consent towards Evans is clear, but what about the female partner? For all of the claims on the website defending Evans of the victim writing tweets about 'winning big' or being after the footballer's money, there is nothing at all to signify that the woman ever desired or planned to have sex with Evans. He was reckless as to whether she consented or not, and that is why he was convicted.

Now, British law does not allow intoxication as a defence. If you were drunk when you punched poor old Tim, then that's your responsibility. You chose to get so inebriated that people around you were endangered. You're in charge of your own actions. If Tim was pissed when you hit him, it is still YOU that was at fault. Do you see?

JEREMY
Yes.

SARA
Sorry, I forgot you were here. What I am trying to say is that the onus should be on teaching young men how not to rape people when drunk, as it is they and only they who are legally responsible.

JEREMY

Yes, I got that. Anyway, better go, I think I can hear my cat calling me—

SARA

Please stay, I think I have an idea . . .

JEREMY sits down politely and listens like a good boy.

SARA

Being drunk is the new married. It's viewed as a form of agreement or pre-consent and victims of sexual assault are seen as complicit in their experience. 'Oh, did you drink wine near penises? Well what did you expect?' It was Ched Evans who should've known there was such a thing as being too drunk to consent. His website should be blaming his school for insufficient sex education. He should be railing at a lad culture that shouts 'Any hole's a goal' at teenage boys and encourages them to see women as conquests rather than people. And he should be helping other young men avoid prison by educating them about how not to unwittingly rape someone. So this was my idea: do you remember ages ago when Tony Blair tried to bring in sexual consent forms?

JEREMY

IT WAS AN ILLEGAL WAR!

SARA

I'm not getting into that. In the early 2000s there was political discussion about consent forms being a way to combat rape, and although they never really took off there are lots of websites that do help people create them (if you are interested). But I thought, what about if we all had a virtual one in our heads. So that if we are with a partner who is highly intoxicated, we ask ourselves, 'If I was to get out a six-page legal agreement and ask them to read and sign it, would they be able to? Would they be able to focus on the wording, hold a pen, flick through the pages?' If the answer is no, then you my friend have found yourself a non-sexual partner to sleep next to respectfully. GOODNIGHT and I hope they don't puke on you. And here is an interesting fact to remember, Jeremy: when the level of alcohol in a person's blood goes over 0.08 per cent, they become unable to form long-term memories. This is why some people can seem to be functioning and yet not remember anything the next day. And you can spot this if a drunk person repeats themselves or forgets what they've already told you – this probably means they are in a blackout state. You can give them some water and not have sex with them. I also think that sex education with young people should involve hearing from those who have been assaulted. I think if boys and men empathised with certain experiences – being filmed without your permission, being flashed at, as well as violation and rape – then they'd be better equipped to combat the predatory culture that currently shapes them. Wouldn't they be less likely to slip a drug into a girl's drink if they had heard, as a fourteen-year-old, from someone whose life was ruined by a drug rape?

SARA walks around, flailing her arms and pretending she is a lawyer.

SARA

Boys have to be taught to forget 'consent' and wait for *enthusiasm.* Sex is not something males do to females; it is something people do together. One partner's arousal and desire should be mirrored by the other, and in heterosexual sex, like in all animals, receptivity should be signalled by the female – and never taken for granted. Now *get out,* Jeremy!

JEREMY leaves thinking sex education needs to be revolutionised in the UK. SARA knows she is being quite lecturey at the moment but she has all these opinions on this and it feels so important. She does some hula-hooping to calm herself down, then winks at you and beckons for you to follow to the next bit.

How Old Is Old Enough?

When I was fourteen, my mum made me join a drama club as punishment. I'd had a party in our house without permission, she was staying out with her boyfriend, David. It wasn't even *my* idea – Hayley (puke not laxative) told me that if I had a party then Steadman would come and he would kiss me and I was pretty keen for this to happen because I hadn't kissed a boy yet and I needed to, to prove I wasn't disgusting. So I'd agreed and Hayley invited all the popular people from school (she knew them cos she shoplifted on demand) and they all turned up at my house with bottles and cans and this was a terrible, terrible idea because they hated me and completely trashed my house. They were sick everywhere – on the sofa, in the bath, someone was sick in the rabbit hutch and the rabbit *ate* it. A boy called Stuart decided to make a bonfire and started smashing up our chairs for firewood, and next door heard this through the walls and called the police. And when the police turned up Jo Summers went out and shouted that she was going to sue them because her dad was a barrister, and I don't know if that was a lie but it definitely wasn't the truth because her mum didn't even know who her dad was. And I was just walking around feeling nauseous – not from alcohol, nobody gave me any, I was sick with regret and shame and because Hayley had got off with Steadman right in front of me.

I stayed up all night trying to tidy everything up but people had put cigarettes out on the carpet and poured cider on

the sofa and there was too much for me to do. When Mum
and David got home the next-door neighbours ran outside
and told them what I'd done and they came into the house
and Mum turned pale as she looked around and I begged
her to hit me, because pain would be a relief from how guilty
I felt. But she didn't. She was furious and disappointed in
me and David was waggling a fork while he shouted. And the
neighbours were pleased that I was getting told off, but then
they said that they ran a drama group on Wednesdays and
Sundays and that they would let me be in it and that it would
'keep me off the streets'. So it was decided – I did plays and
danced around, I met nice people outside school, I gained
confidence and I realised that I wanted to be famous, and
now I AM FAMOUS so I haven't even been punished. In
your face, Mum, it's too late to hit me now!

One of the things that I liked most about doing drama and
being in plays outside school was that I knew people who were
older. Boys who had cars and houses without parents in them.
When I was fifteen and sixteen I had mates who were in their
thirties and I thought it was because I was so incredibly mature
and wise for my age. But when *I* got older, when I got to the
age they were then and I imagined hanging out with a teenager, I felt completely different about it. Suddenly it was creepy.
Sixteen-year-olds are babies, tiny, little – even eighteen-year-
olds are so small and new – whoever even looked that young?
But I can remember how grown-up I felt then, and earlier,
since about nine. Because we age one way, in one direction,
every age we are is the most grown-up we've ever been. So
you don't know, do you? When I was ten I thought I was fully
formed and completely me and nothing would ever change.
And I've continued to believe that at *every* age and then later

on reflect and laugh at how young and wrong and naive I was before. I feel protective over a past me who was adamant she didn't need or want protecting at the time. What I am trying to say is this: I got off with boys who were actually men, who were in their thirties, when I was in my teens and back then I thought it was a sign of great accomplishment, of sexual connoisseurship, and now I think its super-gross. Not illegal, I was not damaged by these experiences, but YUK.

Age and sex is an issue it's difficult to be definite about. How you feel about it will depend on how old you are, whether you have children and how old *they* are. How your first sexual experiences affected you, whether you felt in control. Imagine if we were all on a staircase and each step was a month and I shouted, 'Everyone stand where you think the age of consent should be' – we'd find it difficult to settle, wouldn't we? If sixteen is okay, what about fifteen and eleven months, and then fifteen and ten months? Fifteen and a half? But you can see you're getting closer to twelve down there in the distance and that is *definitely* too low so we start stepping upwards again. 'Some sixteen-year-olds are very immature,' someone says. 'There is so much sexual pressure on young people nowadays,' says their friend. 'Maybe there would be less teenage pregnancy if we raised the age of consent to something crazy – twenty?' And on we go up the stairs, thinking, 'Of course some people will still have sex earlier but maybe there would be less expectation to do it,' and then we arrive and we're very high up and we smile at each other and snort at how ridiculous we're being – it's just sex after all, just nudity and wiggly rubbing – and down we go again to argue about young people's potential to make adult decisions versus the danger of leaving young people vulnerable to the manipulation of older people and so on all day until our thighs hurt too much to continue.

Personally I think sixteen is a perfect compromise for consent law. It's not perfect and individuals differ greatly, some people are 'ready' a lot earlier, some not until years later, but most of us by sixteen are capable of making the kind of mistakes that will constitute the majority of our sex lives: fancying idiots, obsessing about the disinterested, drunken doing-it that embarrasses you forever, and so on. Of course we're conditioned by the rules and expectations of our society so I probably think sixteen is a sensible age of consent *because* I live in a country that tells me so. Laws that forbid sex and marrying while forcing us to attend school create space for us to be children before the graduated slide into adulthood and its expectations. But in other countries there are different expectations; childhood ends earlier. Children may work and get married before they hit their teens, just like in the olden days in the U of K.

Here is my pretend TED talk about the first consent laws. Imagine I am wearing what you recognise as my sexiest beret and on the big screen behind me emoticons are flashing up to signify how I feel about some of the information.

SARA walks on stage. She seems nervous and is holding a pointy stick.

SARA
Hi guys, thanks for coming, thanks to Sweden for arranging this. Let's talk about the age of consent. The first recorded law concerning age and sex was created in the UK in 1275. The legal age for marriage was twelve –

SARA points her stick at a pukey emoticon with fear in his eyes.

SARA

– and this new ruling meant that 'ravishing' a maiden under this age 'with or without her consent' was now illegal. The words to notice here are 'ravishing', with its connotations of passion and 'he couldn't help himself'-ness that have continued to confuse prosecutions of rape to the present day . . .

Thumbs-down emoticon.

SARA

. . . and the significance of 'maiden'. This first ever anti-rape law only protected virgins. The original judgements on what we would call 'rape' and they called 'ravishing' were a type of property law. A girl's virginity was for her husband; its 'theft' was perceived as a crime against her father and future husband rather than herself. It was the taking of virginity that was a criminal act, not the assault itself.

SARA looks at the screen. There is a delay of a few seconds, then a poop-with-eyes emoticon appears. Light titters from the crowd.

SARA

Interestingly, because male virginity has never had any bearing on male marriageability there is no mention of 'ravishing' young boys. Scarily, male children in the UK were not protected by age of consent laws until the 1970s, when feminist pressure groups/heroes had the wording of statutes changed to protect 'people' and not just girls.

Germaine Greer giving a thumbs-up emoticon.

SARA

From 1275 up until the nineteenth century, creating
doubt that a rape victim was a virgin would be sufficient
to avoid a prosecution – a defence technique that
echoes on in the raking-through of modern victims'
sexual history as a way of discrediting their testimony.

*Sombre clapping. SARA tries to cheer everyone up a little bit by doing
a cartwheel but the mood is still pretty serious.*

I have to stop the TED talk now because I can't think of any
more emoticons. I don't get them on my phone – they come
up as little empty boxes.

The story of how the age of consent was raised to sixteen is
pretty incredible. In 1885 there was an investigative journalist
called William Stead and he went undercover to interview pro-
curesses and the girls they bought and sold. Stead realised how
easy it was to trick a young girl (or persuade a poor and desperate one) into an act of prostitution. From the male customer's
point of view a guaranteed virgin was less risky as a sex partner
because she would be disease-free. Some even believed sex with
virgins cured sexual diseases and sought them out for that reason. Plus we have to assume that the men found the girls' youth
and inexperience a turn-on. So the virgins were worth money
and there was this whole lucrative and evil business going on –
and the women who ran it, who trafficked these girls, had no
sympathy for their victims whatsoever, they referred to them as
'little fools' or sillies'. In his account of his investigations, Stead
asks one procuress, 'Do the maids ever repent and object to be
seduced when the time comes?'

MISS X

Oh yes, sometimes we have no end of trouble.

STEAD

You always manage it though?

MISS X

Certainly. If a girl makes too much trouble, she loses
her maidenhead for nothing instead of losing it for
money.

She then goes on to describe the screaming and fighting
of girls who have changed their minds. Girls that she has had
to hold down. WHAT A NICE LADY. Stead pretends that he
would like to 'seduce' some maidens and then meets all these
girls who are completely naive. They don't know the names
for body parts or that sex can make a baby or what the old
man will do to them. All they've been told is the amount of
money they will get and to expect pain.

The most significant element of Stead's discoveries is his
demonstration that once a girl has been tricked into this first
act, 'once her ruin has been accomplished', she is likely to
prostitute herself again because she has no other choice. She
can never be respectable, may never marry. Her 'seduction'
could have created severe emotional and mental health problems. Or she might be pregnant! What he pierces so beau-
tifully is the Victorian perception that prostitutes were bad,
immoral people. He reports situations that could have happened to anyone. An Irish girl is at the left luggage office at
Victoria station when a smart woman approaches, addresses
her by name and asks who she is supposed to be meeting.
My uncle, the girl says. He sent me to collect you, the woman

informs her, then pops her in a carriage and whisks her off to a west London brothel, where six men force themselves on her throughout the afternoon. Stead outlines instances of girls being tricked into owing money for accommodation or dresses they had thought were gifts, and then pressured to sell sex to pay off the debts. Or drinks being spiked and girls waking up with the deed done. The shame surrounding sex meant that girls were punished after their assault by the attitude of the society around them.

Stead, who'd tried to get the police involved and was frustrated by their uncaring attitude, felt he needed stronger proof. So he bought a thirteen-year-old girl called Eliza Armstrong for £5 from her mother. He had her transported to a brothel and drugged with chloroform. Then he entered the bedroom and waited. When Eliza awoke, she screamed for ages and nobody came to rescue her. Stead let her do this a while and then left, allowing everyone in earshot to assume that he'd 'seduced' her. Eliza was then transported to the continent and protected by the Salvation Army. Stead wrote up what he'd done, showing how simple and easy it was to kidnap and potentially rape a child, and this proved to Parliament that young women were not being legally protected. The Criminal Law Amendment Act 1885 was passed and the age of consent for girls was now sixteen.

HOORAY!

Then William Stead got sent to prison because he had kidnapped that girl. Hang on, didn't you say he paid her mum? Yes, but he didn't pay her dad and that's who owned her, so he went to prison for a bit. Then a few years later he died on the *Titanic*. He was a cool guy, I think. I tried to look up what happened to Eliza Armstrong, but it's difficult to find much.

She seems to have had a few husbands and kids. But I want the inside story, how affected she was, whether Stead was nice to her . . . I want to see her on the front of *That's Life!* magazine: 'BOUGHT, SOLD and NOW THEY'VE CHANGED THE LAW' with a picture of her looking sad but you know she got £250 for her story and that's a lot in Victorian money.

SO sex with someone younger than sixteen becomes a crime and nobody ever does it again, except it happens all the time. And as we've already explored, this issue is complicated. What distinguishes a sex crime? What differentiates a sex partner and a victim? For instance, this headline is pretty incendiary:

'Judge Blames Girl, 16, for Sex with Teacher, 44.'

In January 2015 newspapers reported on the trial of a religious education teacher who'd had sex with a sixteen-year-old pupil in a PE cupboard. He received an eighteen-month suspended sentence. The story was titillating and emotive, hence its front-page dominance; the teacher had been *pursued* by the girl in question, the judge called her 'a stalker' and said that 'if anything it was you that groomed him'. The supposed 'victim' had been active. It was consensual sex that she had wanted and initiated. She had been explicit, texting and seductive; how are poor RE teachers expected to cope?

If you were the judge would you have sent him to prison?*

a) Yes.

b) No.

c) Don't know, can I have a think about it?

d) Princess Diana face.

All of the above in that order.

---

* Oh great, another quiz!

The attraction of youth is sensible biology. The clichés of men leaving their wives for younger women, or middle-aged ladies seducing young waiters on holiday, make great sense for reproductive purposes. Some evolutionary psychologists argue that our ancestors would have found younger females attractive not just for their higher fertility but also because they were easier to dominate, to ensure paternity certainty. When you reverse the genders, mature females who have access to their own resources and do not need the strength or support of a co-parent can opt instead for the liveliness of young sperm. Our sexual urges are often inspired by who our body thinks is most likely to get us pregnant/be impregnated by us. But that is not to excuse any behaviours – urges and drives are separate from actions, loins are not magnetically drawn towards others against our will.

My friend Sarah* teaches GCSE English so spends her working days with fourteen-to-sixteen-year-olds. I asked her how she felt when she heard news stories about a teacher having sex with a pupil and she explained she is aware all the time that she cannot be too friendly or sociable with pupils. She doesn't give out her phone number; she rejects friend requests on Facebook.

SARA

But are the kids *flirty*?

SARAH

Yeah, sometimes aggressively so. I've heard Year 9 girls asking teachers out on dates, or getting them to promise they'll go out with them when they're eighteen.

---

* Her parents could spell.

SARA

And they agree?

SARAH

They might joke about it but it's the only way to get them to shut up. Girls get crushes on teachers all the time—

SARA

And how are teachers prepared for this? What's the training?

SARAH

If a kid approaches you in that way, you have to report it to the union—

SARA

But you must have big conversations about it? Seminars and conferences about the ethics, and to prepare teachers to expect it?

SARAH

Not really. You are just told to report it to the union.

The idea of grown men being attracted to teenage girls is understandably distasteful so it gets ignored. But merely wishing it didn't happen leaves young women vulnerable. The people who break the rules (and law) are seen as bad and lascivious rather than weak and average. Surely anyone working with young people has to be given a proper framework to deal with sexual feelings should they arise? There is a difference between desires and actions – I had a lovely long daydream about Terence Peterson today and that's A-OK.

But if I physically forced a man to come on a country walk with me and threatened him until he pointed out raccoons and kingfishers and then proposed to me? That would be wrong.

While I was talking to Sarah I remembered loads of horrible things I did to male teachers at school. I had a crush on a PE teacher and in the fifth year I told loads of people that I'd got off with him in the basketball cupboard. DEFINITELY nobody believed me. I was always doing things like this. I used to pretend I'd had sexual romances on holidays I hadn't been on and gave myself love bites on the only places I could reach, my upper and lower arms. But now it strikes me that I could have got that gorgeous teacher in a lot of trouble. It has echoes of that real-life case with its PE-cupboard virginity-taking and what unsettles me is how fledgling my feelings were. They were Bambi taking his first steps. If you'd asked me at fifteen, 'Do you really want to have sex with Mr Humphries during afternoon break?' I would have replied adamantly that YES I DID, sign me up and take me there. It was something I desperately desired without knowing what 'it' was. I was completely inexperienced and unable to envisage the reality, hungry for a concept.

Aged about twelve or thirteen, I'd begun to be scared of men. I'd always hated my mum's boyfriends, but as I became pubescent it all intensified and I couldn't be alone with one. Even with my dad – we had to see him once a month and I was always petrified he was going to ask for sex with me and I hated him. Men vibrated oddly all of a sudden. Everyone looked at me all the time. My uncle called me Jezebel and said I would get older men into trouble. Grown men started shouting at me from cars and vans. I was flashed at several times walking home in school uniform. On a crowded tube train a man rubbed his erection on my bottom. I felt threatened and I had no way of communicating how or why. This was all ironically coupled with a period of intense self-loathing and shame. I kept a hand in front of my mouth when talking because my teeth were so disgusting; I planned to have a nose job as soon as I was eighteen. I knew I was fat and I knew I smelled and I knew my body was full of disgusting things like pus and shit and blood. I knew that if I fancied a boy at school and put a letter in their bag they thought it was insulting and were mean. I shaved my love-bitten arms and my disappointing face while fantasising that the PE teacher would make everything better by finding me beautiful.

I have lots of girl friends now (bragging) and they all went through a similar horrible phase with their fathers. The awareness of sexuality in each other is massive but unspoken. I think my dad is still weird with me. He lives in Australia now (to get away from how sexy I am?) and last year I was at the Melbourne comedy festival and he came to stay with me and I offered that he could sleep in the HUGE double bed with me and he reacted so uptightly, saying, 'That's a bit Greek tragedy,* isn't it?' and then he slept ON THE FLOOR. And every time I introduced him to someone the next day he would tell them this as an anecdote: 'She wanted me in her bed and I was like, "That's a bit Greek tragedy!" Ha ha ha.' I didn't think it was weird. I have slept in a bed with my mum, no problem at all, why should my dad be different? I asked him and he said, 'Of course it's different.' But WHY? Because my mother doesn't have a penis?** We are human beings, not

---

* You know, cos Oedipus did it with his mother. My dad is pretty clever.
** Bragging.

puzzle pieces that accidentally slot into each other. I don't really understand it, but incest taboo is a whole other subject for a whole other book. And you'll have to write it cos I'm busy with this one.

My adolescent fear of men did not extend to the ones in Take That. For years I emanated hot love for them constantly, like electric heat escaping from an open window, but hotter, HOTTER THAN THAT. The hours in bed before sleep were so frustrating. I would listen on a Walkman as Mark and Gary sang about how much they loved me while I became more and more alert and twitchy. I hadn't learned to masturbate yet, so there was no relief. It was physically painful. I've had actual relationships with people who I loved less. My feelings were real. My plans were solid – I completely believed I would marry one of Take That because of how my parents had met. I thought it was my destiny.

Our house had a cupboard full of scrapbooks filled with Dad's face. There were Polaroids of my mum sitting outside Nanny Babs's house surrounded by olden-time girls in flares. To know that Mum had just picked him and then found him obsessed us. I decided that's how I would get a boyfriend. Cheryl and I would watch *Top of the Pops* very expectantly, waiting for that 'certainty feeling' to happen, then we'd know: 'There he is, let's track him down!' But we didn't have any epiphanies so we simply selected our future husbands: Cheryl chose Robbie Williams and I chose Mark Owen, because she likes jokes and I'm scared of masculine men.

High-status individuals like Mark and Robbie are attractive because the animal, non-logical aspect to our psychology believes them to be great for breeding – they have power and access to resources, that's the kind of shit that keeps babies safe and fed! When guys have talent or good looks there is the *additional* bonus of great genes that would be inherited by off-spring. Subsequent children would be more likely to become high-status too and then have surviving children themselves. It's a double win. Fancying someone is always a smokescreen for biological probability work; it might feel super-sexy, but it's mostly bodies doing maths. Of course we're not usually consciously aware of it, so we find reasons to explain away at-traction, creating logical explanations: 'Oh, it's because that person is a great dancer,' or 'I love the way he plays guitar,' but subconsciously our bodies are trying to get us mating with those who would make and support the finest children.

Teenage girls getting obsessive about famous people is so common it's a cliché. I could claim it's 'universal' but nothing ever completely is. Some teens may have a rare condition that causes them to believe they are a potato and thus only fancy famous potatoes? I'm sure people who grow up in nomadic jungle cultures without a TV don't lust after pop stars – they might ache for a handsome cloud they saw or a tree with a face carved in it?[*] No matter the target, the passions of pu-bescent young women are understood as a phase in sexual development where feelings are explored for the first time via projection and so within a safe context. I was licking and pressing myself against posters on the wall that could not touch or press me back. It was a one-sided adventure.

These crushes are powerful, idealistic objectifications. Sometimes their object might be a teacher rather than a TV presenter or a musician. Mr Humphries was as distant and unknowable to me as Take That were.

---

[*] There she goes, insulting the very people whose habitat was destroyed for the printing of this book. (E-habitat if you're on a Kindle.)

My dad quit being in his band soon after meeting my mum. He doesn't often talk about that part of his life, but he once told me about having girls chasing him, and the dissonance created when strangers say they 'love' you. It must have been weird for him to see me and Cheryl living that in the other direction. My dissonance was reversed; how could Mark not know me when I loved him so much? How could he not feel it? I know that the feelings experienced are as real as anything, it's the target that's fictionalised. I used to have in-depth fantasies of what would happen if I ever met Mark Owen. There were various lead-ins: he might come in to award prizes at school,* or spot me in the crowd at a concert. Or, most likely, Take That would be driving in a limo through Romford and it would break down on Marshalls Drive, WHERE I LIVED. I would just be walking home in my school uniform and would move straight past the sleek black car, assuming some local celebrity like Frank Bruno to be inside. But then Howard gets out and asks me for directions to Manchester. I am surprised but able to hide it, pretending I don't recognise him. It works because I am a great actor who does drama outside of school. The band are a long way from home; their limo driver needs to find a garage, which will take ages, but Howard really needs the toilet. I invite him and the rest of the band into my house.

'Don't worry, Mum won't be back for ages,' I say coolly and then show them around our two-bedroom terrace. They can't believe how mature I am, and how down-to-earth I make them feel.

---

* 'Simon' from *EastEnders* had done this because his dad was our head of year. Maybe one of the other heads was related to Mark? The gates were open between celebrity-land and Gaynes School.

'Beans on toast, guys?'

The band are starving and haven't had any normal people's food for years, but I make it for them and it is delicious. Luckily Kristyna isn't here or she would come in and spit choc ice at them like when Steve Penfold came round. Everything is going smoothly and the guys all really fancy me and are having a respectful discussion about who is going to have sex with me. I don't tell them I'm a virgin or anything, I just look out of the window and act older and then suggest, like it's just occurred to me:

'We could all get in the bath?'

This would work better if we had a Jacuzzi but we don't. We do have a head sprayer shower attachment that we can use to swirl the water around a bit though. We could stick that on, and then I would let the 'lads' do whatever they wanted to me.

My fantasies were a way of testing what I could imagine letting them do. On my side it was always supplication and subjection. I would envisage acts of hurt and humiliation and reassure myself, YES, I would let Mark Owen do that, that's how much I cared for him. I didn't have any intention of receiving pleasure from him, other than his brief attention. Even if he wanted to do a poo on me. Or put things inside me or kick me, that would be fine because he would know that I existed, and so, for a few brief moments, I would.

I consider my teenage daydreams to be evidence of several things:

1. I had a bundle of very sexual emotions. Lust. Desire. Need for connection.
2. I did not understand those emotions yet. No concept of

consensual sex or my own pleasure and how I might find it.
3. I am lucky I never met Take That.

Not because they would've taken advantage of me but because I would've embarrassed myself horribly by force-feeding them breakfast foods. I did try and meet them. I always wore my best red velvet top to concerts in an attempt to catch their eye. And then, in 1995, ROBBIE LEFT THE BAND. I considered suicide for a bit, then realised, hang on, he's split off from the pack, he's weaker – more *vulnerable*, I'll marry *him* instead! I found out he was coming to LONDON to present *The Big Breakfast* for a week. So I decided to follow in my mother's footsteps immediately after stealing from her purse. Cheryl and I got up at 4.30 a.m. to catch the train to Stratford, where the show was filmed from 7 to 9 a.m. The other girls screamed when Robbie came out to chat and do photos, but I just stared at him, willing him to notice me like an intense, completely creepy fourteen-year-old creep. After a couple of days my mum hid her purse and banned us from going any more in case we got murdered. So I ran away to live by the canal near where *The Big Breakfast* was filmed. I lived there for about five, maybe six hours before it got cold and busy with potential murderers and I came home.

Such inebriating fandom is a childish rehearsal of adult feelings and can be experienced by girls as young as nine or ten. Yet admitting that children can have sexual emotions or motivations can be unsettling. Perhaps the fear is that acknowledging fledgling sexuality might excuse those who believe sex with children is morally okay. But while I would be first in the queue to protest the *sexualisation* of kids (padded bras for eight-year-olds and saucy slogans on six-year-olds'

knickers), it seems to me that by choosing to ignore children's sexual development, we have not worked out what it is:
play. And practice. You know how lion cubs fight and tumble
with each other all the time? That's part of the training for
being an adult lion. They are building muscles and learning
techniques of attack and defence. It's cute to watch because
they are small and ineffectual but displaying adult actions.
They give bites that don't hurt and scratches that don't pene-
trate. And when they take on a grown lion they are tolerated
or ignored. Adult lions don't fight the cub as an equal and
then claim, 'She was jumping on me like she wanted a proper
ding-dong. What's a guy to do?'

And so we reassess the solitary educator, like the RE teacher
in the news story. It's not a crowd full of screaming fans he is
faced with, but a persistent student with his phone number,
annoying and fervent. And he needs to empathise with young
women like her, who seem powerful and full of agency, but
who are in a formative life stage and vulnerable to damage.
That's why the law must protect young people from those who
have power over them. Not because their virginity is precious
or because they are too young for desire, but because true
consent can only be given between equals. That's why the
moves a student makes on a teacher have no bearing on his or
her level of responsibility. But I think you knew that already
and were waiting for me to catch up.

So far, so Anglocentric. In the UK any adult attracted to
children under sixteen is called a paedophile and feared/
hated/vilified/used to sell newspapers. But that is not true of
all countries. Here is a map with some countries' minimum
age for sexual consent labelled – it gives a good idea of the
range across the globe:

Norway

Canada 16

UK 16

Germany 14

USA 16–18

Spain 13

Morocco 15

Mexico 12

Jamaica 16

Colombia 12–14

Burkina Faso 13

Peru 14

Angola 12

Paraguay 12

Chile 13

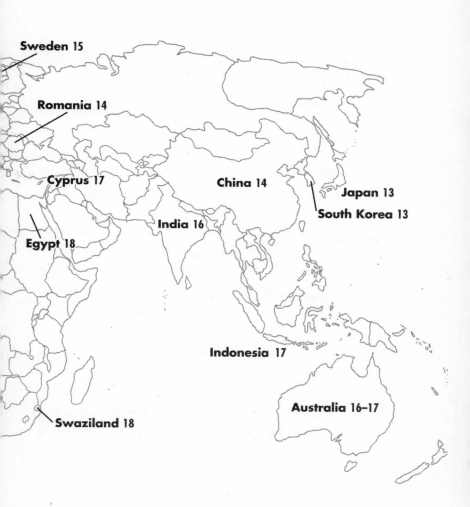

Sweden 15

Romania 14

Cyprus 17

China 14

Japan 13

South Korea 13

India 16

Egypt 18

Indonesia 17

Australia 16–17

Swaziland 18

Even with only twenty or so examples you can see the huge disparity. There are also countries that have no formal age of consent law, places like Saudi Arabia and Yemen. In these countries sex is not permitted outside of wedlock, but there is no age limit on when a girl can be married.

Hmmmmmm.

Of course I'm biased, because I have been conditioned by my culture and society to believe that childhood is a human right. I cannot separate myself from OPINIONATED opinions that children shouldn't work, should be able to go to school and should not be married to men three times their age. And it's this *cultural* difference that prevents an effective conversation about this. Someone might argue, 'If you live in a country where loads of your friends and relatives got married when they are thirteen or fourteen, that will seem normal to you.' But the normalisation of child marriage doesn't stop it causing emotional and physical injury and (sorry to be melodramatic) DEATH.

God it's horrible – it would be easier to respect cultural differences as none of our business and not talk about child brides. I am so tempted to skip it, write about something flippant instead. I've got loads of stories left, I haven't told you about the time I accidentally took speed or about this guy Ben who could only have sex to the *Cheers* theme tune – why would I talk about something I have no experience of? Should I be barging in, giving my unasked-for judgements on a situation I don't understand? Then I remember I don't care, I have the microphone, *I* worry about this and if I'm completely wrong then you are allowed to disagree with me in *your* book.*

---

* Congratulations on your book deal, it's about incest if I remember rightly?

I read about a young woman from Yemen called Najood Ali. When she was nine she was married to a man in his thirties. On their wedding night he beat and raped her, and this treatment continued for months until Najood took a taxi to the courthouse and demanded a divorce.

Yemeni law allows the marriage of children, but forbids sexual intercourse until they have reached the wonderfully vague age of 'suitable'. Najood's lawyer managed to successfully argue that she hadn't, and while the judge suggested she go back and live with her family for three years until she was of appropriate age (this is a common solution granted to young girls who are badly mistreated by their husbands), Najood said no and was granted a divorce. She was ten. It was the first case of its kind, and it has strengthened the movement against child marriages in her country.

Around fifteen per cent of Yemeni girls will be married before they are fifteen years old. There is a respectful understanding between families that mature men who get married to pre-pubescent girls will not have intercourse with them until they are menstruating; however, there is little policing of this and, until Najood's case, no blame for those men who disobey. In 2013 an eight-year-old died from uterine rupture and internal bleeding after her forty-year-old husband had sex with her on her wedding night. I think we can agree arguments about cultural conditioning weaken when children are killed by penetration. The physical damage is an unquestionable sign that their bodies are not prepared for sexual intercourse. The statistics speak for themselves. Girls aged fifteen to nineteen are twice as likely to die in childbirth as those in their twenties; girls under the age of fifteen are five times more likely to die. Giving birth as a teenager, particularly below the age of fifteen, carries an increased risk of obstetric fistula because the pelvis is smaller.

Najood Ali's story of mistreatment is horrific but not unique. Beatings and forced sex are used to subdue and oppress young brides, who are understandably upset at their new lives. Their experience is no less traumatic for being common. What happened to Najood also illustrates the economic reasons behind child marriage. Her family were poor. By marrying her they gained a bride price and lost the expense of feeding and clothing a female child who was never going to be a financial asset. In every country in the world the worst problems faced by girls and women are connected to poverty. Studies and statistics demonstrate that the more education a female child receives, the later (on average) she will marry. Education opens up her earning potential as an adult and it is only through this process that women will have a more equal role in their societies. 'So that's that solved,' say the UN, 'thanks Sara, we didn't realise it was so *easy*.'

I know they're being sarcastic.

History shows us that morality and attitudes to sexuality evolve slowly through a process of discussion and sharing ideas. We won't all agree, but that shouldn't stop us talking about how we feel and listening to each other. We have to lead this. And we will confabulate and we will assume and we'll be subjective but we mustn't let a fear of making mistakes keep us quiet. Writing this book I've realised a really obvious thing, that GROWING UP DOESN'T STOP. The changes, the unrecognisable past selves – it doesn't even slow down. I've learned so little. The extra years of adulthood only really gift me some resilience of experience. When I was young I didn't realise how young I was, and now I am old and I can't believe how childish my life is or how foolish my decisions are – like when a guy tells you he needs the *Cheers* soundtrack to get an erection and you still sleep with him like an idiot.

I think about what my life would be like as a mouse; it would be so much simpler and perhaps easier. But mice can't play the trumpet.

Mice can't write books and be grateful to their readers. And a mouse can't be filled with hope for the future.

Afterword & Charitable Organisations

I have changed how I feel about people. Consciously, I made a decision. Now I think about people how I think about dogs. What I mean is, I like all dogs. Love them, automatically. Never met one I didn't like. Can't imagine one I hated. Sure, oh yes, a dog might bite me or growl like he hates me, but I would instantly forgive it. Perhaps it is hungry or had a difficult childhood? Maybe I'm standing in its nest? And so this is how I've decided to feel about people – every behaviour has a cause, be it chemical or environmental or evolutionary or genetic or whatever. I have decided to be interested in these causes as well as the effects, I have decided to forgive people like the dogs—

I AM NOT AN APOLOGIST.

I am not saying all of the horrid human behaviours are okay because we are animals and can't help ourselves. But maybe all of us understanding more about why bad things happen can help us stop them? I read somewhere that humans are a 'self-domesticating' species. What we did consciously with wolves to provide all those lovely cuddly dogs, we have unknowingly been doing within our own species – we reward teamwork and love and generosity in our relationships and with our sex. We are gradually evolving out of our brutality. Which is nice to think about.

But remember those glow worms shagging away on the street lamps? Just as they could not have evolved the ability to differentiate between electric lights and lady glow worms, so we did not evolve for a world like this. We did not know we were going to be expected to empathise with people in other countries who we will never meet, that we would need to care about people who don't even exist yet and whose planet we are destroying. So we suffer from empathy failure. We retain selfish attributes – a tribal sense of ownership, a greed for resources and looking after our own. But we also have pleasure centres in our brain that reward us when we share. We get dopamine hits when we help others and when we give and receive knowledge. A human being is a balanced creature: we ensure our own survival at all costs, but survival has always involved each other. Empathy is a muscle that can be improved if you work at it.

So let's help each other. Sorry to be a capitalist scumbag but money underwrites everything; without it there is no freedom. Here's a T-shirt slogan for ya: 'Those without cash are trapped'.

Here are some brilliant charities to support across the world, and why:

This list is not exhaustive but includes a variety of charities who work in the UK or abroad tackling some of the issues that I have touched upon in the book. The websites are full of information if you are interested in reading further, and many have campaigns that you can get involved with or share online. They all have pages where you can donate or, if you can't, guilt-trip someone else into giving – perhaps while they are eating a cake or enjoying an episode of *EastEnders*.

www.actionaid.org.uk/ These guys work on behalf of the most
    vulnerable women and children in the world, those who are
    affected by extreme poverty or natural disaster.
www.girlsnotbrides.org/about-child-marriage/ Lots of information
    on the age of consent, child marriage and the various countries
    where young girls are not currently being protected by the law.

http://rapecrisis.org.uk/ A UK charity offering counselling and
advice as well as running campaigns that raise awareness and put
pressure on government. They have up-to-date statistics and links
to similar organisations.

www.microloanfoundation.org.uk/ These great guys give small
loans for women to start their own businesses in sub-Saharan
Africa. All research shows that supporting women to become
independent and self-sufficient is the quickest way to rebuild
damaged societies.

www.fistulafoundation.org/ This charity works to help women in
developing countries by repairing fistulas. They also provide
education and training and are just amazing.

www.refuge.org.uk/ Refuge works to protect and support women
escaping domestic violence. This sector of charitable work is
much needed in the UK and is drastically underfunded by our
current government. See also www.endviolenceagainstwomen.
org.uk/ who run campaigns and raise awareness.

The following charities provide sanitary products to women
in developing countries or places that have been affected by
war or disaster:

www.path.org/projects/sanitary-pads.php
www.daysforgirls.org/
www.afripads.com/
http://lovinghumanity.org.uk/ This organisation is working to give
women the means to make sanitary products so that they can sell
them – so clever.

Charities working to end FGM include:

http://28toomany.org/
http://forwarduk.org.uk/
www.thecruelcut.org/ – there are tons of videos and educational
resources on this one.

That's enough to be getting on with.

Selected Reading

I found some amazing books while researching for this book and if you're at all interested in learning more you should check some of these out:

Sex at Dawn by Christopher Ryan and Cacilda Jethá
Evolution and Human Sexual Behavior by Peter B. Gray and Justin R. Garcia (a text book really, so full of info)
The Origin of the World: Science and Fiction of the Vagina by Jelto Drenth
Curvology: The Origins and Power of Female Body Shape by David Bainbridge (sports bra anyone?)
Fat is a Feminist Issue by Susie Orbach
Bonk: The Curious Coupling of Science and Sex by Mary Roach (funny and facts too)
Sperm Wars by Robin Baker (dubious science and much debated but lots to think about)
The Equality Illusion by Kat Banyard
The Descent of Woman by Elaine Morgan (aquatic ape theory!)
Rape and the Culture of the Courtroom by Andrew E. Taslitz
The Maiden Tribute of Modern Babylon by William Stead (the age of consent/died on titanic guy)
Transforming a Rape Culture by Buchwald, Fletcher and Roth
Why We Love and Lust by Dr Theresa L. Crenshaw (all about all the hormones!)
Zero Degrees of Empathy by Simon Baron-Cohen (talks briefly about anorexia and self-empathy)
Rape on Trial by Zsuzsanna Adler (a bit out of date but great overview of rape laws)
Sex, Drugs and Rock 'n' Roll by Zoe Cormier
Come as You Are by Emily Nagoski (women and sex and pleasure and I can't recommend this enough)
The Circumcision of Women by Olayinka Koso-Thomas

Perv: The Sexual Deviant in All of Us by Jesse Bering

The Case of the Female Orgasm by Elizabeth A. Lloyd

Get Me Out: A History of Childbirth from the Garden of Eden to the Sperm Bank by Randi Hutter Epstein M.D

Sex and Punishment: Four Thousand Years of Judging Desire by Eric Berkowitz (great for witches and vestal virgins)

The Mating Mind by Geoffrey Miller

I am Nujood: Age 10 and Divorced by Nujood Ali (she wrote this with the lawyer who got her divorce)

Survival of the Prettiest by Nancy Etcoff

The Science of Love and Betrayal by Robin Dunbar

Sex on Earth by Jules Howard (where I found out about the glow worms!)

Heretics by Will Storr (how I found out about confabulation and the experiments that proved it a GREAT book)

The Technology of Orgasm by Rachel Maines (history of vibrators)

The Story of the Human Body by Daniel Lieberman (excellent for fat info)

The Red Queen by Matt Ridley (an amazing evolution overview)

The Female Brain by Louann Brizendine M.D.

Delusions of Gender by Cordelia Fine (sex bias in science testing)

Anatomy of Love by Helen Fisher (and find her TED talk too!)

On my website www.sarapascoe.com I have created a page with more *Animal* related stuff, links to relevant articles and new studies as well as some interesting online resources and what have you.

Shouty Appendix

We need to change how rape is tried in courts.

You will be aware of the very low conviction rates for this crime. Only 5.7 per cent of reported rapes end in a guilty verdict. We're all familiar with this, we mutter and complain and shrug our shoulders – or we are furious with the unfairness of it, but we don't know what to do.

The system has to change. We have to demand it.

Rape cannot be tried like other crimes, it is not like theft or driving without a licence. Juries and judges already understand the clear-cut rules of property ownership or traffic law, it does not confuse them. Conviction rates for rape are stupidly low because (as with all criminal charges) guilt has to be proved beyond reasonable doubt, and with rape, doubt is too easily created. There are very often no witnesses; it is her word against his. To create doubt the victim is denigrated, she is attacked, she is insulted. This does not happen with the victims of other crimes, and it should not be permitted when trying rape.

There is a widely held assumption that some women lie about being raped for attention or to exact revenge. Such cases are often reported in the media. They capture the public imagination. All the legal statistics show that the rates for false claims of rape are exactly the same as false accusations of any other crime – about two per cent. Yet people saying they were robbed or hit by a joyrider are not routinely accused of lying in court They're not *all* called liars because a very small percentage of people sometimes lie.

There should be separate courts for crimes involving sex.

The current system is a failure. It punishes all victims and very few offenders. It is unjust. With specialised rape courts, perhaps more people would report the crime and would be willing to seek justice.

In these new courts, judges and juries and magistrates must be given specialist training in the behaviour of victims so they understand how fear and shock affect the body and the memory. They must be taught the ranges of response to personal violence. They must be addressed by experts so they become able to assess trauma. The people working in the new system must all understand that fear often makes people unable to fight and scream. That shock often means a victim does not report a rape, or even tell anybody for a period of time.

There must be adaptations to the burden of proof that are specific to crimes involving sex.

During rape trials, defence lawyers should not be able to directly cross-examine victims. There should be mediators who are able to put the questions across, making them less emotive and painful. The lawyerly tactics are an unnecessary part of rape prosecution and should be removed. Words are used as weapons to discredit – to pressurise women into dropping their charges. No part of a woman's sexual history is relevant to a rape case. Lawyers should be given heavy fines for any type of sexual shaming or insinuation. If they repeatedly offend they should be struck off, sent to prison, thrown in the sea. People who report their car being stolen are not questioned about how often they'd let someone borrow it. A boxercise class would not be brought up to discredit you if you were claiming you'd been punched.

Our culture's misunderstanding of female sexuality is being used against rape victims.

Children's sexual education needs vast improvement.

Every year in secondary school children should be taught together about consent. The lessons could involve analogies, philosophy and ideas. They should involve questions about empathy – how do we know what other people feel? How do we know when we have hurt somebody? Older children would then have lessons that extended these ideas towards sexual behaviour, discussing complex ideas of right and wrong and how to respect boundaries while giving and receiving pleasure. They should be taught about the difference between active wanting – desire and arousal – and passivity, allowing somebody to do things with your body. Children of fifteen should then be allowed to debate the ethics of pornography and prostitution: what is consent when it is paid for? Can consent be bought? If someone is financially desperate and someone else pays them to do something they don't want to, was there consent or was there coercion? Or force?

Societal attitudes to sex could be changed within a generation. And it would be interesting too.

Acknowledgements

Here is where I get to thank everyone without even winning an Oscar!

Thank you to my agent and friend (and future wife?) Dawn Sedgwick, my career mum, who changed my life and shouted at everyone until they gave me a book deal. A thousand thank yous to Faber for believing I could write a book and giving me so much time; eternal gratitude to Sarah Savitt for getting my ball rolling. And Julian, dear Julian, my editor, who twinkles nicely as he sits in a chair while I tell him spooky facts about the female reproductive system. Thank you for being so super-chilled and relaxed while I frippered about and missed a million deadlines. Thank you to the brainboxes Robin Dunbar and Anne Miller for fact-checking and reading at the draft stage and for your ideas and cautious corrections. Thank you to Eleanor Rees for copy-editing and knowing much more about everything than I do. This book was a group effort, yet I have selfishly insisted I was the only one on the cover. Thank you to everybody who made this book physically possible.

Soppier thanks go to my sisters, Cheryl and Kristyna, for making me laugh and making me proud. And for those brilliant nieces you made for me to play with, for Rosa and Hollie. I learned new things above love when I became an aunty, and it's for them I want the world to be a bit nicer. Thanks and love to my dad and my Kirsten. Thank you for always understanding creativity and anxiety and for being supportive without constraints. I love you both so much and it meant the world when you checked in to see how I was doing or let me gabber on talking through ideas.

Thank you to my best friends, Cariad and Vanessa. Thank you for a friendship so intense it would shame most romances; thank you for all the conversations and opinions, for your emotional bravery and cleverness and for inspiring and stimulating me for over a decade. Hayley, thank you for letting me tell some of our secrets and for being my first proper friend and for never ever being shocked at the world or its inhabitants. You are continually interesting and I am lucky geography and a parental punishment gave you to me.

The best thing about stand-up (apart from all the pounds and claps) was that I got to meet the most incredible people – Josie Long, Bridget Christie, Jess Fostekew, Roisin Conaty, Katherine Ryan, Aisling Bea, Tiffany Stevenson, Sarah Millican, Shappi Khorsandi, Lou Sanders, Tania Edwards, Celia Pacquola, Sarah Kendall and Felicity Ward. Thank you for positive words when I was thirsty for them, for the best chats, for *understanding* and for making me laugh my wobbly arse off whenever you perform. It's all love from me.

John-boy, my idiot in crime. Thank you for writing me letters when I lost my confidence and for making me get back to writing when I was having too much fun. Thank you for a million adventures and a love so huge I had to write about it.

Thank you to my mum, Gail, the hero of the piece. The woman who loves me even while I subjectively edit my childhood and who respected my need to write such personal things about her life. After all those teenage years of yelling 'I wish I wasn't even born', can I now say thank you for making me and for sharing your life with me so openly? Thank you.